CROP CIRCLES — HARBINGERS OF WORLD CHANGE

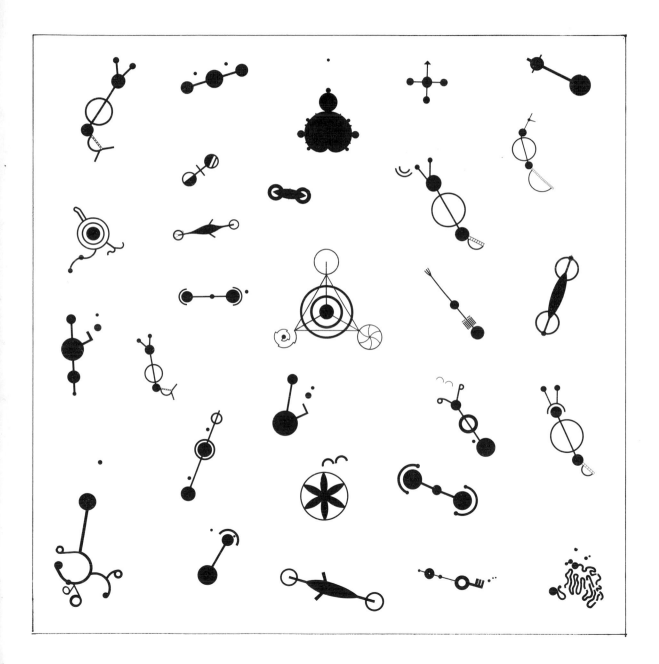

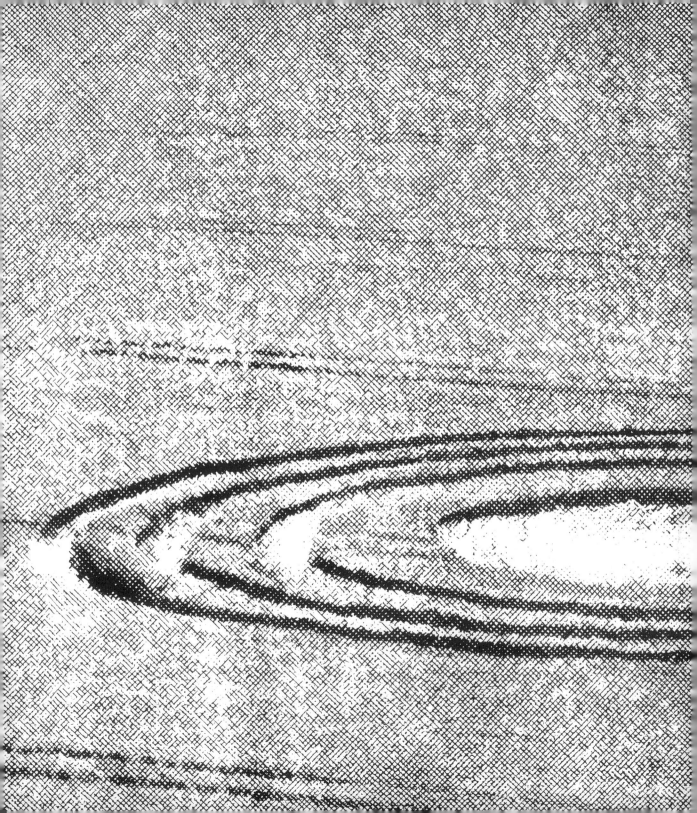

CROP CIRCLES~

Harbingers of World Change

Edited by

ALICK BARTHOLOMEW

First published 1991
by GATEWAY BOOKS
The Hollies, Wellow,
Bath, BA2 8QJ, UK

Distributed in the USA by
ATRIUM PUBLISHERS GROUP
11270 Clayton Creek Road
Lower Lake, CA 95457

Cover design — Studio B of Bristol
Front cover photo — David Potter/Science Photo Library
Back cover photo — George Wingfield

Set in Sabon 9½pt on 12 by
Ann Buchan Typesetters
of Shepperton, Middlesex

Text printed and bound by
Butler & Tanner of Frome
Colour section printed by
Tabro Litho of Huntingdon

British Library Cataloguing-in-Publication Data
A catalogue record for this book,
is available from the British Library

ISBN 0-946551-89-8

CONTENTS

The extraordinary 'weaving' that can appear in grapeshot – this at the Kennetts. (*Paul Dexter*)

List of Colour Plates

These are photographs of some of the extraordinary designs found in the fields of England in 1991. We make no claim that every one is genuine, but we hope so, as they are all so beautiful.

*Pictures marked * are available from the publisher as postcards at £2.50 for 8 cards (incl post). Larger quantities by application. A selection of 8 cards from The Crop Circle Enigma (1990) is also available at the same price.*

Notes on Contributors

Alick Bartholomew has worked in publishing for nearly forty years. His last imprint was the Turnstone Press, which he founded in 1971 (its first title being *Jonathan Livingston Seagull*), and is the publisher of Gateway Books. He is a graduate of Cambridge University in geography and geology, followed by graduate studies at the University of Chicago. Active in several organisations concerned with healing and the environment, he is also a founder member of the Centre for Crop Circle Studies. He is a grandfather who loves mountains, motorcycles and wild places.

Beth Davis is a conservation officer dealing with historic buildings in Cambridgeshire. She lectures on building history and more particularly on landscape history. She also uses her dowsing skills to identify and interpret ancient sites with groups of students. She is a watercolourist and photographer, and is a founder member of the Centre for Crop Circle Studies.

Michael Green, RIBA FSA, a professional archaeologist and architectural historian, was for long an Inspector of Ancient Monuments for English Heritage. He took the initiative in calling together those who founded the Centre for Crop Circle Studies, and is currently its chairman. He writes, lectures and broadcasts, not only on archaeological topics but also on related matters, such as dowsing, which orthodox science is only slowly coming to recognise. He is preparing a study of the ancient mysteries in north-west Europe under the title *The Celtic Zodiac*. He lives in London.

Dean Holden travelled from an early age, educated in Hertfordshire and Bremen, Germany. In Totnes, Devon, in the 1970s, he set up a company promoting concerts and cultural events and a community magazine, serving also as a school governor. He was an active member of the early Ecology (Green) Party, was a candidate in two elections, and was a founder of the Green Collective, which ran influential Green Gatherings in the late 70s and early 80s in UK. As co-director of a marketing company, with Paul Scott, in consultancy, importing and exporting he landed up in the USA and is currently in Hawaii.

Palden Jenkins is a historian, astrologer and teacher-educationalist. He is founder of the Glastonbury Camps (1983) and the OakDragon Project (1987), holistic educational, initiatory and community initiatives in Britain. A student dissident of the 60s (LSE), he has been notable in the alternative movement in UK, Sweden and USA, involved with Tibetan Lamas, anti-nuclear campaigning, radical midwifery, community ventures, counselling, astrological research, esoterics and earth-mysteries. His book *Living in Time*, and a forthcoming book *Cycles of History* (Gateway Books) expand on the logic behind what he has written here. He lives in Glastonbury, Somerset.

Isabelle Kingston was a psychically-sensitive child, growing up in Marlborough, Wiltshire, the daughter of a local doctor. She had a successful career in finance and banking before she developed her spiritual and healing gifts to a greater degree. In 1984 she was drawn back to live in Wiltshire where she has made a study of ancient sites and their link with the crop circle phenomenon. She runs workshops on psychic development, regression and personal potential, as well as individual counselling. She lives in a Victorian vicarage with her son and her mother who is a healer.

Stanley Messenger is an esotericist and philosopher. He was trained in medicine, has worked in religious drama and repertory theatre, as a teacher in Steiner schools, as a salesman, in social and housing work, and as a family violence officer. He is now retired, is a grandfather, and lives in Glastonbury, Somerset. He has long been dedicated to studies of butterflies, and is co-founder of the Gatekeeper Trust, a pilgrimage organisation working with sacred sites. He lectures on sacred sites and Mary

Magdalene, and spends time in Languedoc, France, working with Cathar history and memories.

John Michell has written on many topics at the edge of present understanding, ranging from earth mysteries, ley-lines, prehistoric science, Glastonbury and West Penwith, through the meaning of number and measure in scared buildings and ancient cosmology, to anomalous and curious phenomena and simulacra in all their variety. *The Flying Saucer Vision* and *The View over Atlantis*, published in the 1960s were seminal books to which many owe much for the initiation they gave into ancient and paranormal mysteries. He is a founder member of the Centre for Crop Circle Studies, and is editor of *The Cerealogist*, a regular journal devoted exclusively to the crop circle enigma. He lives in London.

Lucy Pringle was educated in England, France and Switzerland and has travelled widely, spending twelve years in Jamaica, where her two sons were born. At present working for a finance house, she is also the Hon. Treasurer and Membership Secretary for the Centre for Crop Circle Studies. She nevertheless finds time to pursue life-long interests in books, writing, art, gardening, horses, tennis, bridge and backgammon, people and lively conversation. In addition, she has recently begun to practice channelling. She lives in Surrey.

Paul Scott was educated at Downside and Durham University. He has been active in the alternative movement, helping to found Windmill Hill City Farm in Bristol, and contributing to Cruisewatch as a peace activist. Latterly he has been marketing director for a company importing and distributing products from USA. He is currently living in Arizona, where his favourite occupation is watching Sedona sunsets!

Busty Taylor is born and bred in Wiltshire, with a knack for mechanical gear of all kinds, learned from his father. Since the 1960s he has run a thriving driving school, but his two private passions, flying and photography, have gained him an international reputation in cereological photography. A major discoverer of circles, he is periodically seen balancing an unwieldy camera atop a tall pole or flying one-handed while filming with a video camera! He and his work have appeared frequently on TV, or illustrate conferences or books. He is a founder member of the Centre for Crop Circle Studies and lives in Hampshire.

Peter Cedrowen Taylor is an environmentalist, with specialisation in radioecology and nuclear matters. He was educated in South Wales, studied natural sciences and social anthropology at Oxford, and has worked for Greenpeace International, and as a consultant in the negotiation of international treaties and conventions for protecting the world's oceans. From 1978-90 he was director of the Political Ecology Research Group, Oxford, conducting the kinds of ecological research which governments and companies omit to do. He has a personal dedication to inner growth and spiritual traditions, and lives with his family in North Wales.

David Tilt is dedicated to archaeological and cereological dowsing, and writing and lecturing. He has worked in photography, and in radio, tape and video manufacturing in England and New Zealand, and has a private interest in electronics and short-wave radio. He is a countryside lover, and has written many pieces for the British Society of Dowsers and RILKO on energy-leys, sacred sites and previously-undiscovered henges and other sites in Sussex, where he lives with his wife and cats.

George Wingfield was educated at Eton College and Trinity College, Dublin, graduating in 1966 with an MA (Hons) in natural sciences. He worked briefly at the Royal Greenwich Observatory, Herstmonceux, on stellar spectra and the earth's magnetism. He worked for many years at IBM UK Ltd in systems engineering. He is a founder member of the Centre for Crop Circle Studies, and has written, lectured and broadcast extensively on the crop circle phenomenon. His interests span a wide range of other phenomena with research in paraphysics and ufology. He lives near Shepton Mallet, in Somerset.

Introduction

ALICK BARTHOLOMEW

WHAT IS IT about these circles? People either seem to get all starry eyed about them, or else they get very irritated. There is now a third group, who thanks to some farmers in 1991 being more generous in letting people into their fields, have come away with genuine curiosity or interest in what this strange phenomenon is all about, or who 'recognise' the symbols. Maybe you are in the last group and would like to check out your feelings with the *new* insights of some of the researchers.

I stress the word *new*, because the phenomenon is moving so fast that any theories that do not take into account the quantum jumps of 1990, and more especially of 1991 (and that includes almost every book currently available), are either largely misleading, or at least out of date. The main problem that the phenomenon has had to contend with is that of *conventional* wisdom based on preconceived notions and an unwillingness actually to study the evidence first hand. Academic science really has no way of dealing with hundreds of beautifully spiralled sculptures of intricate design in the grain-fields. The response is either of cynicism ('they're clearly all hoaxes') or some other unscientific form of evasion. The media tend to report the phenomenon in a similarly superficial manner, often feeling they must trot out a cooperative 'scientist' to give a rational and uncontroversial opinion of the event.

The hoax theory has an interesting origin. It seems to come from a need in our relatively materialistic society to *explain* everything, to analyse and to pigeon-hole data. This is a left-brain or more masculine rational function, compared with the intuitive or feeling, right-brain function. If you say "I don't know" in answer to the question "How are the circles formed?" many men (and some women) will look at you scornfully. (See Cedrowen Taylor on our need for 'order'.) Our rational society does not feel comfortable with mysteries and unknowns, only with unsolved problems. Interestingly, now that we have created unsolveable problems, the mysteries are appearing! The hoax theory is an easy way to put the whole thing out of mind.

We are a schizoid human society. There is a part of all of us which is materialist, seeking security in these uncertain times — we need order, predictability and control. But we are all also partly spiritual, hungering for meaning and magic. This polarity sets up tensions in us, but also in society. Those in power represent the status quo, but those attracted by a new way of seeing the world are also fearful of change.

The crop circles represent mystery and magic, but by their very nature also imply a massive shift in consciousness and understanding, which must be threatful to the status quo. It is to be expected therefore that the hoax will be encouraged by those in power as a way of discrediting those who are associated with a change in society.

But how about the hoax as a solution to the mystery? It just isn't on! With over 2000 events in the last few years, in the height of the season perhaps 20 a night, and latterly occurring on four continents, often in quite inaccessible places. It has been shown that the hoax of a *simple* configuration takes several hours to make. To avoid detection, it would have to be made at night, without lights.

Hoaxes are usually claimed after the harvest when it is difficult to check the evidence. With the tremendous increase in numbers of the circle events in the last two years, there just are not enough people who can recognise a genuine circle to check them all out over enormous distances. If the culture were not so schizoid, the hoax claims would be challenged. As it is, these claims only confuse the research, for the media usually treat them as fact when actually they're rarely corroborated. It often gets quite silly — one of the few events that was clearly a hoax in 1990 was three circles at the Brattan (Wiltshire) crop-watch. No less than six separate groups claimed credit for it, though there is reason to believe that the real perpetrators did not.

Until the end of the 1991 season, hoaxes were not taken seriously. Then the claim by two people within the crop circle research groups that they had made the circles was widely publicised. It soon became clear to those doing the research that these two were not just the moralistic tricksters they pretended to be, but the pawns of a disinformation campaign. It is unimportant who is behind the wish to hoax — government or rich industrialist — they are initiating something that is already in the collective unconscious. We need to see that this paranoia represents something in all of us because of our fear of change. Until that is clearer, more organised claims of hoaxes will continue to happen. But, don't despair, the real 'Circlemakers' will have the last word, for they are on the side of evolutionary change.

The attempt to 'explain' the phenomenon scientifically has been dominated by the plasma vortex meteorological solution (electrically charged wind funnels). This ingenious theory had appeal for some before the shift towards greater complexity of the 'pictogram' dumb-bell formations of 1990, since when very few of the researchers will give it any time.

That is, excluding the *only* group of academic scientists who have shown any interest in research — some plasma vortex physicists from Japan, who might be motivated by a search for a new cheap form of usable energy (see Isabelle Kingston's information). Interestingly, the few scientists who seem to be better equipped to deal with such an unpredictable, almost mischievous natural phenomenon are the likes of the biologist Rupert Sheldrake who looks at the world holistically rather than in a blinkered, specialised manner; but then he is no darling of academe.

A feature of the crop circles is that one has no sooner noted a repeating pattern and started to form a theory, than that pattern is contradicted almost the next day (*literally*, in some cases). This, and the uncomfortable, for some, realisation that there is a psychic, or at least non-physical, component to the phenomenon has scared off conventional research, but also changed the emphasis from 'how are they made?', because the causative factors are so elusive, towards 'what are they?', and 'why are they appearing?'

1990 saw a quantum change in the crop circles. From the pretty patterns of 'quintuplets', 'triple-ringers' and beautiful 'Celtic crosses', there suddenly developed these strange dumb bell 'pictograms', the big ones reminiscent of ancient rock carvings. These put paid to the meteorological causation theories, for the most part, but they also looked much more made 'according to a plan', as though there was a *mind* behind them. At the same time there was a body of evidence building up of a non-random happening, one sensitive to time, to location, even sensitive to human beings, and possessing a kind of intelligence, as in some of the apocryphal anecdotes George Wingfield describes well in his article. Most, though not yet all, of the researchers by now have agreed that we are dealing with some kind of intelligence.

In 1991 came a quantum change of even bigger proportions. The appearance of the Barbury Castle configuration in Wiltshire on 17th July (see front cover) blew a lot of minds. Here was a masterpiece of cosmic geometry, something of incredible precision, and clearly of meaning. Three weeks later, pointing towards Cambridge, a centre of 'chaos' research, came the incredible 'Mandelbrot Set', a mathematical pattern which shows the order in chaos. The Circle-makers are at last communicating in an unequivocal way, showing the kind of intelligence that radio astronomers have been waiting for for years. And what of the strange 'insectograms', and the very feminine spiralling designs that have begun to appear for the first time? In 1991 several schools of 'circle-makers' were identifiable (see Isabelle Kingston's contribution). We are now being given symbols of a different order, but also perhaps, we have begun to respond to them in a more imaginative way.

While our first book on the phenomenon, *The Crop Circle Enigma*[2] emphasised a rational approach, it is the purpose of this book to focus more on meaning, on the intuitive and the symbolic, while yet attempting to remain grounded. Its inspiration came from White Bear and Thomas Banyaca, two Hopi shamans in Arizona, who were both very moved on seeing a photograph of the first dramatic 'double pictogram' formation at Alton Barnes, of 11th July 1990, and said that similar symbols have appeared before at times of Earth change. Don't forget that the Hopis' memory goes back thousands of years.

So I invited thirteen co-authors to participate in a search for meaning along those lines. As you will see, they all share the strong conviction that the circles contain an intimation of imminent changes that are to affect the whole planet. Each writes from a different perspective, which gives a multi-faceted view of our present situation. Though not all of us are equally involved in the crop circle research, we share the feeling that we are on the edge of a truly momentous change for humanity.

It is interesting that the crop circle movement is dominated by men, even though they may be seeking unconsciously to connect with the feminine within themselves. Men do have a way of wanting to *analyse*, and, in this light, many ingenious proposals have been put forward to interpret the symbolism that is so seductive. Yet the interpretation of symbols requires hooks to hang them on. These are almost by definition one-way streets. So a Celtic scholar will interpret them in terms of Celtic symbols, an astrologer by the planets, a numerologist by the esoterics of number and so on. It is another of these predominantly left-brain rational modes, in which you can keep on going around in circles. How are we to interpret symbols? We in the West have a lot to learn from our wiser brothers from other cultures, who have much more experience than we in working with symbols (see Holden & Scott on Ute Indian comments about Westerners).

On the other hand, several of our authors speak of the psychic happenings connected with the crop circle phenomenon. George Wingfield shows how the sheer body of anecdotal evidence transcends any reasonable suspicion of wishful thinking. Isabelle Kingston provides other-worldly intelligence about the circles. Other researchers have had premonitions of design, location and even the likely time when an event would occur. There is a seductive fascination in the paranormal phenomena that are occurring with greater frequency — coloured lights, UFO sightings, strange sounds, physical and emotional reactions of individuals to visiting circles, and more. Some are learning that over-exposure to circle energy can have disagreeable effects. It seems that too much emphasis on the intuitive and the feeling (right-brain modes) can be as undesirable as too much rationality. Perhaps a lesson the circles have to teach us is to find *balance*. One of the most interesting themes that comes up several times in this book is of the intuition of the different indigenous peoples of the world (whom, thank God, we have not been allowed completely to exterminate) that we are now on the threshold of a new partnership between their wisdom and our technology.

I was manning the Centre for Crop Circle Studies

gate at the urban Bath pictogram in 1991, which received over a thousand visitors, when one asked "Why do you think these circles are here?" It was suddenly obvious: all these city-dwellers were coming out to marvel at the natural wonders, some with their world-views being changed by what they saw and felt! Wasn't that a good reason for the circles' appearance?

Most people ask "How are the circles formed?" All we can say is that they are a natural phenomenon being manipulated by an apparently intelligent source. Beyond that statement, all options are open. This is a highly complex phenomenon which is not amenable to any *one* solution, partly because it is not limited to the physical dimension. For example, I'm sure it's misguided to say "It's got to be the collective unconscious" or "terrestrials must be the answer" or "devic energies and elementals are doing it'. All of these may, however, be involved in different ways. Above all, what is called for is an open mind, and a discerning approach balanced between common sense (grounded reason) and intuition and heart. You may, for example, not like the 'plasma vortex' solution, but that does not mean that some of Terence Meaden's ideas may not have important relevance.

In a sense, it *had* to go this way. The mystery is not going to be amenable to simple answers. The cultures of the developed countries of the world are supremely self-confident in their ability to control their environments, yet are managing to make a complete mess of everything. Might this have something to do with their divorce from Nature? Stay tuned to developments of the next few decades!

The gradual spread of the circle phenomenon to other parts of the world has yielded an interesting pattern. It is appearing, albeit mostly still in simple circle arrangements, in countries like the USA and Canada, Japan, USSR, various continental European countries, Australia and New Zealand. Why not in any undeveloped countries? Is it possible that it is the developed countries that need to get the message, not the underdeveloped?

Cedrowen Taylor points out how the ecological crisis is closely related to our identification with the material and with our obsession to control the Earth. The key to this is what all the ancient peoples are saying - "The Earth is our Mother". The Kogi[3] regard us Westerners as 'the younger brother', not out of condescension, but out of real pity, as one might the profligacy and blindness of the teenagers who, when their parents are away, have an abandoned spree regardless of the consequences.

Palden Jenkins takes us into a detached look at our place in contemporary history, as might a visitor from another planet, warning us of the fragile nature of our hallowed institutions (like the banking system), and how so much of our economic structure is dependent on growth and spend, spend. It reminds one of Hans Andersen's story of "The Emperor's New Clothes" where here we all agree not to tell that it is all a big lie. The trouble is that we are colluders; otherwise, how could France, Britain (and others) get away with the arms sales to the region continuing after a major Middle East war? In one way or another we are supporting a degenerate society that is built on greed rather than compassion. We condone appalling levels of violence. It is about our own family that a sickening statistic was released — that one in four men would kill another for a million pounds! (British poll, July 1991). The crisis of values has reached a really critical point.

The implications of prophesy, biblical or Hopi[4], or from other spiritual sources, is that there has to be a reckoning, and the indications are that it is very close. Certainly public confidence in our political and economic institutions is rapidly failing, as the hollowness and hypocrisy of 'the system' is exposed.

We don't need to look for scapegoats; our leaders don't seem to be aware of what is happening, but we get the leaders we deserve, so it is we who have to change. It is just that we have lost our way, as 'the elder brother' is trying to say. This, I believe, is part of the message of the Circles.

Stanley Messenger takes us into what, for some,

will be unfamiliar territory — though not to students of Carl Jung. It opens up a whole new perspective on our view of life. The prevailing view is that the physical is the only reality. The nonconformist view, on the other hand, is that all of humanity (including the dead) coexists on another dimension called the 'collective unconscious', which is not bound by time or place, or by individual importance — this mirrors concepts of early Christians, of Buddhists, or of many of the indigenous peoples. Many people today are finding that through meditation, or being aware of their dreams, they can be in touch with a more detached part of themselves ('God filled'?); they can thus help to balance out the excesses of their our sensory existence. The collective unconscious (also 'God filled'?) fulfils the same function for the whole human community. What Stanley is suggesting here, is that, at some level, we are creating the circles.

Orthodox Christianity, like its brother religions, Judaism and Islam, has an essentially male quality, compared to the more instinctive and female systems like Buddhism or the beliefs of the indigenous peoples. I have never felt very comfortable in a Church where structure and dogma were dominant (the male controlling element). Having spent all my youth dutifully going to church with my family, I remember well, while a conscript at a Highland barracks in 1948, being inspired by a Scottish minister who must have had strong Celtic chromosomes in his system. He would tell me how *all of Nature is suffused with the Holy Spirit* — and did I respond with joy! Then two years ago, there was an informal series of services on the radio celebrating the holiness of Nature; one such was in Windsor Chapel, in which the Duke of Edinburgh took a prominent part. Times are changing; already there are new initiatives within the churches seeking to restore the balance — like the creation-centred spirituality of Matthew Fox which my Highland minister would surely have welcomed, or liberation theology.

This is not a religious question. Religion is associated with doctrine and power, and by its very nature is divisive. While the party politician will say "My way is best", the religious dogmatist will insist "Only I have the truth!"

It seems to be part of the rationalism of modern man, which glorifies the individual, to want to anthropomorphise everything. So God has to be a person. Angels (if you believe in them) are men. Beings from other dimensions have to be funny looking *people*, and because we are not in touch with our own unconscious, we are continually projecting our guilty feelings onto other people. We are not in touch with our own sickness.

Even last century, scientists used to believe in other dimensions of being, or in a hierarchy of existence[5]. Michael Green in his article talks about other beings, and Isabelle Kingston about the knowledge other dimensions have of our crisis, and of why the circles have appeared. In the 1960's a small community in the north of Scotland[6] discovered how they could transform their garden with the help of elementals or devas. It is important to allow and ponder what Glen Wall speaks of in his article in this regard, for the implications for our future on this planet are enormous.

A particularly interesting feature with the crop circles that has become clearer in 1991 is their involvement with people. George Wingfield has researched this particularly. Some will say that this is wishful thinking, but the synchronicities are now becoming beyond a joke! This is a familiar idea to many, who may talk of "maybe the Universe is trying to tell me something", or a Christian may say "God spoke to me today." Another curiosity is how the same idea can grab different people simultaneously: at the Bath pictogram, three people at different times, out of the blue, volunteered their 'original' thought that perhaps the circles were being created by the human collective unconscious (see Stanley Messenger's article); this is an example of Rupert Sheldrake's theory of morphic resonance[7].

Cedrowen Taylor and Palden Jenkins take us through the present situation of the world and the imperatives facing humanity. Changes do not happen randomly in our highly complex and interconnected universe. There are the principles of cause and effect and of the need for homoeostasis or balance. If humanity has developed its rational side at the expense of its intuitive, its individuality at the cost of cooperation, immersion in the material to the loss of spiritual awareness, then nature will have the balance restored, willy-nilly. Many feel that the crisis is truly upon us, and that an imminent breakdown of our human culture is inevitable.

It is in the nature of being human to be optimistic. Why won't we muddle through this crisis, as we have in the past? The trouble is that we have little time. Our economic and political, even our social systems have become non-sustainable. They are supported by vested interests — by people who don't want to change. I'm not speaking of 'people power' à la Soviet, but of a change of consciousness. People *can* change; many see life differently after visiting a magical corn circle. But that change is not fast enough. The prophesies say that the period of change that we must go through will be traumatic, but the result will be renewal — at a higher level of consciousness. (God knows, how necessary that is!)

So we must be ready for change of an unexpected nature. Think of the Cambridge cipher. Chaos, as Cedrowen Taylor reminds us, is a very feminine and creative way that Nature has of renewing itself. But change also has a note of promise, not only fear. It is rather like the Chinese ideogram which means both 'crisis' *and* 'opportunity'. Take the thought that the crop circle symbols are there not just for interpreting — they are actually doing something magical without our needing to know about it!

What this book is suggesting, then, is that there may be many levels of influence at work with the crop circle phenomenon. It is accelerating a social and spiritual change that has been taking place over a number of years. Beings from other parts of our universe may be concerned that we do not destroy our planet (there is an ecological inter-dependence also in the Universe!), working with the devic energies at the level of Nature, the collective unconscious may have an undreamed-of wisdom, while God (the Great Spirit) suffuses all of existence with meaning and balance.[8]

Whether or not you agree with all these speculations, I hope you will be stimulated and enjoy the book!

REFERENCES

1. A film director recently gave the view that if he were to set his entire team of scenic designers on to the task of creating an artificial replica of the Barbury Castle pictogram, it would take six weeks! This was because the surveying and logistical difficulties involved in dropping designers into the crop-field, leaving no trace at all of trampling or errors, would involve large-scale structures, and helicopters flying at such a height as not to destroy the crop with down-draughts. He suggested that, while such a project would be a fascinating challenge for his team, he would not use up such time and resources as were needed, and he would certainly not be able to carry out such a feat behind the back of a farmer.

2. Noyes, R., (ed): *The Crop Circle Enigma*, Gateway 1990.

3. Ereira, Alan: *The Heart of the World*, Cape 1990.

4. Timms, Moira: *The Six O'Clock Bus*, Turnstone Press 1978.

5. Ash, David & Hewitt, Peter: *Science of the Gods*, Gateway 1990.

6. Hawken, Paul: *The Magic of Findhorn*, Fontana 1976.

7. Sheldrake, Rupert: *Presence of the Past*, Collins 1988.

8. Bailey, Alice: *Initiation, Cosmic and Solar*, Lucis Press.

ACKNOWLEDGEMENTS

Publishing a complicated book in one third of the normal time in order to meet a specific need causes immense headaches. This feat would not have been possible without the dedicated help and expertise in sub-editing and computer skills provided by Palden Jenkins.

And to Mari, my appreciation of her patience and support.

1.   Towards an understanding of the nature of the circles

GEORGE WINGFIELD

STANDING ALONE in a dewy cornfield in Wiltshire in May of 1990 the casual observer could easily be forgiven for failing to see anything of particular note. Certainly not anything of remarkable significance or something which in time may well change our whole perception of the world about us. Yet here were unmistakable signs that the crop circle phenomenon, which had slowly crept up on us through the 1980s, could not possibly be a hoax.

Earlier I had flown over this field in a light plane and photographed a vast crop circle concentrically surrounded by three narrow rings. The geometric precision of this immense formation on Roundway Hill near Devizes was quite staggering, but it was something that could only be seen from the air. It had been discovered, from the air, three days earlier by Busty Taylor. Scattered about the 200ft diameter circle and its elaborate ring-system were no less than 28 'grapeshot' circles with diameters ranging from 2ft to 10ft.

On the ground it had been really quite difficult to locate the circle, but after walking along several successive tram-lines I suddenly realised that I was actually *within* it. So lightly imprinted was the pattern, with the upper part of each barley plant gently bent in the general direction of swirl, that one might have failed to notice it altogether. This seemingly lightly-brushed imprint was, of course, quite unlike the unequivocal flattening of green, and also of mature, wheat which we were to see later in the season in the dramatic pictograms. Nevertheless it demonstrated the sheer impossibility that this formation could have been a man-made hoax.

So too did the narrow rings which were no more than 6 to 8 inches wide, perfectly geometric, and quite impossible for an adult human to have trodden out. And likewise the grapeshot. Each of these, a tiny work of art almost like a corn dolly, swirled gently and precisely into the crop with no tracks leading to them or other sign of human visitation.

Naturally the scoffers and skeptics were nowhere to be seen, and certain scientists, journalists and other all-purpose pundits who would emerge later in the year, following the Blackbird hoax debacle at *Bratton*, to assure a gullible public that the circles were all hoaxes, might have been somewhat put out by such proof positive of the reality of the phenomenon.

Having said that this constitutes proof positive, it must be added that with all crop circles there always lingers a small sliver of doubt, since the vast majority appear mysteriously and silently without any witnesses and usually at night. This is the nature of the beast and it means that 100% certainty of what has occurred is denied to us.

A REVISITATION

In early June I flew over the formation on Roundway Hill for a second time. This time I was a passenger in a military Gazelle helicopter which was fortuitously made available to myself and John Haddington on that day. Looking down at the giant circle I gasped in sheer amazement as I saw that the huge design now sported four thin concentric rings. The new ring enclosing all that had been there previously was immaculately geometric and must have been about 1000ft in circumference. Additionally there were at least twenty new grapeshot circles. (See *The Crop Circle Enigma*, p.93)[1]

Examination of the aerial photographs showed that this revisitation, converting the triple-ringer into what was then a unique quadruple-ringer, must have occurred on about May 26, a week after the original event, but it had not been noticed until my helicopter flight. The revisitation of particular formations was a well-known facet of the phenomenon, but it had been ignored or disputed by those seeking an explanation in terms of atmospheric vortices. This new episode provided dramatic confirmation. Also the slender new ring whose average width was no more than 6inches would have been, like the three original ones, virtually impossible to hoax.

Careful consideration of what had occurred must give substantial support to the view that an invisible energy-blueprint, in accordance with which the circles are scribed, is present and is something which remains *in situ* long after the original event. This is the pattern of ley energy-lines which dowsers detect — and the fact that we are currently unable to detect it with scientific instruments is indicative of the shortcomings of our scientific knowledge rather than proof that it does not exist. The visible pattern may be revealed in more than one stage, as it had been at Roundway Hill, and this was very evident with some of the formations in 1991.

Researchers who ignore these basic facts and attempt to rationalise away what is becoming increasingly obvious can only be described as *totally unscientific*. To paraphrase Prof.Archie Roy, "Many a fine theory has foundered on one small unpalatable fact". The circles develop and evolve, and without a doubt all of the theories which do not recognise this,

and which treat circles as a natural phenomenon subject to fixed physical laws, will be cast aside. The ludicrous declaration which we have been treated to several times in the last few years — that the circles are perfectly understood and are caused by natural atmospheric vortices — has been met with the contempt which it deserves.

THE ADVENT OF THE PICTOGRAMS

In May of 1990 we were presented with a conundrum which moved the whole crop circle enigma forward in what seemed like a quantum leap. This was the appearance of those formations which came to be called *pictograms*, and which initially embodied *dumb-bells*, or pairs of circles connected by a straight passage of flattened crop. The first seven of these were all found in the Winchester area, mostly in the vicinity of Cheesefoot Head.

In view of the nature of the circles phenomenon no one should have been surprised at this departure, but inevitably there was talk of hoaxes and grave suspicion in case someone was pulling a fast one on us. Indeed someone was, but it was the Circlemakers themselves who, at every turn, stretch and test our comprehension. All those who set rules for the circles invariably fall into this trap, and in this instance Dr. Meaden took exception to the rectangular boxes which many of the new pictograms displayed since they were impossible to reconcile with his atmospheric plasma vortex theory. On other occasions when one has made generalisations about the circles, these have been invalidated by events, usually within a short space of time.

Why should this be? Reflection shows that this is part of the very essence of the circles, which are fashioned by an intelligence closely related to the human mind. Time and again this connection is made evident but we can never quite bring ourselves to accept it. "Did that really happen because of what I said, or thought?", we ask. "No, it couldn't possibly be", we reassure ourselves. Nevertheless the connection is there, though usually it is a 'chicken and egg' situation where cause and effect are not clearly distinguished.

To those without first-hand experience of circles events, such an assertion may well seem ludicrous. "How can there be any connection between what is clearly a natural phenomenon," they ask, "and the observers and researchers?" I can only try to demonstrate the connection by taking a few examples.

REQUESTING A CIRCLE

The first recorded instance where this occurred is described in *Circular Evidence* (pp45–47)[2], and most of us probably passed over this, attaching scant importance to what seemed a fanciful account. Busty Taylor, while flying over the Longwood Estate near Cheesefoot Head in August 1986, remarked that "All we want now is to find *all* the formations we have seen to date, wrapped into one, like a Celtic cross . By this he meant a combination of the main formation types which they then had: the quincunxes (which were predominant in 1985) and the single-ringed circles which were the flavour of 1986. The next day, when flying over the very same spot, Busty and his companion, Omar Fowler of SIGAP, found to their amazement that his request had apparently been granted. Down below was a small Celtic Cross formation, which embodied both the single ring, and outside it the four outer satellites of the quincunx. This was the first time such a combined formation had been seen.

Curiously it was not far from this spot, on the Longwood Estate, that a ringed circle appeared on June 18 1989, within a short space of time of my request for a circle, which is described in *The Crop Circle Enigma* (pp104-105). This request was spoken out loud and was made at a time when six of us had been approached by a mysterious 'trilling' noise while sitting in an already-formed circle about 500

yards away. Whatever caused the trilling behaved like a sentient being, approaching and encircling us, although nothing physical was actually seen. Whatever the nature of this presence, it appeared that my heartfelt request for a circle had been granted, then and there.

What can one make of such occurrences? If these were just one-off events they could easily be dismissed as pure chance or coincidence. But they are not, and many more connections of this sort were to follow. To the skeptic such things are unacceptable, rather like the circles themselves, and they can always choose to believe that such stories have been contrived *after* the event, rather than allow us to dent their purely materialistic view of the outside world. The skeptics, however, are wrong. Nevertheless, a simplistic interpretation of such sequences of events in terms of cause (wish) and effect (circle) is probably inadequate. What we have is very much a 'chicken-and-egg' situation, insofar as we cannot say which came first.

THE WANSDYKE WATCH

In June 1990, John Haddington organised a circles-watch lasting ten days between Silbury Hill and Wansdyke. During this, the 'trilling' noise (referred to in *The Crop Circle Enigma*) was heard again by several people, and other strange noises, including a swishing noise, were heard in fields where circles *subsequently* formed. John and a companion also watched on one occasion a yellow luminous object low over one of these fields, and several smaller red lights which seemed to come out of the larger object.

This area near Silbury Hill seems especially prone to such sightings, which are highly reminiscent of the Warminster UFO flap of 1964-79. Again and again one is left with the impression that one's ordinary five senses have been somehow inadequate in their perception of the event witnessed. There is a unmistakable impression that whatever was observed was in some way controlled, and not of a natural or

18

random nature. But what these things are remains a total mystery.

I myself have observed mysterious lights in this area during and after the Wansdyke Watch. These lights were very small and faint and moved slowly and deliberately close to the heads of the wheat at a distance of perhaps 200 to 300 yards from us. At first I thought that this was no more than a trick of the light in conditions of low visibility. But on another occasion together with John and another companion, I watched these tiny lights for more than an hour from a circle formation near Milk Hill just south of Wansdyke. The lights would move about, fade, gather, sometimes brighten and then usually fade away altogether. It was not possible to approach them and if one tried to do so they would just fade from sight.

Certainly these were not glow-worms (with which I am familiar) or fireflies. Or, for that matter, swamp gas, which some people might suggest. Perhaps they were the elusive Will o'the Wisp of old . . . But what I do know is that in each of the fields where we saw these lights, small grapeshot circles appeared at a later date. No circles appeared in the area of Wansdyke during our watch, but pictograms were appearing near Cheesefoot Head at that time.

THE GIANT PICTOGRAMS OF 1990

On July 12 1990 the action passed from Hampshire to Wiltshire with the appearance of giant pictograms, consisting of double dumb-bells in line, at Alton Barnes and Milk Hill. The formation at Alton Barnes caused an unprecedented sensation, drawing people from all over the country to this new temple in the cornfields, and this, more than anything, dispelled the fallacy that the circles could be the mere product of a natural phenomenon. Thousands of people visited Alton Barnes and few doubted that this giant hieroglyph carried some message, albeit obscure, for mankind.

Curiously the location of the Alton Barnes pictogram had been indicated in advance by medium Isabelle Kingston. During the Wansdyke Watch in June Isabelle had, after doing some map-dowsing, assured us that there would be circles below the great tumulus Adam's Grave, which is exactly where the pictogram was found. This was the only location which she indicated to us. Moreover, she drew the shape of this pictogram with uncanny accuracy, well before the formation actually appeared. Only one part of her diagram turned out to be in error. Once more it looked as if a human thought had given birth to the formation which subsequently appeared in the fields.

The other great pictogram which formed that night, at Milk Hill two miles away, received less public attention but was the venue of a quite extraordinary UFO sighting, recorded on videotape, just two weeks later. Steve and Jan Alexander, who had visited the pictogram, were returning along the brow of the hill near the Alton Barnes White Horse when they spotted a small white disk-shaped object flying just above the heads of the corn in the field next to the pictogram. For several minutes they filmed this object with their video-recorder as it moved above the field descending on occasion into the crop and out of sight. The object was said to be approximately 16 inches in diameter and it flashed from time to time as if internally lit.

All this can be seen on their video-recording. Eventually the object flies over the hedge into the field behind where it passes over the head of a tractor driver. He is seen to turn and watch it fly up into the sky where it is lost to sight. This man, Leon Besant, was traced weeks later by Colin Andrews in the nearby village of Stanton St Bernard. He had indeed seen the UFO and had spoken about it only to be met with disbelief and ridicule. When Colin Andrews showed the recording in which Leon is clearly seen on his tractor he was finally vindicated and the disbelievers were forced to swallow their words.

This recording of a small UFO flying over or near

the crop circles was to be repeated in August 1991, when Constantin and Mucki von Durckheim filmed just such an object low over the 'ant' formation near Manton. Once more a small bright object no more than six inches in diameter was seen just above the corn moving in a straight line. It pauses and then moves down into the crop only to re-emerge perhaps thirty seconds later. Once more the movement appears to be purposive and considered. It moves around in a very definite manner and descends for a second time into the standing crop before being lost from view. The circular object is clearly seen in this video though we have no way of telling what it is or where it came from.

This surprising development recalls the white disk which is seen in a photograph of the Town Farm crop circle near Westbury in August 1987, (see *Circular Evidence*, p92). Not apparent to the observers at the time, this was picked up by the camera rather like the 'black darts' which are shown in the Chilcomb circle of August 1987 (see *The Crop Circle Enigma*, p50). These objects do not seem to be solid though occasionally they have that appearance. More likely they are of an etheric nature, though I doubt if orthodox scientists will much care for that term. They are things sometimes visible but more often not, and such things make one aware of the inadequacy of our five senses. Very likely these are related to the dim moving lights which John Haddington and I saw during the Wansdyke Watch and on other occasions. Whether or not they correspond to the agency which makes the circles (or even to that which frequently revisits and adds to them) is something on which we can only speculate.

THE SYMBOLISM OF THE CIRCLES

Amidst all of this mystery there remains a very definite impression among almost all cereologists that the circles carry a message. And also that the message is meant for us. But interpretation of the message is something on which few people can reach any consensus.

Many have looked for symbols or characters which can be directly translated into some intelligible language. Obviously this has to be a language that we can understand, or it is of little value to us, and that would of course indicate that the message was not intended for us in the first place. Hampered by this constraint there has been scant progress with finding any sensible message. Mr Erik Beckjord has deemed that the language of the pictograms is an ancient codification called Tifinag (as described by Dr Barry Fell) and has come up with translations such as "This is the place of the Devil, an evil place". Somehow few can bring themselves to accept the validity of such seemingly trivial messages, which tempt one to reply "So what?".

Ernest P. Moyer of Pennsylvania does rather better with ancient semitic script, which he assures me can be used to interpret the keys and claws of the Alton Barnes pictogram as the Semitic word for 'Eve' or Earth Mother. This sounds more promising, but really, one can make out the English letters E, V and E in the asymmetric protrusions of that celebrated formation. This is, of course, appropriate since the pictogram lay just below Adam's Grave.

The thrust of Moyer's interpretation is in line with Michael Green's identification of symbols representing the Earth Mother in the circles. These correspond to ancient stone carvings of the Earth Goddess and also depictions of the Solar Logos. This connection with ancient rock carvings is indeed persuasive.

However, again and again we find that only a small proportion of the crop pictograms can be intelligibly understood through such an equivalence. There is a multiplicity of potential symbols which seem to have no relationship to any known human sign. Why should this be if the circles solely represent a message for mankind? But quite possibly the majority of the symbols embodied in the pictograms are only capable of being assimilated by the subconscious, rather than the intellectual, mind. They might be, if that is the case, triggers intended to alter our level of consciousness and change us in an evolutionary manner.

Without presuming to answer that question, I can only say that, personally, I find the correspondence of the quincunxes and the crosses to known human symbols by far the most persuasive. In particular the 'quinta essentia' with three equal outer elements, and one unequal, is a symbol that is very familiar to students of symbology, and this has appeared repeatedly. It has particular spiritual significance and its best known form is that of the long-shaft Christian cross. Several quincunxes of this variety appeared during 1991 in Buckinghamshire. That at Butlers Cross (near Chequers, the Prime Minister's country residence) had its satellites connected to the central circle by straight pathways, and one satellite unlike the others, which were circles, took the form of an arrowhead. The earlier giant cross at Amersham had three satellites swirled clockwise and one which was anti-clockwise.

This was particularly gratifying since I had lectured on this aspect of the circles on several occasions during the preceding twelve months and here were the circles actually following the format which I had specified. This is a most unusual thing! But I must emphasise that these variations on the Christian cross were not an interpretation which I sought, since I have no particular religious axe to grind. They were a sign which has been quite clearly imprinted in the English cornfields since 1988 for all to see, and which has been totally ignored by all but a tiny fraction of the population.

But if anyone thought that the Circlemakers were of an entirely spiritual bent and specialised entirely in crosses, they were very much mistaken! Elsewhere in the country different Circlemakers were at work (not the hoaxers, despite their frantic claims) during 1991 and their handiwork looked to be anything but spiritual. Never doubt for a moment that there are many different intelligences involved here and very often their purpose is totally obscure.

THE INSECTOGRAMS

If there is one rule that the Circlemakers can be relied upon to keep, it is *to break any rules that we lay down for them governing their behaviour and development*. Surprises and yet more surprises are the order of the day. If you naively thought that the Circlemakers were but mechanistic vortices amenable to scientific logic, then they will have bamboozled you a hundred times over. And equally, if you thought that they only bore spiritual symbols to uplift the consciousness of humanity, then in 1991 they produced some very odd designs which seemed to relate more to *insects* than to mandalas or crosses.

The pictograms which appeared in June 1991 in Hampshire are what have become known as *insectograms*. I make no apology for this awkward portmanteau word, which merely describes what these latest designs resemble. No doubt I shall be accused, by UFOphobe crop-watchers, of attempting to suggest that the circles are created by bug-eyed monsters from outer space, but that is not my intention! Nevertheless, vorticists, please tell us how a mindless natural phenomenon, to wit a circulating atmospheric vortex, produces the extraordinary 'ladder' feature which is shown in the accompanying diagrams, and which I describe below in some detail.

John Haddington and I chanced on a prototype insectogram on August 7th 1990 when driving between Warminster and Westbury (see plate 21). We had just been visiting a vast crucifix formation (an extended quincunx with three slender annular rings) and were on our way to an airfield from which we were due to fly and photograph the new circles and pictograms then popping up in all sorts of places and at a most alarming rate. Just short of Westbury I spotted this formation in wheat quite close to the road and braked hard to pull into a convenient lay-by.

The pictogram was about 160ft long and consisted of a plain dumb-bell which then extended into a ringed circle from which sprouted two insect-like antennae. Its central avenue coincided with a tramline, with a single box on either side, just beyond the middle circle; these boxes were connected to this avenue by short pathways that appeared to be original features rather than man-made walk-throughs.

All the usual feelings of disbelief and suspicion gripped both of us as we examined this insectogram. Could the absurdly bug-like figure be genuine, or was someone playing an elaborate joke? Having just come from that magnificent crucifix, which seemed charged with a wonderful energy, here was a rapid transition from the sublime to the ridiculous. Curiously I was almost certain that the formation had not been there when we had passed that way earlier, though I couldn't be sure. Despite such doubts, a close inspection gave every indication that it was genuine.

The first true insectogram was found by Matthew Lawrence at Chilcomb Down (near Cheesefoot Head) on June 7th 1991 (see plate 20). This formation had just one antenna but it can be seen to be *archetypal* of the species, unlike our prototype at Westbury. This is because it has the standard insectogram body together with antennae and the 'ladder' feature. The three-part body carries the insect analogy still further: this consists of two circles of about 27ft diameter separated by a large ring, of 66ft diameter, through which runs a central pathway between the circles. Path and ring were about 4ft wide. Now the name 'insect' means literally 'in sections', since an insect's body is divided into three parts: the head, the thorax and the abdomen. These could be taken to correspond to the circle, ring, circle configuration of the insectogram. The large ring corresponding to the thorax is divided by a central pathway. This is curiously reminiscent of a beetle's horny elytra (or two-part wing-case) which further substantiates the parallel with an insect.

The strangest feature of all is the 'ladder' which projects at about 120deg from the line of the central axis and is attached to a half-ring with which it makes a 'D'. The swept lines of crop making up the

sides and rungs of the ladder are all about 1ft wide and these enclose blocks of standing crop approximately 4ft square. The precision of these rectilinear features and the quite undoubted indication of purposeful design is stunning.

The number of rungs in an insectogram ladder varies, and, in that at Chilcomb, Matthew found 14. Other examples have, so far, fewer rungs such as four at Upham and six at Litchfield. Generally the rungs are alternately swept in different directions, but at Chilcomb five adjacent rungs were each swept inwards from opposite ends. Curiously this insectogram acquired a fifteenth rung on the end of the

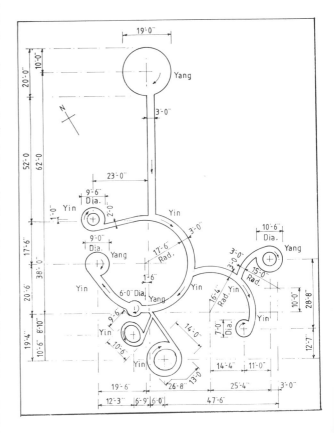

CHILCOMB DOWN, 7 June, the first true 'insectogram' (see also p.76)

ladder shortly after its discovery, but such a revisitation, apparently a genuine facet of the phenomenon, was not unusual among the 1991 pictograms.

To take the insect analogy still further (despite the cries of "Stop, stop!" from those of you who have decided that this thing looks more like a snail), the ladder feature might be compared to an ovipositor or to an insect's sting. There may be no justification for such parallels but all cereologists who have seen the insectograms must ask themselves the question "What on earth are we dealing with, and what are the Hampshire Circlemakers up to?". Of course ladder-like petroglyphs can be seen on the Ilkley Moor Panorama Stone (depicted in John Langrish's article in *The Circular* Vol 1, No 3)[3] these are described by Michael Green in *Enigma* as symbols of the Cosmic Dragon. But I doubt that these correspond to the ladders of our insectograms.

A second insectogram at Upham (plates 22, 23), four miles south of Cheesefoot Head, appeared at about the same time as that at Chilcomb Down. This had two well-developed antennae, terminating in small circles, sprouting from a half-ring around the head of the figure. Sadly this formation in barley was soon severely damaged by rain, wind and human habitation. It was nevertheless strongly dowsable and there is no reason to believe it could have been hoaxed.

THE ORIGINS OF THE INSECTOGRAM

The three-part body of the insectogram was plainly in evidence in Hampshire pictograms during the latter half of 1990. It first appeared at Pepperbox Hill near Salisbury, which is clearly part of the Hampshire Circlemakers' domain despite being in Wiltshire. Then it had two box features within the ring, one on either side of the central avenue. This tripartite body was again seen as part of the beautiful Gallops double pictogram in Hazeley Farm Fields (Aug 3/4 1990) and once more in the Barn Field

pictogram of Aug 11 1990. These are all illustrated in *The Crop Circle Enigma*. The latter formation exhibits oblique pathways emerging symmetrically from each end-circle; these may have corresponded to the developing twin-antennae feature and the half-ring/ladder at the other end. In 1991 the boxes within the central ring have disappeared. One has only to look at the earlier photographs and compare them with the 1991 insectograms to see the evolution which has taken place in this particular species of pictogram. Crop circle evolution is now an established fact of cereological life and anyone whose theories do not admit to this need perhaps to pack up and start again!

At the end of June 1991 we received word of a further insectogram at Seven Barrows, Litchfield, another established circles site in Hampshire, 17 miles north of Winchester. John Haddington contacted the landowner, Lord Carnarvon, who is keenly interested in the phenomenon, and we rushed to the site to carry out a survey for CCCS[4]. Entering this insectogram, which appeared completely fresh and unvisited, we were staggered by the complexity of this great elaborate figure scribed in the wheat (see plate 24). Here again there seemed no question that this was the result of intelligent design — and that those who believe otherwise presumably have their heads firmly buried in the sand. As for meaning, symbolism or understanding of the Circlemakers' intent, I must leave that to better men than me.

Yet another insectogram, this time shorn of antennae and the half-ring/ladder feature, appeared at Cheesefoot Head on July 5. This was in the same field where in June 1989 nine of us heard the strange insect-like trilling noise which was described in *The UFO Report 1991*[5]. For just one moment the bizarre thought occurs to me that perhaps we are dealing with some insect-like alien life-form, but hastily I banish such a heresy!

At every stage the circles phenomenon stretches and tests our perception of reality. Those of us who are unable to escape from the prison of our precon-

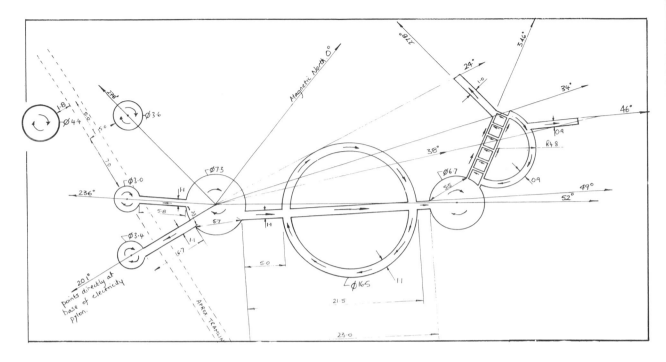

LITCHFIELD (Seven Barrows Field), end of June 1991. This appeared in the same field as one of the dumb-bell pictograms, almost exactly a year later. (*J.F.Langrish drawing*)

ceived ideas will be left hopelessly behind, protesting that the insectograms are a hoax because they don't fit our concept of how crop circles *should be*. And soon no doubt insectograms will be replaced by some new enigma, equally surprising and equally incomprehensible.

THE WILTSHIRE PICTOGRAMS

From about the same time as that insectogram appeared at Chilcomb Down, other pictograms started appearing in the Silbury Hill area which was not unexpected. However these bore no resemblance to the insectograms. Compared with the latter they looked more bold and formal, with symmetry about the long axis, like the Hampshire pictograms of 1990. This clear difference between pictograms appearing in Wiltshire and those in Hampshire was

reminiscent of 1990, when the asymmetrical double pictograms with 'claws' and 'keys' had only been seen in Wiltshire. It was as if the Hampshire Circle-makers of 1990 had moved now to Wiltshire, and an entirely new lot were at work in Hampshire.

To pursue this theme, pictograms also started to appear near Bath, Avon, and two of these exhibited the 'hand' or 'claw' features which were no longer seen in Wiltshire, though admittedly by late July the feature did start to reappear in the Silbury Hill area. This variation of the formation types appearing in different parts of the country at any particular time is indeed very marked.

On July 2nd a huge pictogram appeared at Alton Barnes (plate 59) within 200 yards of the position of the 1990 one. This was a striking formation about 120 yards long consisting of a circle joined to a large ringed circle by a long narrow avenue, which then extended on the other side to, and through, a smaller ring. On one side only two small circles, completely isolated, were positioned equidistant from the central avenue. Again people flocked to see the new formation and the field was opened to visitors at £1 a head.

This configuration, but much larger, was repeated nine days later at Maisey Farm, Ogbourne Maizey, near Marlborough (plates 62, 63). Although in 1990 no pictogram was exactly repeated, here in 1991 an almost exact duplication was to be seen. It was interesting to recall that in 1988 the first giant quincunx formation near Silbury Hill had been repeated exactly in the same field just nine days later.

THE PLOT THICKENS

A few weeks earlier in June, John Macnish and David Morgenstern had run a surveillance operation known as Project Chameleon. This was based on Morgan's Hill near Devizes, and banks of expensive cameras and infra-red equipment were used to keep watch on a field where a magnificent quadruple-ringed circle and a Celtic cross had formed on June 1st and July 5th 1990 respectively. This was essentially the successor to Operation Blackbird which was sponsored by BBC Pebble Mill at Bratton in 1990.

In addition to the video equipment they had a powerful directional microphone pointed at the field which digitally recorded all sound in the range 2-40000Hz, that is, infra-sound, audible sound, and some ultra-sound. Besides this, Mike Carrie, director of Cloud 9, which markets security systems, had set up intruder alarm equipment along both ends of the field so that people entering the tractor tram-lines from either direction would trigger warning indicators in the observation vehicle. It was virtually impossible to gain access to the field unnoticed, and additionally the team had Cloud 9's remotely controlled 'Skystalk' TV camera mounted on an extensible 150ft arm to watch the movements of anyone or anything that did approach.

The night of June 28/29 was cloudy and damp and looked most unpromising. At 3am it grew misty and the mist thickened to fog. A decision was made to keep the cameras running and the directional microphone continued to record. Dedicated circle-watchers are not easily discouraged!

By dawn the unseasonal fog had still not cleared, but at 6am it began to disperse slowly. The dwindling pall of mist over the field being watched was the last to clear, and, as the final patch dissipated, the team caught sight of markings in the crop. They rushed down the hill to check for signs of entry to the field, which now could be seen to contain a dumb-bell

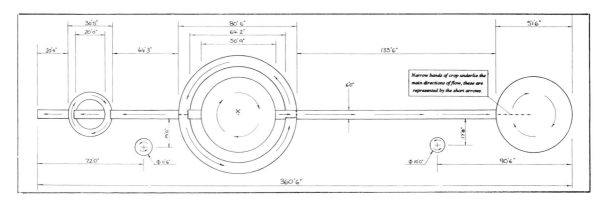

ALTON BARNES Pictogram. Formed in wheat on 2 July 1991 only 200 yards from where the large double pictogram formed in 1990 (see also p.185). (J.F.Langrish drawing)

formation with circles of unequal size. Close inspection showed no sign of human entry or footprints in the wet soil at access points to the field. A playback of the tapes from the directional microphone was found to be blank at all recorded frequencies.

I spoke to Mike Carrie, who was first into the dumb-bell formation (plate 31). He had walked a long way along a tram-line to get there without damaging the standing crop. His trousers were soaked by the wet crop and his boots covered in mud. The circles were perfectly swirled with the crops bent but unbroken. There was no sign of footprints or muddy tramplings in the circles.

He said: "When I was at Blackbird last year I really thought all you people were daft, and the circles were man-made. Now I just don't know what to think." He and the others who were there that night were puzzled and rather thoughtful. It was just as if a conjurer had spread a large silk handkerchief in front of them, waved his hands, and then produced from under it a magical white rabbit. Only this cosmic conjurer was himself invisible.

In July 1990 Mike Carrie was alone in the Etchilhampton pictogram near Devizes one evening after everyone else had left. When he bent down to examine a recess in the soil his head was suddenly surrounded by a powerful whirring noise similar to the 'trilling' which others including myself have experienced in the circles. This is described in *Latest Evidence* (p 66). From that time possibly some element of the circles phenomenon seems to have attached itself to Mike.

The fact that circles had appeared at all in the field which was under observation by Project Chameleon was bizarre enough. This was only the fifth formation to appear in Wiltshire during June and, out of all the fields in the whole of Wiltshire, the odds against it appearing *just there* were astronomically remote. But of course this event was not dictated by chance alone; those familiar with the phenomenon could hardly doubt the conscious link which must have been present between the circle-watchers and the Circlemakers. Just like the earlier examples this was a circle which had been earnestly sought after, but our friends the Circlemakers seemed to have made clear once more that they do not perform in front of the cameras.

A sequel to this strange conjuring trick with the mist occurred when Mike Carrie returned to his home in Nottinghamshire a few days later. When he went to open up his office in Sutton-on-Trent after the weeks spent in Wiltshire, there he saw in fields not far away a further dumb-bell formation in the corn. This was the same shape and size as the one near Morgan's Hill, only the direction of swirl in each circle was reversed.

There is no record of circles at Sutton-on-Trent in previous years. Once again the connection can only be considered coincidence if we allow odds of trillions to one. This is not the first time that a circles-researcher seems to have attracted circles to him, though we are at a loss to offer any explanation of how this could be. Nevertheless the undoubted link between the circles and human consciousness is once more made plainly evident.

CIRCLES FROM THE SKY?

On July 12 1991 at 3am several crop-watchers, including Rita Goold, witnessed a great column of luminosity descend from a dark cloud near Alton Barnes. Although it only lasted a few seconds, this brilliant spectacle greatly impressed those who saw it before it collapsed towards the ground appearing to spread out sideways as it did so. According to Rita it then briefly assumed the shape of a pictogram like that later found the same day at Hackpen Hill (see plate 32), some five miles away due north. No circles were found in the area between Knap Hill and Lockeridge where the column appeared to descend; just the new three-circle 'dumb-bell' formation with haloes at either end down below the White Horse carved in the chalk on Hackpen Hill.

Four days later this circle was revisited. A small perfect circle appeared just beside one of the haloes or half-rings at the end of the pictogram. This kind of revisitation was not in the least unusual with the 1991 pictograms and many of the other formations acquired additions such as small circles, spurs, or partial rings. Close examination gave every indication that these new features were indeed part of the phenomenon, and in general they were dowsable.

THE MOTHER OF ALL PICTOGRAMS

On July 17th the largest and most articulate of all pictograms (plates 5–9) appeared in a wheatfield below Barbury Castle, an Iron Age hill-fort near Swindon. This was discovered at 9am by Nick Bailey, who flies his Robinson R-22 Beta helicopter from Draycot airfield, which is less than two miles away. The field had quite definitely been blank when Nick flew over the preceding night at 9pm.

This formation consisted of an enormous equilateral triangle with sides of about 180ft, enclosing a large doubly-ringed circle. The rings were well separated, each about 7ft wide. Each angle of the triangle is bisected by straight pathways leading from the centre of the formation to circular designs, each different, beyond each apex. One design is a plain ring of 75ft diameter. The second is a ring of similar size, like a six-petal flower but with only the left-side of each petal delineated; this is reminiscent of a frequently used sun-symbol. The third design is a spiral which opens out in six steps like a ratchet, each time it winds around a further 90 degrees. This is of similar size to the other designs.

Flying over the formation in Nick Bailey's helicopter later that day, I was amazed at the scale of this huge hieroglyph; also the staggering geometric precision which exceeded any previous design. It was rather like looking down on a great maze and by that time there were people in every corner of the pictogram.

Later that evening I met Dr Meaden in the pictogram. He looked a very troubled man. "Surely, Terence", I asked, "you don't think this was made by an atmospheric vortex?' He was very silent, but eventually said that he didn't like it since he could see stalks that were broken. To a camera team from National Geographic Magazine, who had appeared and insisted on filming interviews with us both together, he conceded that no one could possibly have produced such a vast geometric design during the hours of darkness. This admission was later reported in the Western Daily Press. I agreed, saying that so far as I could see the pictogram showed the characteristics of genuine circles and that if any stalks were broken it was mostly likely done by all the visitors who had flocked to see it — not that many broken stalks were in evidence.

Obviously Meaden's theory that the circles are caused by a naturally-occurring atmospheric vortex could not survive acceptance of this huge geometric design as the real phenomenon, and the next day he made a statement to the media proclaiming that it was a hoax. This was inevitable. However all the other researchers are in agreement that the pictogram is genuine and represents yet another quantum leap in the evolution of the circles. Apart from the physical characteristics being the same, the dowsing reactions were very strong and definite. The whole formation seemed charged with an almost tangible energy.

Not long before Nick Bailey called to inform me of the great pictogram, Brian Grist, Manager of Waterstone's bookshop in Bristol had called to tell of his crop-watching experiences the previous night. He had been with two friends at Beckhampton at midnight when they had seen a pulsing light move silently across the sky. During the next hour they saw five more such objects, some white, some pulsing green, red and white. All were silent though at times they seemed relatively close to where they stood. At one time a dark object flew across the sky, blotting out the stars. The three were quite frightened by this

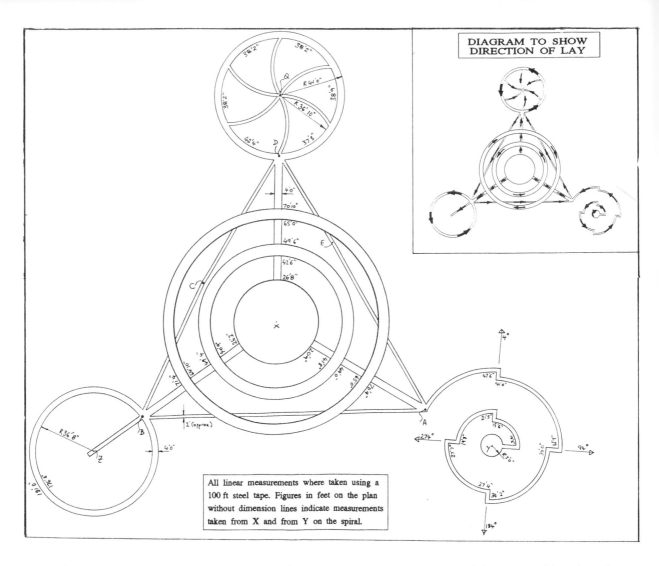

All linear measurements where taken using a 100 ft steel tape. Figures in feet on the plan without dimension lines indicate measurements taken from X and from Y on the spiral.

DIAGRAM TO SHOW DIRECTION OF LAY

BARBURY CASTLE. This three-dimensional tetrahedron, etched on a flat wheatfield was a wonder of other-worldly draftsmanship (see p.15, ref.1). It is a cipher of sacred geometry *par excellence*, and contrary to the Circlemakers' usual procedure, it had no precedents. Instead, it seemed to foretell themes-to-come. The top circle is a half-complete six-petal flower (see plate 12); the lower left circle comes in the 'whale figure' (see plate 38); the lower right hand circle is a labyrinth exactly 333ft long, (a mystical number, but hardly an international measure!). It is oriented exactly magnetic due north. It can yield hours of contemplative reward. This configuration marked a quantum shift in the evolution of the phenomenon, and contains the strongest possible philosophical message. (*J.F.Langrish drawing*)

strange display, and Brian likened what they'd seen to a sequence from *Close Encounters of the Third Kind*. Some of their sightings were in the direction of Barbury Castle, which is just five miles away, but, on first hearing the story, both of us were unaware of

what had been found in the fields that morning.

Other reports were later received of anomalous lights in the sky in the same area. The warden of Barbury Castle, who lives in a bungalow up on the hill, heard the most colossal roar coupled with a pulsing hum at 3.30am that morning, which he described as like one hundred planes going over. This terminated abruptly after a few minutes, but he never saw fit to look outside the house at the time. This is a man who is familiar with low-flying aeroplanes, since Barbury Castle is close to RAF Lyneham. He, too, was quite shaken by this sound and told very few people afterwards.

The verdict on the Barbury Castle formation is that it embodies geometry of the very highest order, and this is a wonder in its own right. John Michell's article on it in the August 1991 edition of *The Cerealogist* is essential reading for those who aspire to understand the importance of this development. To many this was the very high-point of the circles season.

STONEHENGE INSECTOGRAMS

After finding the third insectogram at Litchfield, we concentrated all of our attention on the Wiltshire formations which were appearing every few days at the end of June. It came then as a surprise to hear a report that two insectograms had been spotted in a field to the south of Stonehenge, where no circles had ever been reported. Were the Hampshire Circlemakers now moving westward with their insectograms?

I flew there as passenger in a helicopter on July 14th and was amazed to see no less than three formations in this field, which lay barely 500 yards from the most famous of all ancient monuments. The Circlemakers had crept up on Stonehenge and hardly a soul had noticed. The formations, evidently not visible from the busy A303 road, or from Stonehenge itself, were remarkably undamaged by human visitation.

The most recent insectogram was clearly delineated, and its ladder with seven rungs pointed directly at Stonehenge itself. Beside it lay a ringed circle with a curving pathway leading out of it. These two formations and Stonehenge itself are shown in my photograph (see plate 15). Further back in the field was a more faded insectogram which had probably been there for four weeks or more. But the new insectogram had beside it a new and unmistakable signature. This was a pair of half-rings or 'eyebrows' which both terminated on a tram-line. We were to see this signature from the Hampshire circlemakers (who had now reached the Stonehenge area) many times in the following weeks.

Here once more one saw the doubling-up of major formation types, which is so characteristic of the circles. Almost like cell division, the new types, once established, seem able to proliferate in this way. Then the Circlemakers move on to new designs to supersede the earlier prodigies which were the marvel of yesterday.

The sheer articulateness of the insectograms and the fine detail of the ladder feature must completely rule out the absurd notion that these things are made by natural atmospheric vortices. This has, of course, been perfectly evident all along, but not even a blind man could accept this explanation now. Yet there are still a few *un*scientific researchers who blindly pursue this explanation quite oblivious of the facts. So obsessed are they with their meteorological theories that they reject as hoaxes any new articulate formations such as the insectograms. Dowsing tests indicated that the insectograms were genuine, but the smaller ringed circle was most likely hoaxed.

Meanwhile, over in Wiltshire, ignored by the press and by so-called scientists, further bizarre crop formations were starting to occur. On July 30 a huge 115-yard long formation shaped like a giant fish or dolphin appeared near Lockeridge (see plate 38). The tapering fish-shaped body ran into straight pathways at each end leading to the centres of large rings each 60ft diameter. At top and bottom of the fish-body were straight paths at about 45deg looking like fins or flippers. Two days later an almost identical formation was found at Beckhampton. During August six more 'fish' type formations appeared in the area of the Wiltshire Circlemakers. These came in pairs of slightly different design to the preceding pair and caused great puzzlement to cereologists. What on earth were these Circlemakers up to now?

SIX-PETALLED FLOWERS

The Hampshire Circlemakers of 1991 soon tired of insectograms. Their new design, invariably accompanied by the double-eyebrow signature, was a nest of curlicues which appeared at Chilcomb and was known variously as the 'Harp' or the 'Octopus' (plate 11). A further variant, such as the formation between Amesbury and Stonehenge, became known as 'Mr Curlyman', due to its humanoid appearance. In these curving pathways emanated from the centre terminating in closed loops rather than small circles. These can be clearly seen in the photographs (see plate 14).

Totally freed from the formal linearity of the 1990 pictograms this school of Circlemakers soon found a new form of expression. This was the six-petalled flower. The first of these appeared on Chilcomb Down, not too far from the original insectogram (now accompanied by a second one) on August 6th. Its appearance gave rise to yet another strange story of a requested circle.

Six young men associated with U.B.I. circles investigation went, on the preceding night, to sit and watch in an existing circle formation in the Punchbowl. These included Paul Randall and John Martineau, whom I know. They decided to see whether they could produce through meditation a circle of a particular design. Since there were six of them a six-pointed design was envisaged and the Star of David was the agreed objective. They placed a hexagonal crystal in the ground at the centre of the circle where they lay and positioned themselves equally around it lying with their feet inwards.

An uneventful night passed and when it grew light they prepared to depart. It was then that a travelling man they knew came into the field and asked if they

had seen the new circle. He took them to see a six-petalled flower formation which had appeared during the night 500 yards away in the adjoining field (see plate 12). Not the Star of David they had hoped for but something very similar indeed!

How do I know that this story was not contrived *after* the event? I don't, of course, but I believe that I can trust my informants, and the story bears a remarkable relationship to events which are associated with a similar formation found about one week later.

A second six-petalled flower, rather larger than the first and surrounded by double rings, appeared on the other side of the A272 road at the top of the hill. This was in the field where six people sat in an existing circle and heard the mysterious trilling noise on June 18th 1989, as has been described in *The Crop Circle Enigma*. When I visited this circle on August 20th I was immediately struck by the fact that the new circle was placed exactly where the six of us had undergone this extraordinary encounter two years earlier. Could the six petals of the new formation represent the six who had sat there then, just as the six petals of the other flower seemed to represent the six U.B.I. crop-watchers?

Far-fetched to someone unfamiliar with the circles, but this was very striking to any who had been there. Although hoaxers have claimed that they made this formation, like many others, Richard Andrews and Leonie Starr were cropwatching in that very field on the night that this great 'flower' appeared. They saw and heard nothing. Not long after they found the formation at 5.30am, a motorist stopped and came to see the new circle. He said that when passing by at 2am on his way home from Petersfield, he had seen "a dome of light" moving over the field. Intrigued by the possibility that this UFO might have caused a crop circle, he returned to the field soon after it got light. The others had seen nothing, but had heard his car pass at 2am. The new circle dowsed as genuine.

THE ICKLETON MANDELBROT

As the 1991 circle season drew to a close with the onset of harvesting, the Circlemakers had in store for us one final bombshell. This was to demolish my contention that the symbolism of the circles was something only capable of being understood at a subconscious level rather than an intellectual one. They presented us with a formation which was clearly recognisable and one which appealed to scientists in particular. That is, if they were able to accept that this could not possibly be a hoax!

Beth Davis telephoned to tell me of an unusual heart-shaped formation which had been found at Ickleton in Cambridgeshire on August 12th 1991.

The Ickleton Mandelbrot (Cambridge Newspapers Ltd)

Beth accompanied us to the site on August 17th and I saw that the formation was shaped like a large cardioid with a number of smaller circles attached. But the suspicion that my son Rupert and I both had, soon crystallised into certainty as it dawned that this was in fact a Mandelbrot Set (plates 1 to 3).

Although we were only able to confirm this from diagrams on our return home, we had no doubt at the time what this meant and of its enormous significance. Here at last was a clearly recognisable figure and indeed one of the most complex shapes in mathematics. Moreover there was no doubt that this was part of the genuine phenomenon, since it exhibited all those characteristics which we had come to recognise.

There is no possibility that this was a hoax. All the usual characteristics were evident and the complex swirl patterns and the layering of the crop, which was bent but not broken, could be seen. When I was there very few people had visited the formation and it was in mint condition. This was a place where circles had never previously been reported and it represents a truly extraordinary development in the crop circle saga.

If the public or the media had any understanding of this bizarre phenomenon, the appearance of a Mandelbrot set in this Cambridgeshire wheatfield would have been the first item on national TV news. As it was the majority of those who heard about it in the press, and academics in particular, were quite unable to take such a concept on board, and rejected it out of hand as a hoax by ingenious Cambridge maths students. Such conclusions rested solely on their own preconceived notions and owed nothing to any on-the-spot inspection. The magazine *New Scientist* came to an identical conclusion, again without going to inspect the formation, despite acknowledging that it would be quite impossible to draw (or, implicitly, to fake) such a shape without the use of a computer. Such is the typical blinkeredness of your average citizen of today!

For those not acquainted with the Mandelbrot Set,

the following description is taken from the *Scientific American* of August 1985 :-

"The Mandelbrot set broods in silent complexity at the centre of a vast two-dimensional sheet of numbers called the Complex Plane. When a certain operation is repeatedly applied to the numbers, the ones outside the set flee to infinity and the numbers inside remain to drift and dance about. Close to the boundary minutely choreographed wanderings mark the onset of instability. Here is an infinite regress of detail which astonishes us with its variety, its complexity and its strange beauty.

"The set is named after Benoit B. Mandelbrot, a research fellow at the IBM Thomas J. Watson Research Center in Yorktown Heights, N.Y. From his work with geometric forms Mandelbrot has developed the field he calls fractal geometry, the mathematical study of forms having a fractional dimension."

Fractal geometry is used to study Chaos Theory, and also in the study of growth patterns in the natural world. Why the Circlemakers should now deal us a Mandelbrot set is a mystery, but not unexpected in view of what has gone before. This will still not convince the skeptics, whose minds are eternally closed, but it is perhaps symbolic of the chaos in this time of rapid change in human consciousness, and it is also an indication that even within chaos there is a natural order which permeates both the physical world and the world of consciousness.

Undoubtedly we are dealing with an intelligence, or intelligences, of a high order in the Circlemakers. What form this, or these, take we can still only surmise, but that is probably because we are asking the wrong questions. Such an intelligence, or consciousness, could be entirely non-physical and exist within entirely separate dimensions. Its ability to manipulate physical forces within our dimensions is not something too unexpected, but we should not concentrate such importance on the *method* at the expense of understanding the *nature of the intelligence*. Man, too, in his self-centered way tends to anthropomorphise any concept of non-human intelligence, which is why the media and certain scientists can only speak in terms of alien or extra-terrestrial beings. This is a bogus conclusion which is often paraded for the purpose of ridicule and then shot down.

There are many other ways of considering non-human intelligence, and one example is that of the collective human unconscious or, possibly, the planetary consciousness. This sort of intelligence, which may well be an important factor in the crop circle phenomenon, cannot be anthropomorphised as a single entity. One analogy is to think of this as a vast computer network connecting millions of different processors. Display screens attached to such a network are all capable of bringing forth complex graphic images which represent intelligence. But whenever this occurs, do we ask where such images came from or where the data on which they are based actually resides? The question may be answerable but it is not so important as the intelligence which is displayed. Let us concentrate on the *message* rather than the *means* by which it is imparted.

Having said that, there seems little doubt that if we are looking at some aspect of the collective consciousness, which is a tempting conclusion in view of the close connection of the phenomenon with many of those involved, there is a remarkable change going on in that collective consciousness. Although many millions of the potential 'display screens' remain blank, more and more are springing into life. If we recognise that this process is indeed the raising of human consciousness and the coming of a new age, I think that we would be naive in the extreme to deny that the impetus for this change is something that has penetrated from without and that it is most likely something from a very high spiritual level.

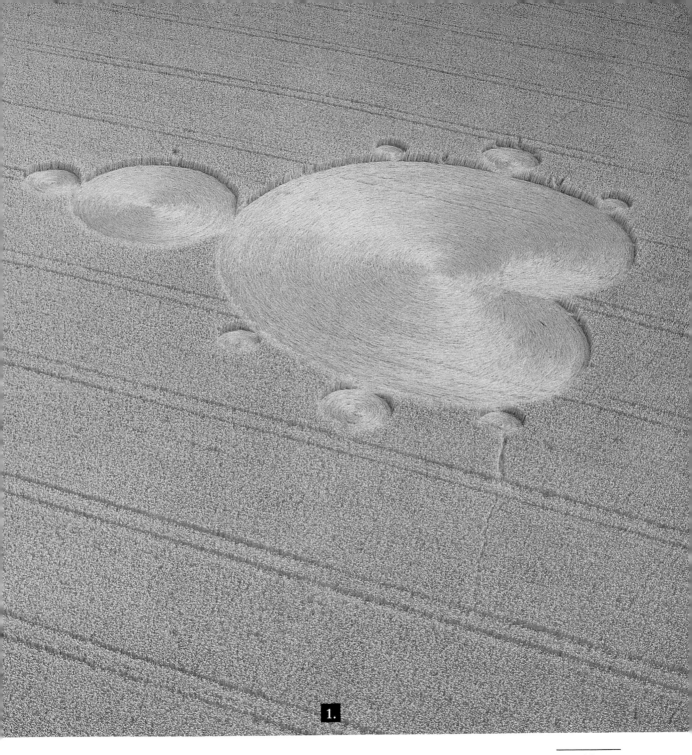

1.

3.

Plate 1. THE MANDELBROT SET, a Mathematical cipher, appeared on 12 August 1991 at Ickleton, 10 miles south of Cambridge (see p.43 for further details). (*David Parker/Science Photo Library*)

Plates 2 & 3. Landscapes at Ickleton, near Cambridge, looking north. (*top: David Parker/Science Photo Library; bottom: George Wingfield*)

Plate 4. BARBURY CASTLE, an Iron Age fort near Swindon, Wilts, stands above the Ridgeway and the remarkable configuration. It is thought an ancient ' white horse' once graced the slope between. (*George Wingfield*).

4.

6.

7.

Plate 5. The BARBURY
CASTLE configuration when
quite new and unspoiled
(see p. 27 for further details).
(*Centre: Calyx Photo Services*)

Plates 6, 7, 8 & 9. Detail of the
centre and the three outlying
circles. Pole shots: (*Busty Taylor*)

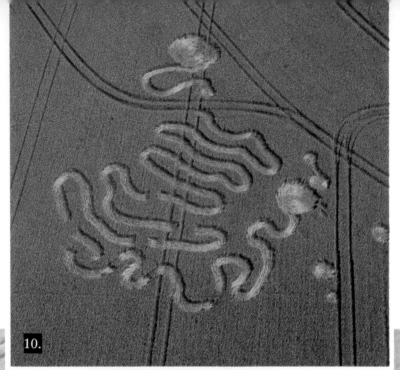

10.

11.

Plate 10. THE SERPENT, Chilton Foliat, Hungerford, mid-August 1991. The only one of its kind. The pathways had strong dowsable energy-counterflows. Notice the discontinuities. (*David Parker/Science Photo Library*)

Plate 11. THE OCTOPUS, Chilcomb, Hants, late July. First instance of pathways which terminate in loops rather than small circles. The 'two eyebrows' signature appears here as it did in the late insectograms in July. (*George Wingfield*)

12.

13.

14.

Plate 12. SIX-PETALLED FLOWER, Chilcomb Down, late July 1991. (*George Wingfield*)

Plate 13. GREAT WISHFORD, Salisbury, mid-July. The discoloration in the crop is due to uneven use of chemical sprays. (*Busty Taylor*)

Plate 14. Mr. CURLYMAN, near Amesbury, not far from Stonehenge, late July. One of the most ingenious designs of 1991, though some are not happy about its authenticity. (*George Wingfield*)

REFERENCES

1. Noyes, Ralph (ed.): *The Crop Circle Enigma*, Gateway 1990.

2. Delgado, Pat & Andrews, Colin: *Circular Evidence*, Bloomsbury 1989.

3. *The Circular* (ed. Bob Kingsley), is published four times a year free to members of the CCCS (see below), but can also be obtained from 58 Kings Road, West End, Woking Surrey GU24 9LW, UK.

4. The Centre for Crop Circle Studies is the principal interdisciplinary and international organisation researching the crop circle phenomenon. It welcomes membership and affiliation; please apply to the CCCS c/o Specialist Knowledge Services, 20 Paul Street, Frome,Som't BA11 1DX, UK.

5. Good, Timothy (ed.): *The U.F.O. Report 1991*, Sidgwick & Jackson 1990.

6. Delgado, Pat & Andrews, Colin: *Latest Evidence*, Bloomsbury 1990.

7. *The Cerealogist* (ed. John Michell), is published three times a year: 11 Powis Gardens, London W11 1JG, UK.

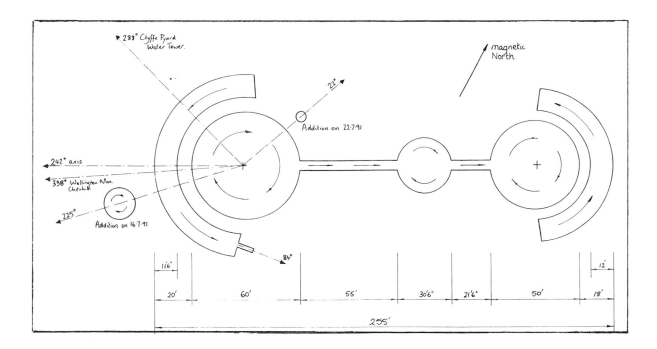

HACKPEN HILL, nr. Marlborough. Formed 12th July 1991, the anniversary of the Alton Barnes double pictogram of 1990. (*J.F. Langrish drawing*)

THE MANDELBROT SET

This is the best known of several mathematical models which are used to describe the way natural things grow. They are part of the science of 'fractals' which is the basis of chaos theory. This helps us to understand better the development of such unpredictables as weather systems, and natural turbulence, wave development, and the growth of plants.

With the development of powerful computers, it is now possible to develop a theory of how natural processes can be described in terms of an unseen or non-physical dimension. For example, by adding a fourth dimension it is possible to describe how alternating electric current works. This is done by applying 'real' numbers and 'imaginary' numbers to a plane according to a given formula, repetitively at speed. Instead of chaos resulting from this process, as one might expect, what results is an area of predictability (the black area on the diagram) and an area of unpredictability outside it. The boundary area just beyond the black shape oscilates continuously producing 'magical' shapes. A colour computer screen will produce here the most beautiful patterns and designs[1], the basic pattern of the Set repeating itself with successive enlargements[2]. The reason I have called it a cipher is that the Mandelbrot Set is a key to chaos theory which is challenging the mechanistic determinism of science. It shows that there is, at heart, (pun intentional!), an order in chaos. Thousands of years ago this was known by the Chinese, who used the same ideogram for 'crisis' as for 'opportunity'.

What could be more synchronistic than, as we were putting this book together for press, the Circle-makers should produce a cipher for the message this book is trying to make — that we are in a dangerous period of breakdown and transition which has within it all manner of opportunities for conscious change, which, if not taken, could lead us into chaos. [*Ed.*]

THE MANDELBROT FORMATION

This beautiful formation near Ickleton, Cambridgeshire, was discovered by a pilot, Mr Cherry-Downes, of Snailwell, Cambridgeshire, who regularly flew over the area on his way to and from work. Mr Cherry-Downes first saw it on the morning of August 12th 1991 — it had not been there the previous evening when he flew home from work.

From the ground, the formation was completely hidden from view, lying on the crest of a north-facing slope above the Icknield Way. A farming neighbour, biologist and agronomist Mrs Wombwell reported: "We know it arrived overnight in a field of wheat 30 inches tall. It would have required floodlights to carry it out. It was incredibly precise. Each circle was perfect, the wheat flattened clockwise, and at the base of the heart-shape, it tapered down to a single stalk of wheat. Every stalk had been flattened one quarter of an inch above the soil. There were no footmarks, and no sign of machinery. It was beautifully done — how, I can't even begin to speculate."

The core of the formation was a rounded heart-shape, with precisely-positioned circles, like jewels, on two sides. Attached to the bottom of the formation were two pendant circles with a third circle beyond, in alignment. Tiny symmetrically-dispersed circles on the perimeter were attached to the heart-shape and the larger circles.

The formation was recognised to be a representation of a Mandelbrot Set. The Ickleton formation is an incomplete template of the design, without 'solar flares'. "Solar flares on the computer-produced designs cannot be eliminated from the formula unless the design is artificially trimmed" was the reaction of Dr David Battison, a computer scientist in Cambridge.

Reactions from Cambridge intellectuals "that it *must* be a hoax because it couldn't be anything else" were offset by some more thoughtful contributions in

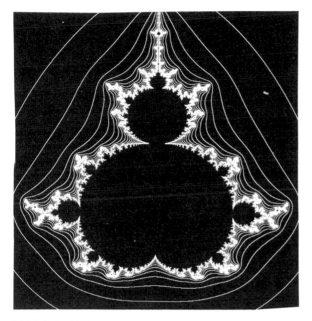

MANDELBROT SET

the local press which considered this to be unlikely, due to the precision and delicacy of the formation.

The structural features of the Mandelbrot formation show all the characteristics familiar to experienced investigators of other crop formations — the swirled floor-pattern with a central node, clear-cut edges to each element of the design, etc. One characteristic which is unique to this feature is the stretching or expanding of each band of laid wheat to accommodate to the asymmetry of the form, with several radii from the centre node. The two pendant circles have anti-clockwise and clockwise floor-patterns. As with other formations, it lies in an area where there are numerous prehistoric barrows and earthworks.

The Mandelbrot formation could be a fusion of two separate paths of human enlightenment: the mystical concept of the spiritual life (the heart, which could be akin to the ancient labyrinth, plus the two pendant circles, suggesting infinity), and the scientific

expression of a numerical paradigm which has infinite potentiality.

The dowsed pattern of the formation showed twelve radii from the node, each of which aligned with a perimeter circle, plus a three-ley negative line along the axis, crossed by a similar but positive line, and also there were 45 concentric rings of energy. Two tumulus sites were identified by dowsing in close proximity to the formation. The powerful Michael Ley line is within two miles to the South.

Beth Davis

REFERENCES
1. A range of the beautiful designs can be purchased on postcards and posters from "Strange Attractions", 204 Kensington Park Road, London W11.
2. See the cover story in "Scientific American", August 1985.

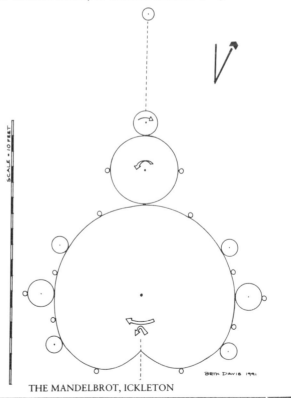

THE MANDELBROT, ICKLETON

2. The age of people

An adventurous assessment of the present and the impending future

PALDEN JENKINS

THE COLLECTIVE UNCONSCIOUS AND ITS POWER TO MANIFEST

A MAJOR KEY to understanding the meaning of current events is the collective unconscious: what humanity is unwittingly thinking, feeling, imaging and believing. Also, in visualising the future, we are dealing not with a simple mechanical extrapolation of events and trends — we are dealing, perhaps more now than in most times, with the Great Unknown. And the Great Unknown speaks in a language of paradox — and paradox building on paradox.

In this sense, there is no major difference between the crop circle phenomenon and overall world events. Both share enigmatic characteristics, where the latest theory has to be perpetually updated or scrapped, and new data comes in hot on the heels of the last lot.

I work on the basis that life and events happen in order for us to *learn*, and are manifested by us — consciously or unconsciously — for the purpose of quickening our evolution. Towards what end is anybody's guess, but it is possible to *feel* when progress is or is not being made. In a paradoxical situation, reality is difficult to identify clearly — and what it has been is no longer a yardstick. For me, *reality is anything which makes a perceptible difference in the lives of people*: history is a strange mix of events, situations, subjective impressions and dispositions, and society regularly has to revise its grasp of things in order to accommodate to new a-rational predicaments. What we *tell* ourselves is happening, or *ought* to be happening, and what *is* happening, are

very different things. The former is the work of the public conscious, while the latter is the work of the unconscious.

A recent example of the public unconscious at work is the 1989 reaction to Salman Rushdie's book *Satanic Verses* — in itself a medium-fair book of no immense consequence, but in its effect, a world-shaking phenomenon. Why such a reaction? Because the book triggered issues already sitting in the unconscious of two dissonant cultures, ready-loaded with charged feeling: Euros and Muslims have roots of enmity stretching back through many chapters. The book was the *event*, while the charged issues, dating back at least to the Crusades in the 1100s (if not earlier) formed the real *energy* behind this chunk of history. Resolution of book-publishing details did not fundamentally heal the deeper charge: rather, it left the issue unresolved, festering there for future use.

The Islamic-Jewish-Christian cultural triangle is a historical minefield — the deepest, most insidious bomb being the prophecy of the Last Judgement, buried neatly under the city of Jerusalem. One of the biggest choices available to humanity is to change this program: do not each of these religions teach how humanity can live in peaceful coexistence? Why has territory become identified with security? Security is a *chosen feeling*.

EVEN IRON CURTAINS CAN FALL

Since 1986, we have moved into something of a different dimension. Deeper issues and unconscious factors have surfaced, announcing themselves in the shape of frequent and intensely-tricky catalytic events. Since 1986 (this is written in May 1991), examples of such events have been Chernobyl, Ethiopian famine, the Stock Market crash, various disasters, *Perestroika* and potential civil disorder in USSR, the fall of the Iron Curtain, Tiananmen Square, the Palestinian *intifada*, Gulf War and Shia and Kurdish rebellions — to omit many.

Underlying shifts during this time have been:

• growing environmental awareness;

• subsiding economic aspirations amongst the affluent;

• realisation of many details of the immense global task ahead;

• European integration and Soviet disintegration;

• the shift of world power from two powers to a patchwork of formative continental and cultural blocs;

• the ending of command-Socialism as a viable system;

• emergence of a new Second World (industrial and oil-producing developing countries);

• the outbreak of contagious nationalism, regionalism and Fourth World (disadvantaged minorities) influence;

• the failure of development aid, and growth of North-South differences;

• rising crisis in the Third World (disaster and disunity);

• and the integration of many ideas and initiatives born in the 1960s, and technologies born in the 1890s.

Many noticeable *non-happenings* have also been around:

• continued oppression of minorities (Tibetans, Uighurs, Timorese, Mayans, Palestinians, Kurds, Islamic women, children everywhere — the list is large;

• dangerous unchangingness in China and India (this might shift soon);

• ongoing use of torture and coercion in many countries;

• the absence of fundamental world economic reform or preparations for it;

• continued environmental degradation (despite campaigns and tinkerings);

• continued avoidance of new technologies and solutions (such as soil remineralisation, sustainable energy-sources, desert afforestation, decentralising technologies and permaculture) and continued propagation of wasteful and toxic technologies (atomic and fossil-fuel power-generation, monoculture, urban expansion, automobiles, etc.);

• the lack of major progress in disarmament or arms-trade de-escalation;

• media and governmental trivialisation and evasion of major issues;

• and much more.

In the 'civilised' (town-dwelling) world, fed by up-to-the-minute media coverage, events are examined, analysed, edited and archived — such that they remain separated, unconnected, uncontextualised. Yet, things have accelerated to a pitch where many people are establishing connections, perhaps uncertain, yet *sensed*. A *sense of history* has crept up. Together with a sense of future appearing like a gaping void ahead as we sail toward a daunting anticipated precipice.

Notice how I moved into using *imagery* in that last sentence: imagery is the language of the unconscious, and it is not just visual, but total, charged up with underlying emotion — of a wholesome and productive, and/or an indulgent and blocking kind. The imagery in the collective unconscious derives from the past experiences (especially traumatic ones) of social groupings, nations and races. But it also contains the dreams and solutions of each land and culture as well.

When the turbanned, scimitar-bearing Islamic Arabs threatened Europe in the 800s, they scared the disorganised Europeans deeply. When the Crusaders entered Jerusalem in 1099, massacring every inhabitant in a five-day holy bloodbath, they set up a shadow which Nasser, Arafat and Saddam Hussein, nine centuries later, found easy to play on — imagery of the unconscious. Yet also, human hope can attach itself to pandas and dolphins, libertarian students in the streets, Mother Theresas and Nelson Mandelas: the power of potent symbolic representation is immense. And different sections of humanity can see the same figure or situation in totally opposite ways — Mikhael Gorbachev and Margaret Thatcher both enjoyed popularity abroad and distrust at home, and their magics worked accordingly (for a time).

THINGS ARE NOT WHAT THEY ONCE SEEMED TO BE

The shift in 1986 was subtle, but also critical. Until that time, it was possible to get away with all sorts of outrages and half-truths, and to believe everything was alright (with a few exceptions): after that time, truth has had a nasty habit of prevailing, even against the best-protected and most unlikely figures and organisations. Up to 1986 the collective psyche had been labouring through a nuclear winter, a dread of evil-empire end-games. After 1986, a new wind started blowing, howling by 1989. It was blowing from the most unexpected quarters — who would have guessed that the Soviet Union was to be the source of world reform initiative?

The two mass-psychological events of 1986 which most symbolised the new time were the Chernobyl melt-down (causing a shiver of fear worldwide), and the worldwide Live Aid concert (which caused tens of millions of people to *think positively* for one day — possibly enough, according to the '100th Monkey' hypothesis, to catalyse a deep tidal swing in the world unconscious).

Chernobyl invoked a rumble of the fear of death (and change), while Live Aid invoked a feeling of hope, a sense that we might have the power to *Feed the World*. This combination of dread *and* hope was lethal to the existing worldview. They were the first clear signs of the *beginning of a process* of inevitable change. Their form was symbolic too, underlining the toxicity of unregulated high-tech progress, and the plight of masses of people beset by man-made adversity. Modern folk were reminded how privileged *and* vulnerable we are.

WAVES IN HISTORY

Deep history doesn't manifest in single events, however: it unfolds over periods of time, in the streets and fields, in the forums and kitchens of the world. Yet, at times, it also intensifies and accelerates, and people are stretched and shaken by a mixture of circumstance and tides of collective feeling. These periods I call *power periods in history*, and the logic of how I identify them is outlined in my book *Living in Time* and a forthcoming book *Cycles of History*. If you cast your mind back to the atmosphere of May-December 1989, you have an example of such a period. They don't happen often. Historically recent *power periods* have been:

- 1792-4, the French Revolution and outbreak of the democratic urge;

- 1818-21, the steam engine, industrial lift-off, and the colonial race;

- 1850-51, extension of industrialism, capitalism and social movements, growth of USA and Russia;

● 1891-1910, a deep historical mega-change (the previous being the 1390s): the final European zenith, global exploration and colonial integration, development of electricity, flight, motor vehicles, plastics, allopathic pharmaceuticals and medicine, socialist parties, atomic physics, psychoanalysis, tinned fruit, telephones and theosophy (amongst many other things!). Plus, a cultural transfer to all parts of the world: everyone came to wear trousers! This was the beginning of the modern global village, and a zenith in industrialism;

● 1932-34, crisis: Depression, Nazism, New Deal, social democracy, Keynesian economics; jazz, cars, films, automation;

● (note that the two world wars did **not** take place during power periods);

● 1945, world peace, reconstruction, United Nations, World Bank, welfare systems, world carve-up, Israel;

● 1965-66, a new awareness, in new conditions (supermarkets, jet travel, satellites, TV), together with new thought-forms later to move into mainstream (feminist, pacifist, green, self-help, dietary, third world liberation, minority and citizens' rights, internationalist and inner-growth movements), plus high-tech advances such as the microchip and genetic engineering, plus new social realities — help-lines, social workers and aid agencies; plus a growing discomfort with the escalating bizarrity of modern life. A new question arose: "is humanity going to survive?".

● 1986-96, with peaks in 1989 and 1993 (about which this chapter is primarily written);

● power periods to come are:
+ 2012-15 (opening test-point of a 140-year cycle beginning in 1965-6);
+ 2039-48 (opening test of a 170-year cycle beginning in 1993, and climax of a 140-year cycle starting in 1965-66);
+ and 2061-65 (opening test-point of the 500-year cycle beginning in the 1890s).

The purpose behind giving these dates is to put the current world evolution into a time-context: an emergency is with us, yet there is time in which to handle it. Since these dates represent the *critical* points of cycles, the periods of buildup and aftermath can expand either way by a decade, if not several — for these periods deal with seeds and longterm evolu-

tionary developments. We are living through one such critical point now, around the year 1993.

ORDER AND STRUCTURE

Let's go back to 1989, which was one of two connected waves in a bigger wave — the other being in 1993. 1989 was a year when the collective unconscious was twanging strongly. A shift of perspective emerged within the collective unconscious, causing some ideas and images to mature, and others to become obsolete. Of maturing ideas *Freedom and Democracy* (the urge for pluralist liberalism and self-determination) formed the core: a growing social readiness edging close to critical mass. A new picture, green and humanitarian in basis, but as yet lacking a full profile and method, was surfacing. 1993 and 2012-15 should also be notable in this evolution.

Marxist-Leninism became obsolete, largely through its incapacity to deliver the goods. This shook the world. Meanwhile, the West, having created a mass of discerning consumers, was forced to begin to rein back unscrupulous business-political practices, to *appear* more caring — though there is far more to come. In 1989, we witnessed simultaneous collapses and arisings of *belief*, sufficiently strong to change social systems — and to turn the spotlight on *all* countries' weaknesses. This will not go away. It was but a beginning.

Everywhere, the slate was suddenly wiped clean of illusions, and nothing solid took its place. Attention fell on social and international structures, since these are the means by which things are changed, and are proving more part of the problem than the solution. A surge of power arose within the collective hearts of people, aware that they had a chance to affect things. The cruxpoint was practical *viability*, and the issues were constitutions, law, the negative effects of vested interests, the ecosystem, its use and products, money, financing and trade, technology itself, health — and for most people, sufficiency. Ecology and economics began to fuse together. All were practical issues, demanding widespread, thorough, global reform, for practical reasons.

The dramatic growth in the number and complexity of crop circles at this time was not at all out of phase with this: tangible, measurable things which posed more mysteries than answers! Synchronous events and trends, even if logically unconnected, cannot be separated from one another.

THE EXPANSION OF EVERYBODY'S OWN BACKYARD

The wonderful thing about the human psyche is that it's wiser than it knows. The busy intents and thoughts of our thinking minds are one thing, and the deep longterm tides of human destiny are another. While humans have been striving to conquer their environment and each other, the deeper collective heart has been unconsciously dreaming a *'one earth, one human family'* potentiality, which has been weaving its web of preconditions behind the stage-show of history. Hmmm, that's a bit far-fetched . . . or perhaps not.

The funny thing is that we're having to *trick* ourselves into meeting our future: that is, in conquering the world, people have created circumstances and adversities (war, pollution, distrust, cancer, poverty, injustices, you name it) which only globally-coordinated effort could end. Not only that, we have tricked ourselves to the extent that there is *no alternative* but to end ancient habitual ills and mal-practices — for the price of failing can be extinction. Very simple. Within our civilisation we have developed both the sources of destruction *and* of salvation — the latter often as a by-product of the former. The nub of the Big Trick is the *global village* — we're all in the same boat! Seers saw this in the 1960s: ordinary thinking people saw it in 1989. It's here.

It fell upon the Machiavellian, alcoholic, nit-ridden, energetic Euros of the Renaissance and after-

wards to colonise the world (although the Chinese and the Arabs were possible contenders) and to transfer their economic and political legacy to all cultures and corners — whether or not it was welcomed. Yet this was not merely the expansionist urge of one race over others — although it had grave symptoms of coercion and devastation. It was the world psyche unconsciously creating the infrastructure for a global village, and production-line industry gave the tools.

Yet we have stepped over a threshold without knowing what the purpose of the next step is — except the somewhat perverse purpose of healing the ills of past. The world is finding out what its purpose *is* by finding out what it is *not*. It has created the conditions for a new world order, but a lot of obstructing obsolete dispositions must first be shed: the social 'dominator model' (rulers and ruled), schism of gender, culture and race, parochialism and xenophobia, environmental and human rights abuse, prejudice and alienation — again, to name but a few. In other words, the habits of millennia need dismantling — not for idealistic, but for practical, survival-oriented reasons.

Here's another thought: have you ever considered that, while we evolved from the lap of mother Nature, we are still in her lap? That is, have you ever thought that Nature is using us as a way of mutating? We are restocking her species, altering her topography, geology and ecosphere, introducing some things, removing others. *Potentially*, we are turning planet earth from a wondrous wilderness into a garden, potentially balanced according to new laws, managed by us. On behalf of nature, which we have changed, and which we are. It might be that we're part of a larger plot to change this whole planet into something other than the heap of plastic-encrusted cinders it looked as if we were creating. Think about it — it doesn't matter if it's true or not. Or does it?

PSYCHIC QUANTA

The 1989-1993 period has qualities of dream-nightmare to it. Time stretching and skidding wildly. Things going awry, the rules of the game changing — and, most unpredictable of all, masses of people expressing it. Yet this slippage of reality is part of a reality-shift: so many people are aware of the need for fundamental change in the world, yet are unable to conceive of how it can be brought about. We're directionless, approaching global gridlock. Resignation is one of our biggest diseases, cancer-producing and cholera-inducing. Such a seized-up situation, such a sense of needed change unlikely or impossible to actually occur, is a characteristic symptom of the imminence of *quantum* change.

In a quantum shift, energy rises to a critical point where it can no longer contain itself: systems become overloaded and fuses blow, until a new circuitry evolves, channelling flows efficiently. Things suddenly become *easier*, even though *more* energy is moving. It's like discovering your car has a fourth gear. The whole world looks different, and previous problems can become subsequent solutions, even to questions no one knew were there.

Mikhael Gorbachev took the world by surprise by changing the rules of the international game, and all nations of the world had to reconfigure to a new constellation, as if he had waved a magic wand. His success in altering the world's thoughts lay in his speaking the message of the time: something which was already close to the surface, to which people simply needed to say 'Yes'. The magic left him by the end of 1989, and he became a normal politician, with bloodied hands. The thought-form, like a virus, had used him as a transmitter. Where did this virus come from? Possibly the same source as crop circles.

What Gorby set in motion was more than he could have imagined: he set up some evolutionary goals and principles (from which backtracking in shock is a natural part of real forward progress), but also he created some allopathic side-effects. One of these was the 'nationalities question', which arose as soon as he lifted off the post-Stalinist pressure. A typical social situation arose: when the focusing influence of oppression is lifted, people, inexperienced in

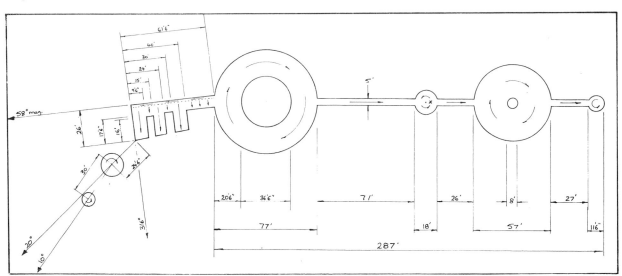

ALTON PRIORS. Formed in wheat, 19 July 1991. The main formation was 349ft long (*J.F.Langrish drawing*).

co-determination, reach out in a hundred directions for solutions, real and imagined, and thereby undermine the very liberation which has occurred. We are likely to see much of this in future, in many countries, as realities flip. Yet, this is a key part in social education: to determine our lives effectively, we must be collectively mature enough to do it — and continue doing it.

stage to deliver to us the consequences of our secret wishes. This is a temporary mass-psychic phenomenon which never lasts: once their message is broadcast, such leaders lose the magic influence quickly — and rarely are trained to recognise this. Saddam Hussein embodied a different archetype, threatening horror: such archetypes exist and have power only as long as we *need* them to be there.

MIRACLES

In this *power period* of the 1990s, we are stepping into globalism — or perhaps, at last, acknowledging that we have already irreversibly done so. We have realised that we are one humanity sharing one small world — and now we're in a kind of shock at the thought. For we are faced with a profusion of interrelated mega-questions, all resulting from erroneous and myopic actions in the past, and we are threatened with chaos, hardship and devastation if we omit to rise to our full potential. What a wonderful situation! It is the sort of stuff which miracles are made of — the necessary precondition for a miracle being an *absolutely impossible situation.*

I'm quite matter-of-fact about miracles. They are, quite simply, breaches in our understanding of things, oiled by faith or depths of despair. Solutions come when we've given up finding them. Most people who choose to read a book like this will have experienced them in their own lives, particularly in crises. But there is nothing mysterious or mystifying about a miracle if witnessing or participating in it brings a change in the way we see things — such that the miracle becomes part of a new normality. Going back to Gorby, his strength was the utter plain *sense* which he was exercising in 1985-9 — it was a miracle-working of the magic of appearances, yet it all seemed so *obvious.* Why hadn't anyone else done it?

I'm harping about Gorby because he is symptomatic of the kind of figures who walk on to centre-

DEMOCRACY

The general recent demise of outright dictators (Franco, Marcos, Pinochet, Ceausescu, Galtieri, Duvalier, Zia and more) and parent-figures (the Gandhis, Mao and Deng, Khomeini, Ronnie and Maggie) is an example of a declining collective need. You might think it's a bit extreme of me to say that people *need* such people as dictators: nevertheless, until people are able to take matters in their hands and deal intelligently with social and political choices, we do need *abusers* to teach us (by aversion-therapy) how to exercise our rights — and duties. Even in the western democracies, where abuse is subtler, vested interests and lobbies pull the major strings.

Freedom and Democracy, so movingly called for in 1989, by so few on behalf of so many, is more difficult to actualise than it looks: it is a generational evolution. Getting rid of an old order is but the first step. The second is establishing a new order. The third is the test of challenges, and the fourth is the test of time. To succeed, a liberal democracy requires sharp and intelligent vigilance and mass study of the issues and alternatives. Without these, democracy is but a whitewashed oligarchy with a pastel eggshell finish.

The hijacking of the new East German democracy by the West German parties and PR machinery in 1990 demonstrated clearly the poor state of democratic health of the West: it results from the cynical complacency of the public, short-term political objectives (usually money and votes), and the loose confederation of business, media, political parties and other vested interests who define the ballgame, and even the score. However, this mercifully is not a watertight hegemony, since no single lobby steers the democratic-capitalist world. Other forces periodically impinge — like people, volcanoes, market fluctuations or ghosts of the past. As Margaret Thatcher once said, "The greatest problem for a prime minister is *events*".

The solution for the world is not specifically *democracy*. It is genuine public participation in decision-making, on local, national and global levels — *especially* when the acts of decision-makers come into question. As Kung Fu-tse (Confucius) said, the people have the final right and obligation to withdraw the 'Mandate of Heaven' from the Emperor. However, each country and culture has its own ways of effecting this — and democracy, as such, is useful only for some.

What is needed is for people at the periphery to be *heard* by people at the centre, and for people at the centre to be visible to people on the periphery — *organisational transparency*. A government is the communication-centre for people, no longer the institutional overlord, and we are likely to see major changes in the basic philosophy and method of governance in the coming century — out of expediency as well as higher principles. For public opinion and popular will are the shaping forces of our time, be it through consumer preferences, migrations of people, issue-campaigns or uprisings.

Nowadays we are treading a fine line between chaos and repression. It is ethically less acceptable to mow down people than it once was — yet, conversely, order needs maintaining if a society is not to degenerate into disintegrity — everyone relies so much on everybody else. Here comes the liberal dilemma: how to create workable consensual reform, keeping its pace fast enough to meet needs and slow enough to be assimilable. The answers for this will be evolved through *force of events*, and both the competence and popular legitimacy of governments and international organisations will be crucial — especially since this is an era of precedents. But even more crucial is the capacity of people in crowds to make intelligent decisions when they vote for, pressurise or unseat governments.

SOVEREIGNTY

The world is rapidly integrating. This is putting nations in a new light. Nations, by force of circumstance, are increasingly having to surrender sovereignty to treaties, international and regional organisations — and to global emergencies which rage, like tsunamis, into people's own backyards. Yet, paradoxically, the growth of large-scale organisations will become top-heavy without a mirroring growth of local communities and nodes of activity.

This is not all. Nations have been cobbled together for diverse reasons, and not all nations reflect a genuine national identity — especially those created by colonial powers. While regional and minority autonomy grows, established borders come into question, since they often divide peoples and regions arbitrarily and ineffectively. In some cases, the very *existence* of borders is the problem — the variegated peoples of the Middle East have frequently lived under one empire (Umayyad, Abbasid and Ottoman), and different groupings occupied neighbouring villages frequently coexisting on the same territory. Then came the Europeans, with their maps and theodolites, drawing lines across the lives of people. It's perhaps up to Europeans to catalyse and guarantee new solutions.

It emerges in our day that *every* social grouping which identifies itself as a nation or people has *some* right to determine its way of living, should it feel the need to do so. A nation can willingly enter the international order only if it has the sovereignty with which to enter it. Coercion and force are not the means by which an international order will thrive and survive: people will no longer accept this. Thus, each region and nation which needs sovereignty (a subjective feeling as much as a state of law) needs to be drawn into the world community by assuming and guaranteeing self-determination — to itself and all others. And disputes must be sorted out internationally, with safeguards for enforcement. A chain is as strong as its weakest link.

This rise of nationalism, particularly in countries where national identity has been suppressed, is surely healthy for the world, for true globalism is a 'trickle-up' process, bestowed, in the end, by *people*, not governments. In the long term, we are likely to see an entirely new world pattern emerging: people will inhabit places not so much because of blood and traditional ties, but because of preference and identification — this process has already started for the growing number of refugees, expatriates, asylum-seekers and world-people of the late 20th Century, be they users of flimsy boats or jumbo-jets. Yet, rootedness to land or kin will then become a *choice*, potentially strengthening indigenous and local cultures within the protection and context of an international community. Regional boundaries will need to adapt to new situations. The Antarctica World Park is the first major challenge.

CULTURAL INTERWEAVING

The decline of great powers in the world has led to a rebalancing — the first sign was the fluxing of OPEC in the 1970s. Oil-producing and industrialising countries (notably the Persian Gulf nations, Japan — Taiwan — Hong Kong — Singapore, and China, India, Brazil, Chile, Argentina, Venezuela and Mexico) have gained an economic and cultural clout which gives them potentially as much influence on the world arena as the industrialised sphere. The world is gradually turning into a new patchwork with no inherent centre or dominant regional culture. Even New York and Geneva, as UN capitals, are beginning to look peripheral. But the global village isn't just a political-economic phenomenon: it is now becoming a cultural issue. Culture is the stuff of people's minds and hearts. The question is, whose culture? Or a new one? Or a pluralist patchwork of cultures?

In the last few centuries, European culture has been imposed or emulated, and is now retreating — or adapting. It is taking time for Third World nations and groupings to mature, held back by combinations of debt, adverse terms of trade, infrastructure-deficiency, mis-applied aid, ill-governance, war and internal division — yet current weakness becomes future strength, for the resolve and creativity of people creates the progress in a rising culture. Yet there are cultures with an identity which has withstood colonialism — Islam and China, particularly — where concepts, practices and moral codes can be more relevant for the future than white-*men*'s ones. Tibetans are demonstrating the resilience of a culture — in the logic of the unconscious, the quiet suffering of Tibetans guarantees that they might well be catalysts of change in both China and the world. While Islam itself seems destined for an internal reform process, it also has a lot to teach the world on law, politics and ethics: the Western world has double-standards which will bring it into increasing trouble in decades to come. Also, which nation has more experience in questions of governance (and mis-government) than China? The most oppressed peoples of the past are likely to be the most exemplary peoples of the future.

Globalisation is happening *anyway*: the focus is on our capacity to keep up with it. The business world has created worldwide linkages, but now the onus lies with people — and especially our capacity to get on with each other. Everything has changed as the world has grown smaller. Our best friends no longer live next door — they're the other side of the world. Which is next door.

MONERGY

When people take certainties for granted, it's a sure sign that the collective unconscious anticipates them to be uncertainties. Arrogantly, as the Berlin Wall fell in 1989, people in the West smugly felt we had won some sort of historical football game: in this was a warning of downfall. For the market-based 'free' world rests on ground as shaky as the Soviet world did — its advantage is simply that it has more flexibility than the command economies had. To a degree.

Nowadays we have vast computer-networked international financial markets, for which no one body is accountable, resting entirely on the confidence of its participants, whose allegiance is primarily to themselves rather than to the markets or the world as a whole, and whose primary objective is to maximise profit. The assumption is that if any change is needed, it will become profitable to bring it about, and unprofitable to avoid it. Unfortunately, this is rarely the case: it pays financial operators and governments to collude in defining what is permissible as a profitable possibility. Meanwhile, institutional investors, ruling the markets, maintain the status quo until such time as they are forced to change.

From a short-term viewpoint, this self-maintaining system makes sense: the sheer scale of debts and economic ties, rooted in *promises* to pay, backed up by guarantees which are frequently unrealisable in cash or usable resources, makes any system-change virtually impossible — a vast settle-up would be necessary, demanding realisation of funds into cash, bills or commodities of *guaranteed* value. Since banks and financial bodies lend far more than they can realise at any time (this *usually* works!), since the markets rely on a backed-up system of zillion-scale trading without up-to-date account-settling, and since the values of guarantees are themselves fluctuating the whole financial system cannot fundamentally change.

Until such a day arrives when confidence in the system is hit on a substrative level. The Gulf War of 1990-1 was brought about over financial market stability: Iraq was temporarily capable of dominating the economies, energy-supplies and currencies of the whole world. Saddam Hussein touched a deep nerve in the international financial system. Unfortunately, the medicine applied was military, and thus solved little.

Many other exposed nerves exist. To name but a few:

• the computerised markets, providing instant market responses, are programmed to parameters based on relatively normal market conditions — what happens when a 'spike' shakes the system, and the cause is not found fast enough to override it manually (as in the 1987 crash)?

• if an earthquake wrecked Tokyo or California, currently-inflated collateral values of property there would crash, and with them guarantees, insurance and confidence — affecting the world;

• debt levels are far higher than sustainable in a crisis, and massive calling-in of debts and settling of contracts within a short time is impossible — be they national, governmental, business or personal debts, or simple unsettled accounts;

• the whole system relies on *confidence*, a subjective and volatile factor, resting its stability in the shared beliefs of investors, institutions and traders;

• market confidence is no longer directly related to real factors such as trade, output, employment or true economic indicators, making the markets resemble a closed system, generating confidence on the strength of its own behaviour, not that of the world at large;

• political factors, such as the unwillingness of governments to lose elections over tough economic measures, or to change ideas, can skew the markets to a precarious degree;

• immediate considerations override longterm ones, leading to an increasing dissociation between the markets and the real world situation.

In other words, we have a sophisticated system which works while rules and conditions of this system hold up. What is called for now is a sustainable system which is responsive to the real needs of people and which reckons in the *whole costs and benefits* of transactions and investments, and assesses profit in social-environmental terms rather than private ones. This sounds like an impossible ideal, but from a survival viewpoint, it is absolutely imperative: thus, force of necessity is likely to precipitate such changes. Money will continue to be used (as long as there is confidence in its value), but the values given to everything must change.

Accounting in terms of *whole costs* and making choices reflecting *real benefits* will immediately slow or stop many common economic activities — bringing a risk of worldwide economic seizure. But it will bring upswings in other activities: preparations and research for a new economy need already to have started. In the developed world we have, for example, developed a sophisticated and expensive medical care system, yet disease has not declined, only changed: thus, we have been expending vast resources on an activity which has not achieved its aims. The resources to be released from ending wasteful practices are immense. The Big Question, simply, is *How fast can we adapt?*

We return again to *force of circumstance* and *crisis*. The wonderful thing about the former is that it concerns reality, and the wonderful thing about the latter is that it throws whole bundles of issues into question, demanding solutions to *all* of them, simultaneously, since they are interrelated. During a crisis, action is necessary, and pandering to lobbies and conflicting interests is suicidally lengthy and compromising: the challenge is to respond rapidly, and to create mega-solutions which appear, at least at the time, to be the best option. And the best strategy, for

now, is to begin *now* with researching the options.

During the 1990s, we are likely to see our world economic system start restructuring *itself*. Many of the ideas which can form the basis for restructuring exist already: they remain hidden to avoid undermining market confidence. Such restructuring is likely to come in waves, where paradoxical, seemingly irresolvable events put the system under stress, to the point where restructuring is unavoidable. 1993 is likely to be critical. This will not affect economic affairs alone, for the consequences reach out in all directions. The crux is likely to be debt problems, insolvency-overload, excessive insurance liabilities, social crisis or excess market volatility, which at some point would lead to a situation of seizure similar to that of 1989 in East Europe:

• a collapse of faith in the system (leading from the past catching up on the present), leading to paralysis in government and finance;

• spontaneous measures being taken by individuals, which demand that regulatory bodies act quickly and fundamentally enough to plug leaks;

• rapid personnel, conceptual, legislative and systems changes;

• dislocations in society and of delivery of goods and services — by what degree depends on many factors;

• problems in dealing with perpetrators of 'economic crimes' — also compensation and organisational questions;

• gradual readjustment of society, capital flows, industrial processes, economic factors, technology and all areas of life — not least public ideas — to the new conditions.

This *can* imply short-term collapse of many economic activities, but it does not *have* to do so: disruption-levels depend on the sense of timing, the skill and clarity of new decision-makers, and on the willingness of people to trust, support and make sacrifices in the short-term. Longterm, many things which we have taken as normal are likely to disappear or change, to minimise waste, adjust consumption and production levels, increase equity and reallocate capital and resources to where they are needed. If anything, the main problem will be to keep up with the sheer breadth and depth of shifting present in all strata of society, and all countries. Paradoxically, armies have a good future in rescue and logistics — they are, after all, trained to achieve their objectives, and there will be operations a-plenty to deal with.

ALLAH AND GAIA

All religions and religious bodies are going through transformation. The secular world also has a moral crisis in front of it. Old historical shadows remain, deeply embedded, bringing friction and schism, even where religion has been overridden by TV-culture. How can there be One God, how is God Great, how is God Love, when a believer looks at the infidel over there as being without God? In the global village, such unneighbourly thinking comes into question.

The Salman Rushdie affair was a manifestation of the Islamic-post-Christian collective psyche purifying itself. How can prejudices become healed unless they are permitted to come to the surface — and if necessary frighten us into movement in whatever is obsolescently fixed? Many are the spiritual crises which will emerge over the next century, as the most fundamental illusions — religious ones — are burnt out, in friction against life-as-experienced. Traditional churches, preservers of the Faith, lose their congregations; evangelists become exposed for manipulative rackets; *Allah Akbar*, invoked in war and threat, fails to serve victory upon believers; Leninism collapses; Buddhist nations lapse into violence — and politicians, high-flyers and TV stars, the lesser gods of the secular world, err and fall with credibility-destroying regularity.

And yet, the Big Frontier of our day is not territorial, neither primarily technological: it concerns the very heart of religion, the very heart of human life. The intensity of world events leads virtually every human alive today, in some way or another, into a crisis of consciousness. A major dissonance grows between life-as-it-presents-itself and our beliefs — even the most modern ones. And, as with dissent in the Soviet bloc before 1989, such deep doubts and conflicts are frequently held privately, until such time as they attain critical mass, to break out as public changes — Catholics using contraceptives, Jews making friends with Palestinians, or Hindus forgiving Muslims.

The frontier is one of *consciousness*, and the catalyst of consciousness is *real live* experience — of which there is plenty to be had nowadays, of a blatantly contradictory and ungentle kind. When raw experience rubs us up, we blame others, or circumstances, as our escape from taking responsibility. But in doing so, our problem is not solved, and the experience becomes even more abrasive — the government might change, but the problem is still basically the same. Sooner or later, a major crisis comes — tragedy, unemployment, marital breakdown, setbacks — in which the blaming turns into questioning and disorientation, even breakdown. Internal struggle ensues, leading to catharsis or exhaustion, then silence, emptiness. Followed by rebirth, a new reality. Even if the situation is unchanged, the *experiencing* of it has shifted radically. This is, at root, a spiritual reorientation, a nuclear fission, a quantum shift. All over the world, such changes are going on in the personal sphere, and now are leaking out into the public domain. People are being forced to form their own conclusions, for the traditional authorities in the definition of Truth are themselves experiencing crisis — and the truest spiritual leaders are those who can show it.

From two directions — from our social-ecological environments and from the collective unconscious — the Big Picture is shifting. Deity takes on many forms, and forms are transforming. The new religion has no doctrine, no church, no priesthood. But it has soul and spirit. In the earthly sphere, the Quest is now Survival, and the Victory to be won is over ourselves, and our fixed conceptions. This is the new frontier. Crop-circles, as but one omen from the heights-depths, form entirely new patterns, new codes for decipherment. And perhaps it is the case that we will decipher them at the time when we have *already* come to understand their message.

Intelligent faith is liberating, for it takes us beyond ourselves and our humdrum daily realities. All of the greatest teachers have exhorted followers to examine their belief in the light of personal experience — doctrinal, unquestioning faith has arisen through insufficient communion with the spirit, inadequate personal examination of the *essence* of the faith. Prejudice arises out of *authoritarian followership* — a psychological, not properly a spiritual issue.

The breakthrough humanity needs to make is on the human level. And the bringers of the breakthrough are those who most feel the pathos of humanity and the instinct of nature . . . women. *And* the woman, the *anima*, within men. Without this feminine influence, no rebalancing. Without this, no future worth embracing. For it needs to be a co-created new world.

The Big Solution is very simple: forgiveness, understanding, compassion. If the Holy Land is truly holy, it will be a place where love and trust in the human family is demonstrated. Yet the simplicity of this transformation is, in the current context, not quite so easy, for we are in the deep-historical habit of avoiding it. We have to be stopped in our tracks, and only two things can do it: awareness, which stops to take stock of the situation *as it is*, or crisis, which comes at us from outside to pin us down, thrashing and cussing, to accept the reality we have created.

CATASTROPHE

There doesn't have to be catastrophe in the world. But the avoidance of it requires a conscious, intentional effort just as strenuous. When wars are declared, nations are mobilised to enormous lengths: without needing to create war, we need such mobilisation. Kalashnikovs and Patriots contain valuable metals and components with better uses.

As revolutionaries have found, people take time to change, but there's nothing better to catalyse change than *force of circumstance*. And there is no better circumstance than crisis. The grating of circumstance with human delusion creates *pain*. As Sakyamuni Buddha once taught, the experience of pain is the beginning of enlightenment. The darkest hour is just before dawn.

The underlying fear pervading the 1990s is: if we accept, embrace and legislate for change, will we unleash forces which are beyond our power to handle? The answer is YES, but such an unleashing will also unleash genius, energy and cooperation. Omission to unleash such forces will bring even greater suffering. This is a risk — a step into the Unknown.

When Death is trying to take us, things become simple — you live, or you die. *Before* a transformative breakthrough, change looks difficult, complex, even impossible. When change is rife, however, it comes easier than expected, and in unexpected ways. It is the *buildup* to change which is most nightmarish, not change itself.

In any change, some people rise and others fall, and dislocations and wrenchings exhaust and irritate people. Mistakes are made, some problems seem irresolvable, others get overwhelmed by bigger ones following, and others simply take a long time. But the difficulties of change are not, in our time, as great as those of stability: we expend vast amounts of energy and happiness maintaining our *status quos*, carrying our burdens of civilised normality. *Status quos* are habitual, while transformation needs courage, heart.

The *status quo* in the world is not working, and things *are* changing. We're *in* it. The only choice we have is to make it easy or difficult for ourselves. If we *facilitate* and *allow* changes before the final need arises, we will find time and energy enough to adapt, to use crisis positively. If the historical default pattern is continued — walking backwards into the future, changing only when forced — the chances of catastrophe grow.

There is a way to deal with this: START NOW. Two major preparatory undertakings are now imperative, over and above meeting immediate issues: a serious assessment of the *means* by which the world can be restructured, and a compiling of an inventory and timetable of world strategy for the coming *century*. Followed by *commitment*, as we do with warfare. The assessment will train the spotlight on international institutions — UN and its agencies, the World Bank, multinational corporations and the world legal system. If these bodies reflect but paradigms of the past, they will not be able to solve the large-scale questions of our time. They will also obstruct the grass-roots solutions which arise from ordinary people in their areas of abode. The strategy will give a starting-place for concerted, overall action.

If there is no inventory and timetable, there is no perspective, and we remain imprisoned in the short-term and the parochial. We do not now know the full extent of the world 'problem', but we certainly can attempt a full assessment, fearlessly. We do not know the extent of possibilities available to us, but we can invest in researching them. We do not know the timetable or order of appearance of major issues, but we can certainly hypothesise a timetable, to clarify our ideas and priorities — even if it must be revised each decade.

The dividing line between catastrophe and transformation is very thin. Yet treading that line is the probable reality of the 2000s. Danger and impossibility is the precondition for miracles. Governments will need to attract the very best people to serve in them,

and to serve in ways which stay urgently close to the pulse of the time. Often, there will not be opportunity for consultation, for much of the work of government will be *competent response to events*. But people must feel they have a say. And grass-roots solutions must be acknowledged and supported, for the revolution needs to move from bottom-up and from top-down. If people do not have a say, they will exercise it in other ways. This is the age of people. Year 2000, there will be 6 billion of us.

The onus lies with *people*. People the world over. You and me and the person over there. Do we meet the intensification of world energy with fear or with willingness? Do we avoid the Big Issues or welcome change? I can answer this only for myself --- and the same goes for everyone else. But if, in a specific knotty circumstance, sufficient of us decide to make a step forward, a tide lifts off, and the contagion spreads. If sufficient decide for doubt and fear, human evolution is blocked.

When something utterly new and incomprehensible presents itself to us, it can be exciting or terrifying — an increasingly common experience for all. Eitherwhichway, preconceptions inevitably turn out to be inaccurate: the Great Unknown eats them for breakfast. Now, a crop circle or pictogram, in relation to the vastness of our world and its problems, is physically like a peanut in Antarctica: yet, on an inner level, it is a paradox of continental proportions. That's why they have come to us — a zen *ko-an* (answerless question) which can be measured and photographed. They — plus our reactions to them — are symptoms of our time.

What I thus propose to you is that, if we looked at world events as a kind of educational game by some power (call it what you will) which seeks for us to evolve through learning, then we might perceive and understand the chaos of world events in a much more useful light. As in the case of crop circles, if we cease trying to effect the quick fix, the mystery grows deeper, and solutions, paradoxically, might be more easily found.

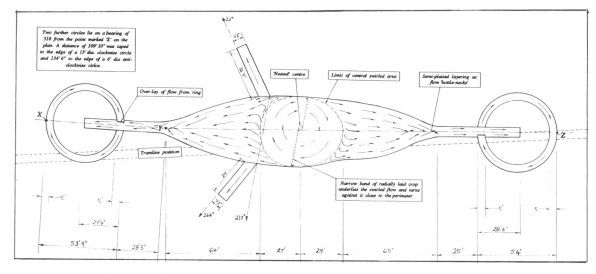

Within the diagram, the following labels appear:

Two further circles lie on a bearing of 318 from the point marked 'X' on the plan. A distance of 109' 10" was taped to the edge of a 13' dia. clockwise circle and 134' 6" to the edge of a 6' dia anti-clockwise circle.

Over-lay of flow from ring

'Nested' centre

Limit of central swirled area

Semi-plaited layering as flow 'bottle-necks'

Tramline position

Narrow band of radially laid crop underlies the swirled flow and turns against it close to the perimeter

LOCKERIDGE, new Avebury. Formed in wheat, 30 July 1991. (*J.F.Langrish drawing*)

Circles and pictograms are a first-class mind-bender: there's no way to feel comfortable with them except by changing our way of thinking, seeing and being. It's the same question as *What to do about China, Khmer Rouge, Sudanese refugees, intractable Afrikaaners, Party apparatchiks, disposable nappies, nuclear waste?*, or *What to do about the people down the road?* or *What to do about myself?* There is no easy solution, yet we can start now in sincerely seeking it out. Yet, as Kung Fu-tse (Confucius) once said: *"The Creative works through the Easy, the Receptive works through the Simple"*.

Resolving the future of the world, and answering the questions crop circles bring up — these are but two fields of enquiry amongst many. Yet they are the same question. And we have perhaps fifty years in which to crack it, before bare survival and tragedy render investigation useless. The writing is clearly on the wall. My own sense of what lies behind the crop circles is that we perhaps do now have to acknowledge that we earth-humans are not alone in the universe, and are not the most advanced beings around — I believe that the taboo, even amongst relatively enlightened thinkers, against ascribing this

phenomenon to an extra-terrestrial source is something we will have to overcome. Not only this, but also we perhaps need to identify that there are several intelligent sources of these pictogrammatic designs, probably working with different motivations. But this remains for us to sort out another day — tomorrow rather than next century! This matter is too urgent for us to sit in our little conceptual holes, deeming that this or that is impossible: the universe is a large and unfathomed place, at which we are peeking through a scarcely-opened door.

There isn't one big, simple Answer for the future. Yet the answer lies inherently within the *heart* of humanity, within our memory — both of the past and of the future. We shall, I believe, uncover it, through wrestling our way through what is to come, and answers will come quicker and easier if we cultivate an attitude of *learning*. Force of circumstance will lead us to the solutions we need to make. But it is *we* who, in our decisions, can turn problems into solutions. We have *no alternative*: this is the beauty of the mess we've got ourselves into! Never before have humans lived through such an enlightening period of history — this is it!

3.   Earth changes, ocean dawns

PETER CEDROWEN TAYLOR

THE EARTH IS SICK. Her fragile and balanced ecosystems are being systematically destroyed by man's activities. The oceans are polluted, the regional seas of Europe and the forests of its continent are dying; the tropical forests, lungs of the planet, are being cut down at a rate that will see them gone by the turn of the century; the waste gases of our industry and households are destabilising the atmosphere, and already the weather patterns are changing, bringing death and destruction by flood, famine and hurricane winds.

In the face of this headlong rush to destruction, a global ecological consciousness has dawned and a new imperative has emerged: we must 'reclaim the Earth', protect Her, replenish Her, and save the planet. For the less poetic, it is a matter of protecting 'the environment' and creating the conditions for 'sustainable development' and 'rational use of the biosphere'. Common to all is the call to live in harmony with Nature's cycles[1]. Nature, when unaffected by Man, is seen as a complex harmonious web of interdependent species, balanced and sustainable communities[2].

This planet is not sick. It is not fragile. It is not called Earth. Seventy percent of its surface is water with an average depth of 4000 metres. In the darkness of the abyssal plains of the sea floor are the planet's only stable communities — species that have changed little in hundreds of millions of years. This planet is called Ocean.

Ocean is dynamic and powerful, ever-changing, ever moving, impossible for man to dominate. She it is who creates wind and rain, she the lungs of the planet, she the cradle of evolution, and her crowning jewels the whale and dolphin. The apotheosis of harmony has been reached, was reached, millions of years before man. Our story is not this.

If Earth is Mother, Ocean is Consciousness. Many claim to know their Mother, to love and cherish her, very few to know themselves, the extent of that consciousness. Yet the Mother cannot be truly known other than through that gate of perception, and all that we now hold to in our deeper ecology is still projection. We see her as sustainer, yet fragile. We would walk lightly upon her, out of reverence, yes, but also from fear of damaging that fragility. We are still in awe of our own seeming powers.

What kind of Mother is this who must fear her children? We are still locked into our Judaic birth, we cling to Mother as unfailing sustainer of the Christ-child. The highest of man needs no wisdom of Her, He bathes directly in the light of his heavenly Father. In the Christian canon He has no need of her once the breast is finished. She becomes onlooker, unquestioning, but knowing the pain to come. She is the pale mother. The dark mother he knows not[3].

This terrible error now leads us to our destruction. This is our story. All creation is looking on. Unseen intelligence draws signals we cannot avoid, as if prompting from the wings to players who are not even conscious of the stage.

THE PALE AND THE DARK

If we flee from the evil in ourselves, we do it at our hazard. All evil is potential vitality in need of transformation. To live without the creative potential of our own destructiveness, is to be a cardboard angel.

Sheldon Kopp

The pale is that which flees the reflection of itself. The dark is to meet. We would flee our own destructiveness. The Judaic legacy is an embrace of Creator and Sustainer, and a flight from Shiva, the Destroyer. Human consciousness, amputated by the psyche's desire for a father's omnipotence, for his recognition of the individual growing boy-child as if that were the end of all creation. In this fatal projection it is the Father who recognises and secures that individual consciousness. The pale mother demurs, the dark mother is lost, and the unbalance begins.

 What is this we flee? We have called her evil, Kali, Hecate, Erishkigel. We have left her destitute as hag and whore, witch and crone. Elements of our psyche held at bay in the light of Church. So also it is with our Earth. If we honour her at all it is as provider, her paler role. We do not honour her darkness. This we call chaos. We ourselves would order her seasons. Coal, oil, gas, uranium: her fossil treasures have become 'resources' to be 'exploited' for our 'development'[4]. We would banish the cold and damp of winter, fertilise the soils, eradicate pests and disease, take the effort from travel. We would become master of these.

Vast numbers of mankind now live huddled in cities[5]. Protected from nature's cycles, surrounded by a tamed and simplified landscape, we have lost conscious connections with how our food is grown, from whence the water comes, and few have any technical knowledge of the environmental costs of our fuel and power. For the price of a cold drink and 'convenience' food we could lose our atmosphere's protective coat, and at the unconscious switch of a light, another drop of acid will fall on our dying forests[6]. Our cars will melt the ice caps and inundate our lowlands[7], our washing machines clog the coastal waters with stinking algae[8], and the residues of our constant chemical wars with nature will poison our children and the most beautiful of our animal icons, the dolphin, the seal, the otter[9].

The 'deep ecologists' among us would strive to change all this. We must think like a mountain[10], sing like a whale, talk to the trees, listen and extend our consciousness. It is all us. To harm nature is to harm ourselves. With realisation will come harmony, with knowledge of the self will come knowledge of nature[11]. Gaia has even been reborn as a science, an hypothesis that Earth is a whole being, all creatures in concert to maintain the optimum conditions for life[12]. This is still only the surface story. The Earth as ecosystem, man as animal, consciousness merely philosophy, ethics and logic[13]. Earth as Earth, not ocean.

Think like the sea and we will know the dynamics of land. This millennium, a mountain, formerly a sea, once a coral reef, eventually sea again. Everything changing. Bed upon bed of former lives, shells of ancestors, broken and calcified. Slow death and quick death, asteroids that emptied oceans, tides that raced across continents, volcanoes that rained dust and acid to bury the land, close out the sun, wipe out whole dynasties of exotic creatures[14]. Acid rain, hothouse Earth, rising waters, dying forests, extinction of form: these are all Her, all us, our darker heritage. This is no fragile Earth.

SCIENCE, TECHNOLOGY AND ORDER

For many this sad rampage of mankind across the Earth is a folly driven by science and technology, as if within the scientific endeavour is to be found some germ of disease. Yet science was not always without reverence, and technology not always so rapaciously directed. There is a deeper malaise of which science is an *effect* not a cause. All human endeavour, science included, is affected by hidden motive and unconscious desire, and it is to these we must look. Indeed, if science and technology are to help us re-create what we have destroyed, then it is imperative that we do understand its hidden agendas.

The myth of objectivity is a cloak with a very high collar that science has readily drawn against doubting onlookers. Scientists view outsiders as plagued with subjective opinion and the swing of emotion. The scientific method supposedly cuts through the contingent realities of ordinary perception and creates that which is universally verifiable — the fact. Many scientists believe that this is what they are doing, that this is science. It is not, and the true scientist, of which there are few, knows this. True science does not deal in facts. It does not know certainty, only hypotheses, which stand until disproven. It is tentative, and the method is generative, an hypothesis only of value to the extent that it generates new insight. True science is not popular.

The public, and more particularly, our representatives, do not like true science. For this reason there are few true scientists, which has always been a precarious occupation[15]. To be true is to be free and that requires a somewhat detached paymaster. They are a rare phenomenon. So we must speak of that which *dresses* as science, which is politics under another name, when the community of scientists would have influence, would become managers, would profess to know how things ought to be, or when less ambitious, would become servants directed by the priorities and perceptions of the polity. It has direct relevance.

It is this 'scientific' community that would now persuade us that the Earth is warming up, when little more than a decade ago, they were agreed it was cooling down[16]. However, the current view is not without dissenters, particularly in the USA, where the political environment militates against acceptance of the majority view and its implications for expensive action.

Another community of scientists will tell us that though the oceans are contaminated by all manner of fall-out and run-off from industry and agriculture, none of the changes we see, the dying seals and disappearance of dolphin, the algal blooms and red tides, can be ascribed a specific cause-and-effect[17].

The problem with science in relation to the environment is twofold. On the one hand scientists cannot avoid being driven by their own interests: they will always have a research agenda that requires more study and there is an expensive infrastructure to maintain. On the other there is a complex environment that does not speedily reveal definitive answers, and indeed, has so much natural variability and change that it may be beyond the limits of science to derive such answers. Who would tell their paymaster the latter and not draw out the programmes of monitoring and analysis? And conversely, perhaps perversely, who would offer definitive answers to a government reluctant to act when there are still uncertainties worthy of further research? The history of modern science is littered with examples of those who held to their truth but lost their grants![18]

This leaves the non-scientists (including the majority of political leaders) in a dilemma as to whom they can trust. Is the Earth warming due to carbon dioxide, and if so what will that bring? Are the forests disappearing, and are they necessary for global survival? Are the seas dying? Is the weather unusual, have we done something to affect it, is it irreversible? In all these questions, the scientist has been elevated to soothsayer, yet in truth cannot answer.

It is not that the true scientist has nothing to say, only that it will not *suffice*. In truth the Earth is too complex for our limited science. If we can detect a trend out of the complexity of constant changes, we can seldom ascribe a cause or make out a quantitative relationship. Of the world's effort in marine science, there is only one continuous 'plankton recorder' that goes back a mere four decades: it has detected major changes in abundance and diversity in the north-east Atlantic, but there is no clear cause, only a correlation with the massively variable and little understood Gulf Stream. Against the complex changing patterns of nature's mysterious forces, there is little chance of detecting the subtler impacts of man's activities.[19]

So it is also with global warming. Only fifteen years ago, the scientific consensus was that the Earth was entering a cooling phase, a periodic phenomenon that brings us ice-ages. These periodicities are not to be understated: ice caps several miles thick, ocean levels dropping by several hundred metres, large expanses of new land, new forests, new weather patterns, deserts expanding (the land appears to have been drier during the cold periods), tropical forests contracting, with many species disappearing and others gaining in abundance. All this within a mere 10,000 years. Science does not yet know what drives this pattern, but it does know that carbon dioxide levels change drastically. There is a complex interplay of plankton masses responding to changes in temperature and ocean currents, which sequester thousands of millions of tonnes of carbonate in the deep ocean, but whether this is cause or effect is not known. There are planetary cycles as yet unexplained, periodicities of the sun and perhaps the galaxy itself.

My own reading of the evidence is that we began, in this century, to leave the warm interglacial weather of the past few thousand years and that an ice age could have been anywhere from 100 to 2000 years ahead. What we have experienced in the 15 years since the 'cooling' consensus, could be evidence that man's activities are warming things up, perhaps staving off the ice-age! Equally, at least one of the models predicted just such a warming interval as a natural interruption of the cooling pattern.[20]

Yet, surely mankind *has* transformed the Earth's surface? Surely this has had drastic ecological effects? We are nearly 5 billion and our impact is everywhere. We have replaced forest with pasture or desert,[21] redirected great rivers,[22] reduced the diversity of life

STOP Acid Rain: In 1984 Greenpeace carried out eight daring climbs in European countries to get this combination of letters. The campaign led to promises of 30% reduction of emissions within Europe. (*Greenpeace*)

by wiping out thousands of species,[23] changed the chemistry of the atmosphere and the coastal seas,[24] and we are set to double our numbers early next century[25]. We have been here a mere 2 million years out of Earth's 4,500 million, among species that mostly evolved to their present forms 30 million years before us, and yet not 10,000 years ago we were hardly noticeable.[26]

Even so, we must beware of the emotive drive of perception. There are those of us who are pierced to the heart by the desecration of a sacred wilderness, the near extinction of the whale, the elephant, the tiger; those who cry for the lost cultures of the red man, bushman and aborigine; and there are those who are grimly awed by the advance of concrete dams and motorways, sprawling cities, squared and ordered fields, whilst on the fringes gather the famined millions, exiled by the market, beset by war and disease. Who amongst us does not have a secret wish that the corrupt and arrogant will fall, that the Earth will exact her revenge, that monstrous progress will overstep itself and nature redress the balance? How many hidden desires exploded at Chernobyl? How many now look to dying seals and beached whales for signs of a dying ocean? Each wind, each frost, each torrent of rain watched, recorded vaguely, who cares for statistics? Did we not tell you this would happen? How many of us have a subsurface death-wish borne of a collective guilt and a desire for the humbling to begin?

We must beware our hidden motives and perceptions. Yes, the Amazonian forests, though still vast, are endangered when forest loss may approach 5% per annum in the worst areas, but the Congo losses run at 0.2% per year. Of 15% total forest loss since agriculture developed, only 3% has been tropical — the rest the denuding of huge areas in the USA, Central Europe and the Soviet Union, areas which nevertheless still maintain roughly 30% forest cover. Approximately 40% of the global land surface is still wilderness, even excluding Antarctica.

The soils of temperate regions may be as important in the carbon cycle as the forests. We have degraded vast areas, oxidising the organic content and releasing carbon dioxide. In terms of global carbon budgets, there is three times as much carbon in soils as in trees — so what we in the rich North do to our soils is as important as what others in the poor South do to their forests. Of the 5 gigatonnes (thousand million) of carbon we release from fossil sources (which will be exhausted in 150 years at that rate), the ocean absorbs 2 to add to its 38,000 and the atmosphere adds 3 to the 730 it already holds. We do not yet understand the dynamics, the flux from one compartment of the planet's ecosystem to the other. Our monitoring covers less than 100 years directly, yet via other indicators such as ice-cores and the shells of marine organisms, we know that at different times there have been great changes in these levels and fluxes. We do not know how this complex system will behave as we make our inputs — it could suddenly switch into accumulator mode with changes in ocean currents and down-welling, or it could begin to breathe it all back out, thus accelerating the warming process.

The increased heat could paradoxically lead to more snow cover at the poles (with lower water levels and drier land) if that heat drives more water from the equatorial regions to fall as snow at higher latitudes (a minority view among the modellers); or it could melt the ice caps and flood the lowlands. For all we know the carbon dioxide may compensate for a global cooling originating in the sun cycle and be protecting us from an ice age. Even the sulphur that causes acid rain may act as a moderator by seeding clouds and controlling the build up of heat!

If Gaia were our conscious Mother, as some experience Her, could she not use our ignorance as a self-regulating part of the system? Heretical as this would be to many 'deep' ecologists, if she cared about humankind, she might be thus motivated to protect it from the turmoil and competitive strife that it would fall into if the Earth cooled rapidly. Perhaps we are not ready for another ice-age? Such perceptions would make the identification of enemies rather difficult, and much of modern environmentalism is as demanding of enemies as the system it criticises.

It does not much matter where the perception falls. When the seals were dying, we focused upon the possible man-made causes, but there are natural epidemics too. Who knows or cares about the dying crayfish of Europe, also struck by epidemic? The elm disappeared, hit by a fungus, carried by a beetle. Monkeys have horrific AIDS-like diseases, cats can develop leukaemia, and virtually no living organism from bacteria to giant redwood is free from viral attack.

So we must take care in looking for signs. Science may not help us because it cannot be immune from the desire to see certain things or not to see them. We tend to see what we *want* to see, to find that which we look for[27]. If we are to find a true relationship to nature we must first know what we desire from it and the limitations of our perceptions. At present there is too much projection for us to see clearly.

I will put to you that paramount in our desire is the need for *order*. Our minds are too afraid of disorder. Disorder speaks of uncertainty, of decay and death. Our 'objective' science has arisen out of this desire to know that the universe itself is ordered and subject to predictable laws. In such a universe we can protect ourselves. As we unravel these laws, we can re-order the universe, at least that part immediately available. Technology is the manipulation of the natural laws and cycles of life to our advantage. Science has become the servant of technology.

Here is where we would have order: in our bodies through medicine, we would strike out invaders such as bacteria, fungus and virus, and the renegades of cancer and leukaemia; in birth we would eradicate death, for all must be born and all must live and nothing be left to chance; in food we must have a plentiful and constant supply; in shelter there must be no season, constant warmth; in travel no hardship, no uncertainty, minimal risk; with enemies, at least a semblance of control, a stand-off, a balance of powers; above all, the economy must be predictable, but growing, for things must get *better* and there is safety in growth. If there is no shortage, there is no conflict. Most of science and technology serves these imperatives.

At some deep level we know nature as the enemy of this. If our order did not prevail would she not take our children, render our own life short and brutal, our harvests insecure, our shelter inadequate? Romantics speak of her harmony,[28] but do they sing of her parasites and plagues, of when the rain does not come, when her fires rage, her surface heaves and the sun is darkened? Who welcomes her other face, who embraces her dark side?

No, we would have order. Our technology is the flight from disorder. Our prayers are to that guarantor of order, the Father in Heaven, the constant Light and Spirit, the God that will create a lasting cosmic rest for each struggling personality that has blossomed, forever petalled. Or more furtively, God as the Great Architect, protractor of the Universe, beloved of bankers, generals, and their merchants.[29] Everything that is disorder must be subjugated. Where it threatens to regain consciousness, it must be labelled *evil* and expurgated.

Which brings us to the wisdom of women. Of the estimated nine million 'witches' who perished before the 'light of reason' could dawn, there is little trace. What cultural 'disorder' was so rigorously expunged? The knowledge of herbs and spells, of how to ride with the devil? Was this so threatening? Or did they represent a communion with nature, with that which was not of an ordered consciousness? Did a part of woman die with them, now only fearfully regained and lived in exile from the world of men and half-women? Was there a way through them to the dark and beyond to the fearful limits of ordinary reality?

Dying Forests: spruce trees damaged by acid rain in the Karkonoski National Park, South-West Poland. (*Simon Fraser/Science Photo Library*)

CONSCIOUSNESS, ORDER AND THE CHANGES OF NATURE

In the Hindu pantheon, Shiva, Lord of the Dance, must die to Kali, the Dark Goddess. She dances on his supine form. However, it is a *conscious* surrender: to resist is to die by the sword. What is surrendered is the directed consciousness of the ego, the mind in control. What is surrendered to is the wild and the dark cosmic Mother-of-All.[30] The aspirant must learn that nature in her terrible aspect will claim all lives eventually, that individual consciousness, however one strives to defend its minutes of existence, will be taken away.[31] In life, however, exists the potential for *conscious surrender*. A death, but of the ego. This too is not without terror. It is a warrior's path. Beyond that gate the conscious mind has no power of direction, no certainty of return and the world is not what it seems.

In the early time of our western civilisation there were similar teaching myths. In Sumer, Innana, the goddess of the sun, descends to the underworld to meet her dark sister, Ereshkigel. She dies to be reborn. Hers is a conscious decision to undertake the perilous journey. By the time of the Greeks, Persephone, daughter of Earth's fruitfulness, meets the dark side not by conscious undertaking, but by abduction to the underworld by Pluto. He offers her marriage, but she will have none of him. In her absence, her mother mourns and the upper world becomes barren. The world of fruitfulness is saved only when Persephone finally relents and partakes of Pluto's fruit. The Gods of Justice grant Pluto his desire — Persephone must return to the underworld as his bride for half the year. Thus are begotten the seasons of death and decay.[32]

It is as if we need constantly to be taught: we long for summer to be forever, to banish winter, for we cannot love both life and death. Yet nature is this cycle of birth, of growth, of decay and death. She is constant rebirth. The western mind has sought to break this cycle at the level of the conscious individ-

ual, to perpetuate life at all costs and to hold faith to an after-life as a denial of death. The individual shall live on in another world, a heavenly haven of unblemished egos, non-material, non-matter, non-mater . . . the unlife.

In masonic teaching, the myth of Pluto is not of an abduction, but of a seduction, and the acolyte is warned not to be so enticed. But the Lord of Rebirth is not so easily held at bay. As with the individual psyche, that which is suppressed, resurfaces as outer reality. The unconscious mind is creative of circumstance. Thus it has been that at the culmination of modern science's hunt for the ultimate control of nature, the splitting of the uranium atom and the harnessing of nuclear power, the forces of disorder have made their presence known. As gods they begin to tease us, as we indeed have mocked them.

The radioactive mineral was named after Oeranus, Father Heaven of the Greeks, because it could colour glass a celestial blue. In the reactor, its 'decay daughter' neptunium gives birth to plutonium. This the stuff of deluded dreams: everlasting fuel and awesome weapons for the defence of freedom. The God that was spurned by the isolated psyches of our 'absent' fathers, now tips their missiles and threatens a double-edged reality of control or total destruction. In the astrological mandala, Pluto in transit is held to signify 'the great awakener'. Either the ego awakens and surrenders to the reality of one-ness, or it is destroyed.[33]

We have fled the darkness, but the darkness returns. We have mocked the gods of yesterday: Gaia has become a hypothesis and Chaos a theory; Oeranus a mineral and Pluto a reactor; Hades a missile, Poseidon a submarine.[34] In the dissolution of old power blocs, nuclear weapons begin to lose their lustre. The forces of disorder are no longer controllable by 'superpower' posturing.

Science too, begins to lose its hold on reality. Whilst the technologists were eagerly transforming new knowledge into temporal power, the true scientists were left to explore further nature's secret larders. Beyond Uranium's thin veil of reality lies, however, dissolution. The world breaks up into myriads of particles, forces of attraction and repulsion, uncertain realities that involve the observer in the observed, a move to one-ness and unification (in theory if not in consciousness).[35] As might be expected, the usefulness of this endeavour is now in question! The first redundancies have been served.[36]

In this awakening new science we have perceived the limits of order, but we have called that which is beyond, Chaos. This poetical misnomer must be corrected if we are to go further. What we have perceived is the extent of order and its frontier with dis-order. That frontier is simply the limits of our prediction. In nature there is no disorder, but there *is* Chaos. They are not the same. Only the human mind creates the duality of order and disorder. In nature there is simply *what is*. Chaos is what is not. It is the void. In Chaos is perfect peace and stillness. It is the non-material. Dark matter, anti-matter, before matter, cosmic mother-of-all, she who gives birth to the universe. She cannot be observed or measured, because by definition she is not that. Only her children can be seen, as they are born, galaxies upon galaxies. From her is born the light of the Father and the substance of the Mother, all vibration, all one, the cosmic dance, Shiva and Shakti. The mystic mind may reach her but not return. She is beyond individual consciousness. She is the warrior's home.

And we are not a warrior race. Our future mystic King we would mock. In this age all that matters is the defence of the Economy and the freedom of the Market. The New World Order is not new. It was predicted long ago as the time of the Beast. That which would be worshipped in every land. The beast *is* the material Economy. Its number is 666, without which you shall not trade.[37] The battle of Armageddon is not of angels and demons, but the duality of good and evil in the mind of man. It is not a place, but a time.

THE CIRCLES TELL OF THE END OF TIME

Who can talk of this? Mystics warn that it is close. Babaji[38] and Barry Long[39], medicine men, psychics and yogis. The world as we know it is coming to an end. The Hopi have prophesied of signs: when the Eagle builds his nest in the sky; when the Eagle lands on the moon; when the sacred sites are raided for minerals which the Earth should keep for her balance and man has not the wisdom to use; when they will create of it a gourd of ashes that will bring fire from the sky.[40]

In Revelations, a fallen star burns for days raining bitter poison on the land and is called Wormwood. In ancient Greece the symbol for 'uranium' was a star, and some have held that Chernobyl is synonymous in Russian with the bitter herb, wormwood.

Astrologically, the Piscean age is almost over. The sacrifice was made under the sign of the fish, the surrender of the material body to higher consciousness: but we played out the lower octave, the deluded dream of material reality with the Cross a symbol on marching shields. We failed to enter consciously into that surrender. The great teachers came to show us that beyond lay infinite love, but we could not trust. Now the time is over. A new age beckons, slowly.

We would play this one basely too. The Aquarians have already been at hand: Hitler, Stalin, Pol Pot, Mao Tse Tung, Saddam Hussein. The new social order and its fear of individual creativity. We are not ready for the freedom that Aquarius can offer. Pluto now orbits inside Neptune: the hidden and repressed emotion will out. We are half way through a great cleansing process, for the new and golden age cannot dawn in the thickness of present consciousness.

Gaia, who is not a hypothesis, but a living mother, knows this. She has been waiting, but we have sought only the father's recognition, and for the majority who received no sign, there has been but time and havoc. This was the testing. Love was ever-present and if chosen would have redeemed. As children we have not learned. Now the time of distant mothering is over.

GAIA AND THE REBIRTH OF CONSCIOUSNESS

We have feared and run from the Dark Mother. We have failed to learn that death is a cleansing process. In nature every death benefits the whole: old and worn-out form is destroyed, minerals recycled, carbon released. Cohorts of microbial life lead the process. When death takes the young, it takes the infirm; when it takes adults, the sick go first. In this way the vitality of populations is maintained. Human populations have, for a short time, cheated the 'grim reaper': infant mortality has been drastically lowered, life expectancy has risen, but the consequences are now apparent. Populations have become unbalanced: in the South there are more young people than normal, and they in turn will have children; in the North, the imbalance is with the old who must be maintained by the productive young. In the North the economies will be strained, in the South the ecology is breaking. In both eventually, starvation and disease will redress the balance.

So it is also with consciousness. Death is the opposite, not of life, but of birth. The personality is dissolved, its acts and ideas left to be woven on the loom of culture. The individual soul returns to its source, to merge once more with the one great soul. Were this to be faced, would not the individual ego more readily devote itself to that which had permanence — that which is human, the spirit of man and woman, an evolving love? Individual creativity would still flower, but as with all blossom, it would serve the seed.

To live a culture where death is not feared, where it is welcomed as the sharp edge of life, where suffering is seen to strengthen spirit and elicit compassion, would this not be to live with nature as friend and teacher? In life the treasure would lie in poetry, art, craft, in the love of physical union, and in the exploration into the divine. The warriors' path would be everywhere, in the humility and love of everyday tasks as much as the ascetic and mystic seeking of cosmic realities.

Certainly in past cultures there were times of ignorance where the gods and goddesses of nature were feared and propitiated in ritual and sacrifice. The warriors' path is that of at-one-ment, where there can be no fear. This is not the end of ritual. The great teacher of yogis, the mahavatar Babaji, rose before dawn and with ritual bathing, singing and fire ceremony devoted every day of his brief sojourn in the physical body to the Great Mother of All. Each culture has had its celebrations in love of the divine mystery and has sought through dance, music and invocation to consummate that love.

This much we have lost. This was the life of the red man, the aborigine, the yogi, the sufi, and indeed, the early Christians. A human being seeking to balance the forces of light and darkness within, the deeper masculine and feminine, *yin* and *yang*, will have no need to dominate nature.

How far we are from this spiritual life! The teeming millions on every continent have not the will and wisdom to turn of their own accord. Even those who *know* must still struggle to maintain their focus. In this age it does not come easily. We need help. Without help the future will unfold in a steady deterioration of the ecological support-systems upon which human life now depends. The spirit will grow weaker and human consciousness will be dominated by even stronger material concerns. The rich and safe will stand by as millions perish. Or where they do act, it will be out of consideration for 'international order' and their own safety.

The mother weeps, but not for death, nor pain and suffering. She *is* that. With that she tests our love, hones our spirit. No, she weeps because we are lost to Her, to Life and to Love.

Those who are still sensitive, those who 'have ears to hear', know of Her weeping. They hear the cry of the Earth Mother for they are still close to Her,

The Maha-avatar Babaji conducting the Vedic fire ceremony or *Yagra* dedicated to the Divine Feminine Principle, Mother of the Universe, *Jagat Ambe*. 1971. (*Haidakhandi Amaj*)

uninsulated, at one with her cycles. Divine intelligence speaks directly through channels still open, through the allies and mediators of crystal or plant kingdoms and totem animals. In the western world only the true poets hear the Earth.[41] Thus it is that we need such powerful signs, symbols the mind cannot *understand*, but cannot fail to *see* and to be stunned into a new listening.

When the masters, prophets and sensitives foretell of a great cataclysm that approaches, they tell of a great cleansing. The upheaval of the Earth that will destroy the great majority of peoples. The forces unleashed will not be physical alone.[42] There will be waves of earthquake, flood and fire, and an energy that will cleanse the minds of those who remain. There will be left a great humility and awe, and a great love. Human consciousness will be cleansed in rebirth and the dark mother will have done her work. Of this the circles speak.

REFERENCES
1. Even Margaret Thatcher, during the last years of her term of office, entreated the world to "respect the cycles of nature".

2. Economists and ecologists are currently engaged in developing conceptual frameworks which might mimic natural ecosystems, especially with regard to materials-use and waste. At a recent seminar, Robert Costanza, editor of the journal *Ecological Economics*, outlined the process of learning from 'stable, sustainable, ecological systems' which he presumes, rather uncritically, are the natural state of affairs.

3. There are those who believe that Mary and a number of other women around Jesus were rather more active than the early Church wished to acknowledge, that they were possessed of a high level of esoteric training, and that additionally the Magdalen, far from being a 'reformed prostitute' was an adept or temple priestess, a partner with Jesus in the exploration of sexual union and higher states of consciousness.

4. Within the current paradigm, to *conserve* a resource has come to mean 'rational exploitation' for 'sustainable economic development'. Virtually all ecological science and international politics is directed towards this goal, to be formulated at the UN Conference on Environment and Development in Brasilia, 1992. Any other paradigm is regarded as irrational, yet current depletion-rates of key resources will not sustain modern economies beyond the next

30 years for oil and natural gas, and 150 years for coal and most metals (UN Environment Program, Environmental Data Report, 1991).

5. Nearly three-quarters of all people in the developed world live in urban areas — an increase of 10% since 1960, and in developing countries a similar 10% rise in that period brought one in three to the cities — by 2000 that is expected to be one in every two.

6. The chemical, CFC, has been widely used as a coolant in household refrigerators (as well as in industry) and its present and future uncontrolled release is a key factor in the 'stripping' of ozone from the higher reaches of the atmosphere. The consequences of this loss could be catastrophic, not only in increased diseases (such as skin cancers), but more fundamentally in the balance of plant life — particularly in the surface waters of the ocean, upon which the whole planet depends for climate-regulation. With regard to fuel use, as fossil fuel is burned, it produces acids which travel great distances with cloud and rain, gradually acidifying sensitive soils, and not just killing trees, but also depleting lakes and upland streams of insects, fish and birds. Large areas of north and central Europe, North America and China are affected.

7. Transport use accounts for one quarter of oil consumption and hence contributes to the 'greenhouse' effect through exhaust gases. In the decade 1977-87, 21 countries experienced more than a 50% increase in vehicle ownership. The world total is now over 500 million vehicles, and is growing at an average annual 5%, faster than population, and if maintained, this vehicle population will double by 2030. As the globe warms up, the sea-levels will rise and flood many lowland areas, where much of the world's population lives. The twelve most industrialised countries account for 70% of the greenhouse effect.

8. Most non-ecological washing powders use phosphates, which in conjunction with nitrates and more phosphates from agricultural fertiliser, runs into the sea via rivers. These act as nutrients, and coastal waters are experiencing 'algal blooms', the excessive growth of small phytoplankton, which then rapidly die and decay, depleting the water of oxygen and making other areas unfit for other sea life.

9. Residues of persistent chemicals from pesticides and synthetic industrial liquids such as PCBs are now found in virtually all living organisms from the Arctic to the Antarctic. The effect of these contaminants is the subject of much scientific controversy, but the data is now showing subtle effects at low doses — in particular the suppression of the immune system in mammals, making them more susceptible to disease and stress, and impairing reproduction due to hormonal imbalances and damage to ovaries. Hundreds of thousands of tons of PCBs still exist in electrical equipment worldwide, much of it too small to account for and collect (eg. fluorescent lighting tubes) and some authorities hold that if all this goes to landfill it will eventually leach through rivers to the sea, and we could see the extinction of all marine mammals.

10. See in particular John Seed's *Thinking Like a Mountain*, Heretic Books, London.

11. Arne Naess's *Ecology, Community and Lifestyle*, Cambridge Univ Press, contains the original philosophical framework taken up as deep ecology.

12. James Lovelock, *Gaia: a New Look at Life on Earth*

13. Although it is evident from later work of the 'deep ecologists' that the expansion of consciousness becomes less of a philosophical or ethical quest, more a ritualised extension of self in drama and psychotherapy — see Naess's chapter in *Thinking Like a Mountain*, and Joanna Macy's *Council of All Beings* in the same book. Seed also works with powerful yogic breathing techniques ('rebirthing') to transcend ordinary conscious reality.

14. For most of this century science has frowned on *catastrophism*, and favoured the doctrines of *uniformity* in interpreting fossil records. However, the last decade has seen a shift toward acceptance that periods of mountain-building and vulcanism, and the periodic impact of asteroids or large meteorites, may have contributed to mass extinction over quite short timescales — including the disappearance of the dinosaurs. During such periods, violent temperature fluctuations, acidification of rainfall, tidal waves and disturbances of atmospheric chemistry would have had catastrophic effects upon land and sea surface life-forms.

15. A glance through the biographies of many of the 'true' scientists — those who extended the frontiers of knowledge, such as Galileo, Einstein, Tesla, Mendeleyev, Reich and Schauberger — will reveal a history of opposition from other scientists, as well as political suppression, repression, harassment, exile and ridicule. In more recent times such opposition could be fierce and effective — read David Boadella's *Biography of Wilhelm Reich* and Alexandersson's study of Schauberger, *Living Water*.

16. In 1974 the science journalist John Gribben visited all of the major centres for climatological and geophysical research in North America and Europe. His conclusions were published in *Forecasts, Famines and Freezes* (Wildwood, 1976), where he presented the consensus view that the Earth was about to enter a new glacial cooling phase.

17. One of the most respected scientists in the field stated in 1989: *Although there appears to be no firm correlative evidence linking residue concentrations in marine mammals with reproductive effects, there is enough concern about possible links to justify more experimental studies* (Addison, Canadian Journal of Fisheries & Aquatic Science); whereas a UN review group (ICES/IOC Review of Contaminants in Marine Mammals) concluded in 1988:

> The DDT family and the PCBs, or possibly some of their breakdown products or impurities, are known to cause reproductive failure, disrupt the metabolism of steroid hormones, and affect the immune system of many vertebrate species. There is now convincing evidence, although much of it is circumstantial, that they have similar effects on marine mammals, particularly seals.

Note that in the latter, the review group are willing to accept circumstantial evidence as 'convincing', a quite unusual step for a scientific committee. The problem is, that faced with enormously complicated interactions, ecological science and toxicology are unlikely ever to be able to deliver quantifiable cause-and-effect statements.

18. In my own personal experience, a colleague working in marine science at the University of California had his grant cut and his laboratory closed following his vigorous and rather successful interventions against the policy of radioactive waste dumping at sea. On the other hand, a rather remarkable exception to this general rule occurred when the British government so firmly backed the analysis of Farmer, regarding the ozone hole over the Antarctic — which was later to have economic implications for British (and world) producers of CFC chemicals. (See page 160)

19. Such data collection is essential to an understanding of natural variations of climate, ocean currents and the abundance of different life-forms, yet recently the British government came close to cutting the funding for this — the world's only continuous recording effort. The same fate nearly befell Farmer's work in Antarctica.

20. See Gribben, op.cit. p97.

21. Estimates made in 1983 of change since pre-agricultural times put total forest loss at only 15%, 3% of which had been in tropical rain forest. The total reduction of tropical rain forest was 48 million hectares (Mha), from 1277 Mha to 1229. (Britain has an area of 22 Mha). 700 Mha of temperate forest was lost. Current forested cover of the globe is approximately 4000 Mha, with 2050 Mha in temperate and boreal zones, 1750 in tropical-moist and 300 in tropical-arid regions. 42% of the tropical zone is still forest, and about 30% of the temperate and boreal zone. Forest loss in the tropics runs at about 10 Mha/annum (thus, the 1983 estimate might be updated by an additional 80 Mha, or 4% of tropical forests), whereas in temperate and boreal regions forest cover is increasing slightly (1.6 Mha 1950-77 in Europe, 10 Mha in Scandinavia and 70 Mha in USSR since 1960). Rates of clearance in the tropics vary from 2-4% per annum in the worst places (the Amazon, Indonesia, SE Asia, NE Africa) to 0.2% in the Congo.

22. In the USSR, for example, redirected water for irrigation has caused massive contraction of the Aral Sea, as well as salinification of soils over a wide area. Worldwide, groundwater use in industrial and tourist development regions threatens to deplete deep 'fossil' water, which will not replace itself, as well as to lower water-tables and bring stress to soils, forests and crops.

23. Current estimates are that the planet is losing species at a rate of several thousands per year, with perhaps one quarter of known species being lost by the turn of the century. In advanced conservation-minded states such as Germany, about 30% of mammal and bird species, 10% of reptiles, 20% of amphibians and 25% of fish are threatened and declining. In the USA, the percentage of threatened and declining species is around 5%. In tropical countries data is difficult to collect, but varies between 10% and 15% of mammals and birds. Over 20% of all species live in Latin American forests *outside* the Amazon, and another 25% in forests in Africa and Asia, outside the Zaire basin. All of these forests may disappear within 25 years at current rates of clearance. In the next century, if present trends continue, one third of all species could be lost (World Resources Institute, 1986 report).

24. The composition of the atmosphere has varied minutely over the past 160,000 years, and these slight changes correspond with major changes of climate — they may be the cause, they may be the effect! Carbon dioxide levels are now at their highest for nearly 200,000 years. In the last great ice age they fell to 200 ppm, and the warm interglacial period of 130,000 years ago was accompanied by levels just under 300 ppm. We now stand at 351 ppm, with an increase each year of 1.4 ppm, or 0.4%. It is estimated that of the 500,000 million tonnes of carbon that fossil-fuel burning releases, half is absorbed somewhere by the global ecosystem, and the rest is driving the atmospheric buildup. However, other gases (methane, nitrous oxide and CFCs) from human activities ranging from forest-clearance to livestock farming and rice paddies also contribute. Carbon dioxide levels are set to double by the year 2030 at a level never experienced in the recent history of our ecosystem.

In the coastal zones of many areas of the world, nutrient levels have risen due to nitrogen and phosphorus inputs from farming and domestic sources, such that marine plant communities have undergone rapid fluctuations of bloom and decay, stripping the water of oxygen and decimating other life forms.

25. This doubling will occur primarily in the tropical moist zones, on the most sensitive soils currently protected by forest. Less humid areas are already in a state of population crash, with a chronic food deficit. The tropical moist zone has a population growth rate of 2-4%, and will double from 2 to 3 billion by 2000. An additional 100 Mha of land will have to be cultivated to provide food under current systems of agriculture.

26. At the time of Christ, world population is estimated to have stood at about 100 million. Its rate of increase was averaging 2% every 1000 years, but by 1970 this rate peaked at about 2% *per year*. The first billion was reached around 1800, with 2 billion 130 years later in about 1930, the third billion by 1960, the fourth in 1975 and the fifth in 1990. Although populations in the industrial North and China have either been stabilised or now grow slowly, and the annual rate of increase as a whole is declining, most projections are of 10 billion within the next 50 years. In the tropics, even recent declines in fertility are offset by the age structure of the populations, where more young women are reaching child-bearing age.

27. Exceptions do occur, but tend to be in the purer sciences. For example, astrophysicists spent many years constructing a theoretical model of the universe according to the theories of 'dark matter', and then began collecting data to support this theory. The data did not fit, and they now seek new theoretical constructs.

28. Rupert Sheldrake speaks of a rebirth of nature in the modern mind, as people turn to Renaissance values, but as with the Romantics, it is her pale side they turn to.

29. A large proportion of the industrial world's professional classes worship in secret under the rubrick of the Masonic Order. In Britain, estimates put the number of members of lodges at 600,000, with the highest proportions in the police, military, banks and local government. See Stephen Knight's *The Brotherhood* (Granada, 1984) and Gurwin's *The Calvi Affair* (Macmillan, 1988) for an analysis of their pervasive influence and control.

30. In the *Nirvana-tantra*, the gods Brahma, Vishnu and Shiva are

said to arise from her like bubbles from the sea (David Kinsley, *The Hindu Goddesses*, Univ of California Press, p122).

31. Consider how we focus on the 'saving' or the 'losing' of lives in endless counting. I once took part in an inane argument over the loss of lives through 'late cancers' as a result of Chernobyl, and heard the precious statement from the nuclear industry that I should not refer to numbers of deaths, since everybody must die someday. It would be more accurate to talk of 'life-shortenings'. Yet in the obscene lies some truth. What *should* count is the quality of life and its lessons.

32. I have no bibliography of these teaching myths. Perhaps it is better to receive them as I did, by oral tradition. They seem to come at times of transformation, and the teacher is part of the teaching. The seminars of Howard Sasportas are transformative, but there is a book too, *The Gods of Change* (Arkana Contemporary Astrology).

33. At the moment of the first atom bomb's fearful ignition in the American desert, Robert Oppenheimer, quoting from Hindu scripture, exclaimed: *Behold, I am become Death, the Destroyer of Worlds*.

34. Kaos was the ultimate dark mother goddess in the Greek pantheon, the void which gave birth to all form. Gaia and Oeranus were worshipped equally as Earth Mother and Sky Father. Pluto, formerly Hades, was guardian of the underworld (the subconscious realm of repressed desires and fears, but also of hidden treasure, vitality and power). The British atomic scientists at Harwell named one of their first reactors *Pluto*, and the French military their nuclear missile, *Hades*. Furthermore, the first atomic weapon tests were code-named *Trinity*, and the first fusion test *Baby Jesus*.

35. There are many writings: Capra's *The Tao of Physics* (Fontana), Bohm's *Wholeness and Implicate Order* (Ark), Davies' *God and the New Physics* (Pelican).

36. For example, British physicists are fighting the closure of the pioneering particle physics laboratories at Daresbury — not that I would wish to defend such convoluted paths to awareness!

37. The nations of the new economic order united in condemnation of the beast they had created in Baghdad, whose soldiers wore their clothes and wielded the weapons manufactured in their factories, and who suddenly played the same game that had made them all rich and powerful in their time. The mirror must be broken. The series of UN resolutions to this end included the number 666, which resolution sought to control the entry of relief supplies to the peoples of many nationalities caught up in the war zone.

38. Oral tradition: he left his body on February 14th 1984, but may still talk to you if you breathe softly enough!

39. There is a rather foreboding tape, *The End of the World*, available from the Barry Long Foundation, BCM Box 876, London, or Box 1260, Southport, Australia. For the antidote, try *Making Love* tapes I & II.

40. Oral tradition, Hopi grandmother in London, 1983: the eagle, of course, is the American state, the nest in the sky is SkyLab and the moon landing; the major uranium mines in the USA are on sacred Navajo and Hopi lands; and the gourd of ashes the Fat-Boy bomb on Hiroshima.

41. Robert Graves defined the 'true poet' in terms of relationship to the divine feminine, the 'White Goddess'.

42. My own teacher, the Himalayan master Babaji, foretold of a moment in time, instantaneous over the whole planet, the 'kranti' or pivotal point, after which all would be changed. It would be a moment of mass destruction and it was very close. There is also a western literature, much derived from the prophecies of Edgar Cayce, which talks of 'pole shifts' and 'cosmic triggers'. There are even some respectably scientific theories of mechanisms that could shift the Earth on its axis. Keep an open mind and a light heart! In the new mathematics of Chaos Theory the boundary of order and disorder can be similarly sharp. For example, a system of flow can be transformed to turbulence in an instant with the slightest change of but one parameter. The Earth with its oceans and atmospheres is such an orderly flow-system with subordinate chaotic elements. As we slowly change the parameters of temperature, or the mixture of gases and particles, we are assuming that we are dealing with a system that will respond linearly. However, it could also respond with an abrupt transformation to a system where the vortex ruled! Intriguingly, the circles are held by some physicists to be vortices of charged air, and to be increasing in frequency. Perhaps the message is in the medium, as much as in the writing.

15.

16.

17.

18.

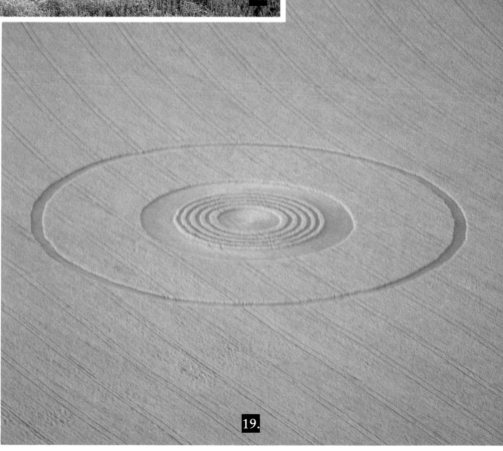

19.

Plate 15. STONEHENGE insectogram, with its 'double eyebrow' signature. The smaller ringed circle is thought to be a hoax; about 10th July 1991. Notice the ladder points north towards the world's best-known prehistoric monument. (*George Wingfield*)

Plate 16. STONEHENGE. The older insectogram here was formed about 18th June 1991, the later one with the eyebrow signature about 3 weeks later. (*George Wingfield*)

Plate 17. A pole shot of the head. (*David Tarr*)

Plate 18. Pole shot of the ladder pointing towards with Stonehenge. (*David Tarr*)

Plate 19. Woodford, near Thrapston, Northants. A wonderful six-ringer at sunset. (*George Wingfield*)

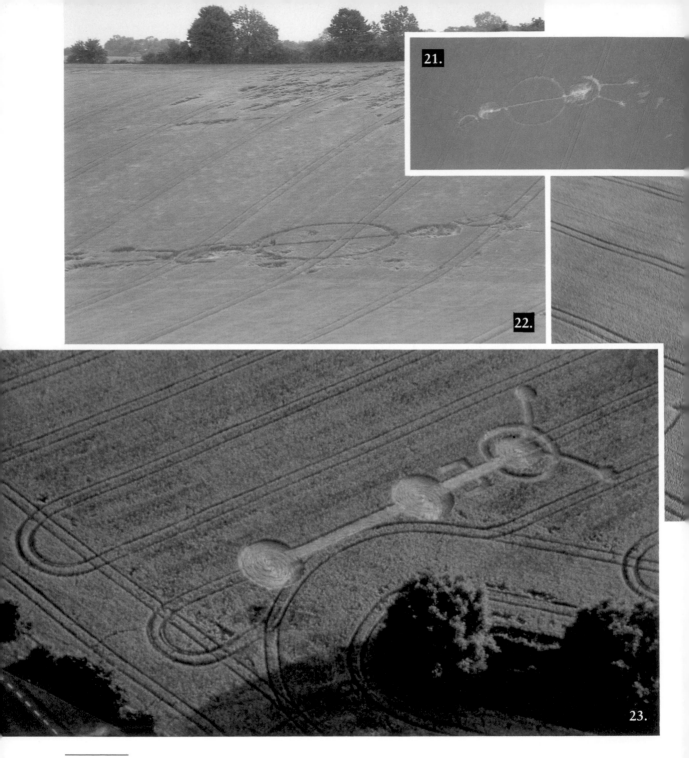

21.

22.

23.

Plate 23. WESTBURY, Wiltshire, 7th August 1990. A pictogram which seems to have been a prototype insectogram — note it still has its boxes. (*John Haddington*)

Plate 24. CHILCOMB DOWN insectogram, June 1991. (*John Haddington*)

Plate 25. UPHAM insectogram, June. (*Busty Taylor*)

Plate 20. Centre: CHILCOMB DOWN insectogram, near Winchester, the left on 7th June and the right during July 1991. (*George Wingfield*)

Plate 21. LITCHFIELD, near Whitchurch, Hampshire, late June. This was the third insectogram, in barley. (*Busty Taylor*)

Plate 22. UPHAM, Hampshire, early June 1991. This and the insectogram at Chilcomb Down were the first of this type in 1991. (*David Tarr*)

26.

Plate 26. THE PUNCHBOWL, Cheesefoot Head: a 'snail' formation, July. The variety of fauna was widening, but this motif was not repeated. On the right, the two insectograms on Chilcomb Down can just be seen. (*Calyx Photo Services*)

Plate 27. The LITCHFIELD insectogram from the air. (*John Haddington*)

Plate 28. Pole shot of the Litchfield pictogram. (*David Tarr*)

Plate 29. NEWTON ST LOE, near Bath. Formed by the side of the railway. It has been termed a 'violinogram'. (*Busty Taylor*)

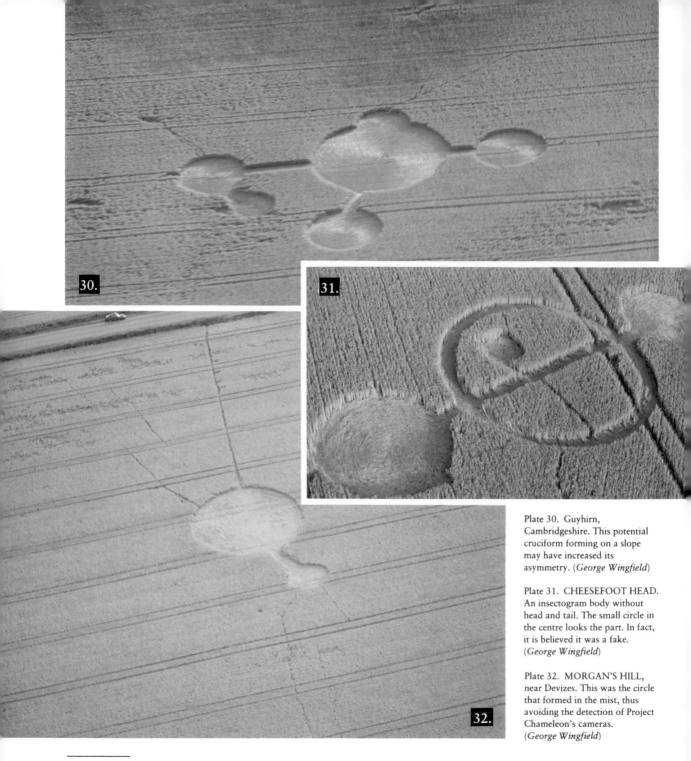

Plate 30. Guyhirn, Cambridgeshire. This potential cruciform forming on a slope may have increased its asymmetry. (*George Wingfield*)

Plate 31. CHEESEFOOT HEAD. An insectogram body without head and tail. The small circle in the centre looks the part. In fact, it is believed it was a fake. (*George Wingfield*)

Plate 32. MORGAN'S HILL, near Devizes. This was the circle that formed in the mist, thus avoiding the detection of Project Chameleon's cameras. (*George Wingfield*)

4.   The circles spread worldwide

GEORGE WINGFIELD

DURING 1990 THE CIRCLES PHENOMENON was reported in many countries from which we had never previously had reports. There can be little doubt that this was an actual increase in the geographic distribution of the phenomenon rather than an artefact of observation created by enhanced interest in what was happening, though admittedly investigation showed that circles had been appearing in very small numbers in a few of these countries in earlier years.

A curious but not unexpected aspect of this was that circles started to show up in countries where people displayed particular interest. An example is Japan where, as far as can be ascertained, only one circle had ever been reported during the 1980s. This was a small atypical circle in a rice paddy found after the vivid sighting of a UFO during 1984.

During 1989 several Japanese researchers and TV personnel travelled to Britain to visit and record the extraordinary occurrences of crop circles in Hampshire and Wiltshire. They came to Cheesefoot Head to see what experiments were being carried out at Operation White Crow, and they interviewed Colin Andrews, Pat Delgado and Dr Meaden. TV documentaries on the British circles made at that time were received with great public interest back in Japan. Again in the summer of 1990 the Japanese travelled to Britain, and this time their camera teams meticulously recorded the new formations, which for the first time ever included the pictograms. The Japanese never showed any doubt as to the impor-tance of this work at a time when segments of the British press only covered the subject in a puerile or frivolous manner.

THE CIRCLES APPEAR IN JAPAN

Soon afterwards crop circles began to be reported from Japan. Reports from Fukuoka Prefecture in Kyushu Island were the first to gain worldwide attention. Shunzo Abe, a rice farmer awoke on September 17th to find two formations in one of his fields. He thought at first "that a wild boar had run amok. But there were no signs of footprints to show that anything or anyone had entered the field". Newspaper photos showed a large 59ft circle, and close by a smaller 20ft circle with a single concentric ring around it. Carefully positioned between parallel pathways which crossed the paddy field these looked uncannily like British circles despite their oriental setting. The report said that Mr Abe was bitter because he did not know where to lodge a complaint.

Large numbers of people came to view these circles, and soon tracks into them were trampled by thoughtless visitors just as with the British ones. Whether the populace thought they were caused by wild boar, UFOs or plasma vortices is not recorded. Two weeks later further circles appeared in Kyushu Island, this time near Yoshinogari archaeological site in Saga Prefecture. A 33ft single circle was soon followed by a further ringed circle and four scattered smaller ones of between 10ft and 13ft diameter.

The significance of their proximity to the ancient site at Yoshinogari was not lost on some of the Japanese, but without much previous experience the press and public came up with the usual predictable reactions which had been seen in England for five years at least. Several other Japanese circles were reported in 1990 and we have indications that more circles were appearing in Japan in 1991.

CANADIAN CIRCLES

Ever since farmer Edwin Fuhr found circles in his canola (rapeseed) at Langenburg, near Regina, Saskatchewan in September 1974 there have been reports of crop circles in Canada. It is worth recalling Fuhr's story to contrast the perception of what causes the circles then and now.

Fuhr was driving a swathing machine picking up his rapeseed when he noticed what he took to be a tin duck-hide in the field. He assumed this was some kind of a joke perpetrated by his brother-in-law, so he climbed down with a view to kicking the 'hide' and scaring whoever was in it. But he never got closer than 15 feet. "All of a sudden, I noticed that the grass was moving .. turning near this thing. Then I saw the whole thing was turning. I backed up slow. I wasn't going to turn my back on the thing. When I got back up on the swather I noticed there were another four to the left of me, all revolving. I just froze on the seat and didn't move."

For the next 15 minutes Edwin Fuhr sat motionless watching the five 'stainless steel' hemispheres hovering about a foot off the ground. He wanted to take off on the swather but couldn't make his hand move to the gear lever. He wanted to run but his legs wouldn't move. "I was terrified. I froze . . . couldn't do anything", he said.

"Then they took off . . . straight up. There was a grey vapour coming from underneath them and a strong downwind which knocked the rape down. I had to hang on to my hat." It took two minutes for the objects to disappear into the clouds and a further two minutes for Edwin to descend from the swather. "I wanted to be sure that they were gone." Beneath the spot he had seen the first hovering object was a depression in the foot-high grass of about 11ft in diameter. The grass on the outside was flattened and twisted in a clockwise ring. In the centre it stood erect. Then he discovered four more depressions where the other objects had been spinning. "I felt the grass to see if it was warm. There was nothing you could feel and there wasn't any smell."

Figuring that he'd done enough swathing, he then headed back to the farmhouse for lunch. "I didn't know how to tell my folks. The wife just stared at me and said I was nuts. Mother wouldn't believe it at all but had figured that I'd seen something."

Word soon got around and the next day constable Ron Morier from the Langenburg RCMP turned up at the farm. "They took me out to where they'd seen these things in the slough grass. I saw these rings about 10-12ft in diameter", said constable Morier. "Something was there and I doubt it was a hoax. There's no indication that anything had been wheeled in or out and Mr Fuhr seemed genuinely scared." The RCMP gathered all the information they could, including photographs and measurements, and sent the material to the Upper Atmosphere Research Section of the National Research Council in Ottawa.

A few days later a neighbour's dog started barking at about midnight and kept it up until about 3am. "The people who owned the dog said they couldn't stop it from barking and that it kept looking over here", Mr Fuhr said. No one saw anything that night but on Monday morning when Mr Fuhr returned to the site there was a sixth ring exactly the same as the others.

He estimates that since word started getting around about the landing, 2000 people have trampled through, over and around the circular depressions. "But they are still there and very visible", said

The Circlemakers came to the cities in 1991. Top: Dumb-bell above Bristol. Bottom: Double pictogram just outside Bath, Avon. (*David Tarr*)

Edwin. "It was Friday before Mom would even go and have a look. Everyone believes it now and Mom figures it's about time to move into town." In all about 7000 people eventually visited the Fuhr's farm.

This account taken from an item in Regina's *Leader-Post* is certainly reminiscent of many crop circle events today, and yet now there is an entirely different perception as to the cause. If it's UFOs today, they really have to be invisible; why then in 1974 did Edwin Fuhr give such a graphic account of shiny metallic nuts-and-bolts flying saucers? Perhaps it is humanity that has changed, or at least its perception of the external world . . . or is it the UFO phenomenon itself?

In all other respects the circles phenomenon described here is very similar to what we experience time and again. There are the mysterious rings, the incredulous friends and relations, the policeman (or mountie) who calls, the thousands of visitors drawn by some irresistible compunction, the barking dog, the revisitation of the site, and even the naive supposition that science, here personified by the Canadian National Research Council, will solve it all.

Sixteen years later, in August 1990, circles were still appearing on the prairies in Saskatchewan and Manitoba. Four large circles appeared in a wheatfield near Tweedsmuir, Sask., and soon afterwards further rings were found in wheat in southern Manitoba at St Francis-Xavier, Rosser, Niverville, Lockport and Petersfield. The Tweedsmuir circles ranged from 50-66ft diameter, and were within 200 yards of each other. They showed no trace of human involvement. "The circles are so symmetric; they are done so neatly and with nothing broken, it's like it was so gentle," said Mr Roth, publisher of a local magazine. The largest circle had four 'spokes' emanating in a pattern from the centre. "It has to be a spaceship", added Mr Roth. "The prank theory has been totally ruled out here. We're pretty arrogant if we think we are the only intelligent life form in the universe."

About twenty Canadian circles have been reported since 1974, and there were at least a dozen in the summer of 1990. This sudden increase reflected the worldwide surge of circle reports at this time and many people then became actively involved in this research. Chris Rutkowski, co-ordinator of the Ufology Research Centre of Manitoba in Winnipeg, investigated the summer's sudden outburst of circles in the province with four colleagues.

"In Manitoba we have three active theories," Mr Rutkowski said. "They are either a hoax, a UFO, or some unknown meteorological or weather phenomenon." Mr Rutkowski said he could not rule out the possibility of weather, or a meteorological phenomenon. "But there are thousands of them in England, and this year in particular they have appeared on the prairies. One has to ask why now?"

All of the 1990 circles in Canada appeared in wheat fields and not in barley, flax, canola or hay. Most Saskatchewan circles are swept clockwise, while Manitoba's run mainly anti-clockwise, according to Chris Rutkowski. But some like those at Tweedsmuir are made up of concentric swirls which are alternately clockwise and anti-clockwise.

This pattern was found in a circle at Alvena, Sask., by 57-year old farmer Mike Shawaga, who was swathing his wheat crop early on the morning of August 31st 1990. "My son — he's 15 — says it's the aliens", said Mr Shawaga with a chuckle. "Me? I don't know. Our family's been farming here since 1907. My father — he's 80 — has never seen anything like it." Mr Shawaga does not think wind made the circle in his field. "Sure, we get the odd twister around here", he said. "But it would have to stick around for the hell of a long time to make anything like that. At first I thought it was the dogs who'd got a porcupine — but look it's perfectly round".

The ripening of the wheat in the Alvena circle appeared to have been retarded, as did that in the Tweedsmuir circles which were believed to have formed in mid-July. Most Canadian circles were only found while harvesting and their date of formation was usually estimated by the maturity of the crop within the circle. Mr Rutkowski and his colleagues in Manitoba found no magnetic deviation and no radio-activity within the circles. "We've had a dozen or so UFO reports since the rings began to appear. There does seem to be that connection", he said.

Initial reports from Canada and the USA in 1991 indicated many fewer circles than in 1990, but that may be because most North American circles are only discovered at harvest time.

AN OUTBREAK OF CIRCLES IN THE U S MID-WEST

At much the same time as in Canada in 1990, circles were appearing in the Mid-west of USA, in particular in Kansas and Missouri. Local reactions were very similar, and again the talk was of whirlwinds, UFOs and hoaxes. In general no one saw or heard anything unusual and farmers were confronted by mysterious formations of geometrically flattened crop.

On Roger and Lynda Lowe's farm between Odessa and Bates City, Mo., two circles of 30ft and 50ft diameter were found in sorghum, which is a coarse plant averaging 8ft in height. Dozens of curious farmers and townsfolk drove up at all hours to gaze at the field, take pictures and chat about what could have caused such things. Maybe a UFO visited, some suggested. It has to be freak winds, said others. But many of the local farmers just shook their heads in disbelief.

"I've farmed here all my life and I've never seen anything like it", said Terry Henning who lives two miles from the Lowes. Power cuts were reported in the Odessa area that night, but all was fine at the Lowe farm located in Lafayette county east of Kansas City. The weather was clear and calm, according to a National Weather Service spokesman. No tyre tracks were found near the circles which were separated from a nearby gravel road by a foot-deep ditch.

The larger circle later expanded into an uneven shape that takes up nearly the size of a football pitch.

Whether this was the result of 'revisitation' of the phenomenon or not is unclear from reports; a more mundane solution is that subsequent wind damage was facilitated adjacent to the circle as often happens with British circles. Little of the crop could be saved and the two acres flattened would have been worth about $2000.

"I still think it was the wind, myself," said Roger Lowe. "How it did it, I don't know". The Lowes don't see the circles as a big deal and they quickly grew tired of the attention. "It has been a kinda pain", said Mr Lowe.

Other Missouri circles were found in sorghum at Osceola, and in Kansas more were reported in a grass pasture south-west of Oskaloosa, and one in a field west of Topeka. Again residents joked that this must be the landing mark of a spaceship or else Big Foot had been up to his tricks.

Dangerous heretical opinions of this sort no doubt galvanised the skeptics, and Philip Klass of CSICOP soon got in on the act by telling the newspapers "I am quite certain that we have no alien visitors in our skies. Whatever is generating these circles, it is not an alien spaceship". This reaffirmation of the skeptics' creed, curiously similar to the frenzied denunciations of UFO believers uttered by Jenny Randles and Paul Fuller in England, was evidently insufficient, and another CSICOP spokesman, Barry Carr, delivered a lengthy dissertation to journalists explaining how the circles were caused by atmospheric microbursts or spinning winds that are sometimes called 'dust devils'. Glen Marotz, a meteorologist and professor of civil engineering at the University of Kansas, added, "When the atmosphere is faced with an energy imbalance, it acts like you would expect it would. It tries to get rid of them. One way is to create a spinning vortex."

All this sounded very similar to the meteorological theories of Dr Terence Meaden, though the latter would have us believe that these vortices are caused by the lee effects of hills (at least up until 1991). The snag with these Mid-West circles, of course, is that the areas around Kansas City where they were found are in extremely flat country with no hills anywhere in the vicinity. So why not adopt Glen Marotz's explanation and allow the atmosphere to bombard you with spinning vortices in order to rid itself of awkward energy imbalances? No matter that it has only decided to act this way in 1990; perhaps Terry Henning and all those other mid-westerners have been walking around all this time with their eyes shut. After all, anything is surely better than admitting that there are some things which scientists cannot explain.

Besides Kansas and Missouri, circles appeared in 1990 in several other states where they had not been reported previously. In Milan, Illinois, farmer James Lawson found a perfect 46ft 6in circle in his corn (American corn) while harvesting in October. This crop had no tram-lines like a British crop and there was no sign of human entry to the circle. "I was just making my first trip (on a combine) through the field," said Lawson. "The first thing I thought of was a UFO."

"I thought 'holy smokes, what is this?'. It feels weird. There's no road coming in," said Lawson, 70. "It could have been here quite a while, but the ears are still on the stalks. Maybe it's been a month or so. When I went to tell my wife, she didn't believe me. She said, 'You're goofy'." Lawson has farmed the land for 42 years, and although he did not think the crop circle a hoax, he wasn't quite ready to accept the UFO theory. "It couldn't have been the wind because the dike would have stopped it. And it's a perfect circle. The stalks are mashed in perfect rows," he said. "Maybe it was a UFO that made the circle when it landed and then took off."

A fascinating study of North American crop circles was published in February 1991 by the North American Institute for Crop circle Research (Winnipeg, Manitoba). This categorised the North American circles (or more correctly UGMs, Unusual Ground Markings) into: 1. flattened circles; 2. flattened rings; 3. burned circles; 4. burned rings; 5. burned

and flattened; 6. concentric rings; 7. vegetation missing/damaged; 8. depression; 9. hole(s); 10. other markings or residue.

This distinction is interesting but seems hardly one that is required in England where the vast majority of markings are geometrically flattened crops. In the USA the burned markings have been regarded as 'UFO ground traces' for many years, but such markings are very rare in England. In the USA many circles were in grass and comparatively few in wheat and other crops such as sorghum, oats, alfalfa and corn.

Another distinction is that rings and concentric rings are very rare in Canada and the USA. No pictograms, or anything even approaching the complex circle sets found in England, were reported up to the end of 1990, but an interesting formation at Northside, Saskatchewan, had straight pathways emanating at 90deg intervals from a central circle and crossing two concentric rings. This was found on August 28th 1990 together with two smaller circles. Another formation at Finleyville, Pennsylvania, was a plain double-ringer circle in grass. A formation like a reverse question mark at Leola, South Dakota, is apparently the subject of some doubt.

CIRCLES IN RUSSIA

During 1990 several reports of crop circles were received from Russia. These sounded to be similar to our circles whereas reports in earlier years of burned circles, and ones showing enhanced radioactivity had usually been associated with UFO 'ground traces'.

In June a mysterious circle had appeared in wheat near the town of Yeisk in the Krasnodar Region. A local resident had reported that on June 20th at 3am he had seen a white and blue luminescent object somewhat like a welding arc in the immediate area. The next morning a peculiar depression of wheat stalks in the field was discovered by local inhabitants. These people refused to enter it due to fear of something unknown.

A week later a team of investigators lead by Yuri Stroganov arrived to inspect the circle. Already numerous visitors had trampled the crop. This 'circle' was in fact oval measuring about 35 by 45 metres. In it the stalks were flattened in a counter-clockwise spiral, and in its centre was an oval of standing crop measuring 2 metres by 1.5 metres. The long axis of the large oval comprising the 'circle' was aligned north and south, whereas that of the small oval of standing corn was east and west.

In the oval one could discern two concentric ring-like paths each 40cm wide and separated by the same distance. Their centre did not coincide with that of the oval(s). In these circular paths the stalks were of brighter colour and appeared denser than the rest of the wheat which was green. Radiation measurements showed that the level in the oval was the same as background level, except in the circular paths where the level was null. While Stroganov's team experienced no health problems at the site, others who entered the formation when it was fresh complained of headaches. The investigation team concluded that the strange effects were consistent with the visitation of a UFO.

There were many other stories of Russian circles but little documentation has reached us as yet. Other reports in Russian came from the Tomsk and Kemerovo region of Siberia. These also included photographs and information on mysterious vertical cylindrical holes in the ground which formed overnight and sounded to be similar to those reported from Switzerland in the last few years. One such hole near Tomsk was cup-shaped and measured 4 metres diameter and 6 metres deep.

EUROPEAN CIRCLES

Farmer Gert-Jan Petrie discovered Holland's first circle while harvesting his wheatfield in the polder landscape of the Haarlemmermeer, south-west of Amsterdam, in the first week of August 1990. "High on top of the combine you have a great view. At a certain moment I saw a piece that was trampled down. First I thought a couple who had made love there had flattened it. But when I got closer it turned out to be a circle."

"The circle had a diameter of 9 metres," according to Petrie. "At the edges there were five small circles with a diameter of about 75cm. The wheat inside the large circle had been flattened 'to the right'. A sharp clear-cut edge divided the circle from the rest of the wheat," according to the farmer.

A few days later farmer Jan Blonk found a second circle, 7 metres across, in his field one and a half kilometres away. "I have never seen anything like it," he said. "The ears of corn were not damaged at all. It looks as if an air-cushion had landed on the field."

Petrie ruled out intentional practical jokes. "It hadn't rained for three weeks, so the soil was bonedry. But there weren't any footsteps to be seen leading to the circles. It's really something else that must have happened." Possibly the presence of a nearby high-tension cable could have had something to do with the circle.

For some reason we have no reports of anything like a regular crop circle from France. Why this is, is unclear. Of course, it may be because the French, in general, do not believe in them, if one is to go by the tenor of an article published in *Science et Vie*, by a certain Thierry Pinvidic. He is a UFO investigator, and regarding the crop circles, he concludes, in the best CSICOP tradition, that "Like UFOs, there is always some logical or natural explanation, such as a goat tethered to a picket walking round in a circle." For someone who spent much time in Hampshire and Wiltshire in the summer of 1990 investigating the circles and pictograms, the conclusion that these were all man-made (or the handiwork of goats) probably tells more about the psychology of the investigator than the actual provenance of the circles. Nevertheless we have just received reports, as yet unconfirmed, of crop circles near Figeac, in the Dordogne.

Italy has had a number of formations mainly in Tuscany and Emilia provinces. Reports in 1990 came from Grosetto and also there was a report of a circle in the Puglia region in the south. Johannes von Buttlar, a veteran investigator of UFOs, located and photographed a more complex formation in a remote mountain valley in Sicily. This dumb-bell shaped marking was in long meadow grass far from any roads or tracks.

Eastern Europe has not escaped the spread of the circles either. At Drouzhba, near Sofia in Bulgaria, a pattern of four circles joined by concentric rings was discovered in the summer of 1990. Other circles are reported from Romania, Czechoslovakia, and the Puszta region of Hungary.

THE GERMAN CONNECTION

Last but by no means least in Europe came Germany. Despite a dearth of reports before 1991, a bumper crop of circles was reported during that year. Interest in the subject was especially high following the publication of a German edition of *Circular Evidence*, by Andrews and Delgado. In June a conference on crop circles was held in Hamburg at which the speakers included John Michell, Pat Delgado, Jürgen Krönig and myself. This was greeted with great enthusiasm and I joked that I had brought some circle seed to scatter to the winds in Germany.

Within two months reports of crop circles were coming in from every part of Germany, though I cannot claim any causality between the conference and this extraordinary outbreak. A dumb-bell at Idstein-Worsdorf had been reported before the event but after there came at least ten reports from Schleswig-Holstein. Two of these, at Felm and Damp were undoubtedly fakes, and the making of at least one was admitted to by four law students subsequently. This was the large ring formation at Felm which anyone can see is wildly irregular and nothing like the real phenomenon. There is no reason to think

that the others in this part of Germany were hoaxed.

Further south there were fine formations at Bornheim near Bonn, and at Sossenheim in Frankfurt. In the former East Germany there was a formation in Sachsen Anhalt near Magdeburg, and further south again ones near Rosdorf and Ulm.

But the *pièce de resistance* was undoubtedly the amazing pictogram found at Grasdorf near Hildesheim. The authenticity of this formation will no doubt be hotly debated by cereologists and at a distance it is difficult to give a verdict on it. The formation consists of thirteen circles of similar size and a ring with a cross in it. These are connected or not by a number of straight pathways. Whatever its origin this hieroglyph attracted much attention from the media and thousands of visitors who were charged 3DM for entry by the farmer.

A curious story was to follow. An unidentified man arrived at Grasdorf with a metal detector and asked the farmer permission to use this instrument in the circles. In front of television cameras and many people he located three places, each at the centre of a circle, where he said metal was buried. With permission he dug at each spot to a depth of 40cm and in each he unearthed a metal plate of about 30cm diameter. These he stowed in his car and said that he would take them for scientific analysis. He was never seen again. Pictures later received by newspapers showed these plates to be embossed with the actual layout of the pictogram, and an anonymous telephone call, supposedly from the man who had dug them up, said that the plates were of gold and that he was keeping them.

Like so much of the folklore which attaches to the circles, this story seems just too good to be true, and perhaps indeed it is no more than an elaborate hoax. But then, in the established tradition of the phenomenon, one is once more left bewildered as to what is actually going on. Again and again circle events stretch one's credulity to the limit, and yet very few of the stories can be dismissed as deliberate deception.

THE REST OF THE WORLD

No reports that we have heard have originated from the third world countries of Africa and Asia. Whether this is because of the lack of suitable grain crops as a medium for the circles to form in, or because of other considerations we cannot tell. There have been some reports from South America but these are mostly of burned circles and are usually associated with UFO sightings.

Australia has long been familiar with crop circles and once more these are mostly associated with UFO sightings. The earliest Australian reports are from Tully in Queensland where a whole series of 'UFO nests' were found in reed-beds in lagoons near that town. These occurrences date from 1966 but continue to some extent even to the present day. More conventional crop circles have been reported frequently in the last few years from Victoria and from South Australia. It is interesting to note that the latter events during the Australian summer are occurring at the time of our crop circle close season in the Northern Hemisphere.

Apart from Australia and Canada most countries had very little circle activity until 1990 and this tends to confirm the worldwide spread of the phenomenon. Where this will lead we cannot say, and we must wait and see whether the huge and elaborate English circles of 1990 and 1991 will in due course spread to the rest of the world.

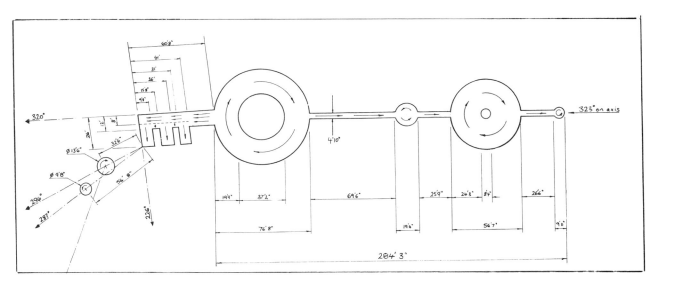

THE KENNETS, near Avebury. Formed in wheat 26th July 1991 (*J.F. Langrish drawing*)

5. Keys to hidden doorways

DEAN HOLDEN and PAUL SCOTT

SUCKED INTO CIRCLES

OUR INVOLVEMENT WITH the crop circles began in the USA, where we were planning to present a radio show for US syndication. The show was to feature European music and was formatted to contain interesting aspects of metaphysical information. We decided that the first show should contain a piece on crop circles, a subject which had recently been gaining some media attention. Our arrival back in the UK coincided with the appearance of the first pictograms.

The radio item was quickly completed, but our interest in the phenomenon continued to grow. Dean had an increasing sense of connection to and familiarity with the circles. On a visit to Britain, his first venture into a circle overwhelmed him with a depth of feeling which he could only describe as recognition — although he could not then say what it was he recognised, just that it felt to be very much part of him. Paul professed to be unaffected by the energy of the circles, but he was fascinated by the puzzle of their creation and moved by their beauty.

A short time later we were back in America, having learned a lot in a short time about circles. We had a sound commercial reason to be in USA, but alongside that, there seemed to be another itinerary which we neither had planned, nor had control over. We were ostensibly there to meet radio executives, media people and the like, which we did with great success — but at the same time we were meeting with a very different sort of person.

Everywhere we went we met clairvoyants and channels, shamans and native Americans who all seemed to have something to say to us on crop circles. We quickly ceased to be surprised at the 'coincidences' which brought us to our next crop circle meeting: a chance meeting in someone's living room brought us in contact with an Ute shaman, a phone ringing while we were visiting someone else gained us an invitation to visit the Hopi — these soon brought no more comment than a resigned roll of the eyes from Paul.

Over the next few months we were, separately or together, to encounter Hopi, Ute, Lakota, Mayan and Hawaiian holy men. What struck us very forcibly was the universal recognition that these people showed for the circles, and for the pictograms in particular. They all viewed them in terms of their own symbolism, and they all seemed to be able to reconcile them with it.

We ourselves noticed many similarities between Native American symbols and some of the pictograms. The sweat lodge, for example, consists of a dome-shaped structure containing a central pit into which are put red-hot stones, heated in a fire pit in front of the lodge. The native Americans believe that there is a straight line joining the two pits which may not be crossed: two circles joined by a straight line — does this sound familiar? The Medicine Wheel is another example — a circle of stones with four lines of stones forming a cross, meeting at a smaller central circle, forming a 'boss' — much like the strikingly beautiful circle at Winterbourne Stoke at the end of the 1989 circle season.

We were very excited and ready to evolve an interpretation of the pictograms based on the symbolism of the ancient cultures — native Americans being relatively articulate, living and accessible representatives of them — but, like all those who think that they have the circles pinned down, we found we had to think again.

DISTANT MEMORIES

There was, and still is, a great deal of interest in the USA in the crop circle phenomenon, people being hungry for more details of this fascinating subject. More or less by accident, we found ourselves being drawn into giving lectures on the circles and appearing on media shows. We soon began to notice something very curious: almost invariably, the people we showed the pictograms to found something familiar about them. We watched with fascination as, over and over again, people would struggle to try and remember where they had seen these things before. Very often someone would get in touch with us days later to say that they could not get a particular pictogram out of their minds. On occasions, someone would be so drawn to a particular pictogram that they would get quite possessive about it. We made a point of photocopying the various pictogram shapes and distributing them at our lectures. We would ask people to concentrate on them and give their reactions, and time and again came the responses: "I know what this is, I just can't remember . . .", "It's on the tip of my tongue . . .". When we showed them to children we were delighted at the response — again we saw attraction and recognition — even young babies seemed to giggle more when in possession of a crop circle picture!

This seemed to us to widen the nature of the pictograms, for they were not solely accessible to the memory of the more ancient and spiritual cultures than our own — they appeared to be meaningful to everyone. Perhaps we were looking at a universal symbolism, a symbolism so deep and so powerful that it can strike a chord in the soul of all who see it.

We have watched the complexity and number of circles accelerate in unison with global change, and we have seen the many attempts to explain them in natural terms falter and fail. Throughout this time, however, the circles have not really suffered the ridicule that one would generally come to expect with a phenomenon as extraordinary as this. While there is not yet a willingness within the scientific community to accept them, in fact they are often viewed with the kind of respect shown to a holy object. There does not seem to be the level of hostility which would prevent serious consideration of the circles at some future time. Could it be that there very existence could act as a forum where the scientific and the spiritual could meet together on equal terms? Could we possibly come to an understanding of the universal nature of these remarkable symbols and, within the framework of this understanding, have the ability to unlock the door to the collective resonance contained within them?

It became clearer and clearer to us that the power contained within the pictograms was operating on a fundamental level in the human spirit. Here was no intergalactic morse code, no message that could be decoded and written out for all to see — it was much more important than that. We felt increasingly that those who desired to understand them in terms of literal meaning were looking in the wrong place. An Ute shaman, Jade Wah'oo, put it into words for us: we were showing him photographs of the circles and he had been silent for some time, concentrating on a large photograph of the second Cheesefoot Head pictogram, and obviously deeply moved. Someone asked him what he thought it could mean, and Jade replied: "This is a symbol. A symbol does not *mean*, a symbol *is*."

From the time that we first became interested in the circles, Dean had found them invading his dreams and even intruding into his waking hours. The entities that he had felt all his life seemed to press closer in on him, as if eager to impart information concerning the circles. Even Paul experienced some flashes of intuition, much to his alarm, but the main information seemed to be coming through Dean. The contact with the ancient spiritual cultures that we had been led to changed us both profoundly, and Dean in particular grew in understanding of the wider perspective and the multi-dimensional aspect of the circle phenomena, and found that his personal life went through many adjustments and his level of sensitivity was expanded. He became interested in encouraging 'energy-shifts' in people, showing how a multi-dimensional perspective can enhance both individual lives and the consciousness of the planet itself.

EARTH ENERGY

As more information became available about the circles, it seemed that they were in some way related to earth energy. The work of Richard Andrews, in particular, demonstrated a clear relationship with ley-line energy, and sketched out a potential mechanism. Who or what was modulating the earth energy to produce the circles was still open to question, but it was at least a theory that fitted all observable facts — something that is very scarce in circle research.

We found ourselves concentrating increasingly on the earth-energy aspect, and the role of sacred sites, such as Silbury Hill. Had the circles happened in that area before, and were these monuments there in order to commemorate them? Were they constructed in order to utilise the energy-concentrations associated with the circles? Perhaps they may even have some part to play in the generation of the circles. When we read *The Sun and the Serpent* we got very excited indeed. Paul Broadhurst and Hamish Miller had set out to dowse the famous St Michael ley-line, and what they discovered was not one but two lines of energy stretching across England — the Michael line and the Mary line. These lines are associated but rarely interact at the south-western or north-eastern ends. In the centre, however, they weave together in a series of beautiful patterns, precisely in the area of greatest crop circle activity. It looks almost like a generator, pulling in power from the rest of the country to drive the activity of the 'Wessex Triangle'.

Hamish and Paul demonstrated a historic and prehistoric awareness of the existence of these two energy-lines. There were of course any number of ancient sites and sacred wells along the lines — that came as no surprise. It is easy to imagine an earlier time when people in Britain were closer to nature and better able to appreciate and accept its powers. It was very surprising to find, however, that comparatively modern buildings, particularly churches, had been built to align with the lines. This suggested that contemporary British society is, on one level or another, capable of comprehending and utilising this energy. There is not some arcane wisdom that they knew and we did not, that we must somehow discover: the knowledge is already there within us and is all around if we look. It seems scarcely credible that there has been a continuity of tradition from Neolithic shamans to Anglican vicars — it is more likely that they reach the same revelations through different means.

Earth energy is celebrated in almost all cultures. The Chinese geomantic tradition, *feng-shui*, visualises it as rivers of force — *ch'i* energy — flowing across the landscape and, in certain places, forming spirals of energy. No Chinese building was erected without first considering how it could be harmonised with the surrounding energy-flows. The Australian Aboriginals speak of 'song-lines' which cross the land, each song-line with its own individual song which they are able to detect and work with. They also believe that everything was dreamed into existence by the Earth, that all creation is linked together by being part of that dream. Unsurprisingly, many of the symbols that the Aborigines use are reminiscent of crop circle patterns.

The two questions which any crop circle researcher is asked are: "Who is doing them?" and "What do they mean?". People are always very dissatisfied when we tell them that they ask the wrong questions, since this sort of preoccupation with meaning and source can actually impede the process of further understanding. The approach needs to be intuitive as well as rational. There is little sense in asking questions of other people when the answer is already contained within ourselves — how else to explain the universal familiarity with the pictogram symbols? How else to explain the link between Neolithic shamans and later church-builders? The acceptance and recognition of the pictograms by people of many different cultures?

The implications of this realisation are profound. Within the industrialised Western nations, many people who are concerned with spiritual development suffer from a sort of metaphysical inferiority complex. They use the ritual and practices of other cultures because they feel that there is poor possibility of inner growth within our own culture. They look to the spiritual traditions of tribal peoples, the past, India or even the alleged superiority of other planetary systems. The effect of this is to divorce spiritual life from everyday existence — the language is different, the assumptions are different and the context is different. The effect of importing other spiritual traditions is also to freeze them — who are we to interfere with these sacred rights? The result tends toward stagnation rather than the growth and change which are essential to a healthy spiritual development.

THE HOPI

When we look at the traditions of other cultures, the lesson we can learn is that we are spiritually linked to the earth, and through the earth, to everything else. The recognition we feel when we look at the pictograms is evidence of our ability to tap into the universal spirituality for ourselves and to express it in terms that are relevant to the society that we actually live in. And the growing connections between our society and ancient societies — in which we were playing one small part — can teach both about the other, positively. A Hopi elder had some interesting things to tell us.

The Hopi live in a very isolated part of northern Arizona. They are an ancient culture, occupying what is believed to be the oldest continuously-inhabited settlement in the United States. They have an Atlantis legend, and claim to have settled the Hopi lands after fleeing from the inundated continent. They are also very secretive, guarding their religion closely, not welcoming strangers easily.

When we were in Sedona, Arizona, we were able to talk to White Bear Fredericks, a Hopi artist and co-author of the *Book of the Hopi*. White Bear told us of the Hopi prophecies and how he thought they related to the crop circles. The Hopi believe that

Thomas Banyaca in the petroglyph cave (*Paul Scott*)

humanity must progress through nine eras or 'worlds' before achieving completion. We are now at the end of the fourth world, and the fifth is already beginning. White Bear saw the circles as being clear confirmation of this. He remarked that many of the symbols featured groups of four elements, and where there was a fifth element it was generally distinguished from the other four. This corresponds with the native American emphasis on the four directions, each with its attributes, principles and powers, and the fifth 'direction' at the centre.

Shortly after this, we were surprised and happy to receive an invitation to visit one of the Hopi elders, Thomas Banyaca, who happened to telephone a person we were visiting while we were there. We drove up through increasingly dry and inhospitable country until we reached the Hopi land. It seemed incredible that anyone should choose to live in such a desolate area. When we got there, Thomas' wife came out and told us he was asleep. We went away for an hour and returned. We were sent away a second time, leaving with the impression she would be just as happy if we did not return. We did return however: on this occasion no one came out, and, in line with Hopi tradition, we waited quietly outside. Eventually, Paul became impatient, and, explaining he was English, and in his tradition you knock on doors that are not opened to you, he went up and knocked, and this time we met Thomas Banyaca.

He told us about the Hopi story of the ears of corn. The Creator gathered all the peoples of the world and showed them a line of ears of corn, inviting them to choose one each. Each of the ears was large and succulent, except for one, which was small and dry-looking. Each tribe sent a representative forward to pick an ear of corn, and all of them avoided the small one. The Hopi hung back, declining to choose until there was only the small ear left, which he then took. The other tribes were amazed and scornful of the Hopi, but the Creator congratulated the Hopi, saying: "You have made a good choice, for all the other ears of corn are illusion, and you have chosen

reality". We took this to be an explanation of why the Hopi had chosen to live in such a desolate-seeming area.

Thomas Banyaca studied our crop circle photographs with great care. After we had shown them to him he sat for a long time and said nothing. He was silent so long that we were beginning to think that he would decline to say anything, and that we would have to leave, no wiser than when we arrived, but then he started to speak. Like White Bear Fredericks, he spoke of the fourth world giving way to the fifth, and he saw the circles as being forerunners of that change. He gave more details about the Hopi prophecies as they relate to the fifth world, and about the story of the red brother and the white brother.

Many thousands of years ago, these two brothers lived together, but the time came when they separated and the white brother went away. The Hopi always knew that the white brother would return, and that he would come with a cross and a circle — if he came with the cross alone, it would mean that the time was not right and there would be much trouble. When the white brother came with the cross and the circle, however, they would be able to combine the lessons that each had learned and enter into the fifth world.

Thomas saw the circles, which are happening in one of the most sacred parts of the white brother's lands, as being a long-awaited sign. He showed us an ancient petroglyph that he had been led to discover forty years ago, which showed the divergence of the two brothers, their following of different paths and their return to each other. He saw the red brother's spiritual development joining with the white brother's technical development to form a synthesis which would be far greater than the sum of its parts. We stood on the mesa together with Thomas, who was dressed in his bright Hopi colours. He told us many aspects of the Hopi prophecy, illustrated by the wonderful petroglyph backdrop. As Thomas talked of our moving from the fourth world to the fifth, we noticed in the four corners of the Painted Desert four

Petroglyph photo (*Paul Scott*)

separate thunderstorms, which seemed a fitting conclusion to such an auspicious occasion.

MATTER AND CONSCIOUSNESS

To begin to perceive the multi-dimensional aspect we must see the fluidity of what we would normally characterise as solid matter. All things are creations of consciousness, existing in an agreed format and operating within universal principles. Western thought has traditionally been limited in its ability to comprehend the concept of many things occupying the same space, although the principles of quantum physics begin to enter that area.

The Maya, in Yucatan and Guatemala, have a recorded history and calendrical system which goes back at least 28,000 years. We spent some time with Hunbatz Men, a Mayan shaman, who told us of the traditional Maya perception of science and spirituality being one and the same thing. Are the crop circles saying something similar, drawing rationalists and mystics together in muddy or sunny fields out in England's green and pleasant land? Hunbatz Men was also very interested in the circles, and pointed out that Mayan symbolism made great use of the spiral — which he interpreted as the Milky Way, our galaxy.

The Mayan culture was obliterated by the invading Spanish Conquistadors, and Mayans such as Hunbatz Men are attempting to reconstruct it by means of research and intuition. He was unable to give us a definitive interpretation of how the circles fit in with Maya symbolism. But he did tell us of a powerful Maya priest, once seized by the Spaniards: just before they put him to death he prophesied that the oppressors would triumph totally for a number of years, and then the spirit of the Maya would return. This time-limit expired in 1987 — the year that crop circles began to be more sophisticated and noticed.

Carved on a rock not too far from Oraibi village is a petroglyph that conveys the prophecy of the Great Spirit. Starting in the lower left hand corner and moving to the right, the petroglyph means roughly the following: "The Bow and Arrow are the tools which the Great Spirit (to the right) gave to the Hopi. He is pointing to the spiritual path of the Great Spirit. The upper path is the White Man's path, with two white men and one Hopi to represent the Hopi who adopted white man's ways. The vertical line joining the two paths (just to the left of the first man and circle) represents the first contact between the Hopi and the White Man since the emergence from the lower world. The lower path is the spiritual path of the Hopi. The first circle is World War I, the second World War II and the third is the Great Purification which the Hopi feel we are now approaching, after which corn and water will be abundant, the Great Spirit will return and all will be well. Notice how the White Man's path eventually becomes very erratic and finally just fades away. The quartered circle in the lower right corner is the symbol for the spiritual centre of the continent, which for the Hopi is the South-west". (*From* The Six O'Clock Bus *by Moira Timms, Turnstone, 1980*)

Apparently this prophecy was recorded by the Spanish archivists of the time. Hunbatz described how the Maya understood energy and movement, and that they were able to chart star systems. He also told us that they are familiar with the concept that everything is energy and vibrates at different frequencies.

We are now beginning to realise that we can only perceive a small fraction of what is going on around us. If we consider, with quantum physics, that physical matter is a vibration at a certain frequency or range of frequencies, how many levels of frequency can occupy the same space — like radio waves, coexisting but not interacting? Do we, when we experience a shift in consciousness, tune in to those other frequencies? Visualise, for example, an energy-matrix in place around the surface of the earth, dimly perceptible to us, and made more detectable by dowsing. An increase in energy widens the 'wave-band', allowing this subtle energy to spill over into physical manifestation. In producing such manifestation in synchronicity with increasing planetary consciousness amongst people, such a matrix serves as a pre-programmed vehicle to assist in our perception of a wider and deeper perspective. Only now are we beginning to understand different levels of reality, and how our understanding of these principles allows us to access what in the past was viewed as 'mystery'. How many doors can be opened by this understanding?

Perhaps the symbols have always been in place, serving their own purpose in the complex inter-dimensional matrix that is woven into the planet, along with other devices already in position in the grid system. These align themselves to the earth's geometric configurations which wind around and within her infrastructure. Consider the universal law

WORLD CHANGE

White Bear Fredericks with Hopi artefacts. (*Paul Scott*)

Is it a coincidence that these remarkable events are occurring at a time of great global change? As people, we go through the birth and death process not only at the beginning and end of our lives but also as we shed old personas and move on to new levels of understanding. Is it not also conceivable that the earth also undergoes a similar process? The earth is a living entity with its own path of development, laws and purpose. This has been the viewpoint of indigenous peoples throughout the ages. Even westerners have perceived and commented on the power of nature and her ways of balancing and evolving. When we shift into new levels of empowerment or realisation, everything in our own lives must fall into place within that new perspective. So it is with the earth. As we move into this new frequency, and the earth claims its own destiny, everything that is part of her must come into a state of realignment. One of the most prevalent common factors shared by ancient cultures and belief systems is that of a conscious natural force. This can take the form of 'gods' who are responsible for particular aspects of the natural world, or it can be a perception of the earth as an entity. The Australian Aborigines, indeed, have the belief that all of creation was dreamed into being by the earth. As she moves into a higher state, we could be witnessing the beginning of a realignment. Everything on earth is a facet of the higher consciousness and therefore has its part to play. Since we are also part of the whole, we cannot remain unaffected by the change, and must also fulfil our appointed tasks.

It is hard to grasp the scope of the immense changes that have already started to take place upon the planet as we move into this shift which is resonating on many different levels: social, economic, political, geographical and individual. How many of us are going through profound changes in our own lives, and how many of our friends are doing the same? If you amplify that, you will see that the scale is enormous.

that all things are part of the whole and reflect different aspects operating within a single framework. What other devices could be in place around the earth's mantle which could also move down into the denser levels, being triggered by the frequency alignments? What other phenomena are we going to witness in the foreseeable future, and how much re-evaluation of the old? Like all aspects of universal symbolism, the circles are probably performing functions on other levels, acting like keys to levels behind the physical. We cannot disregard the consciousness-raising function performed by the existence of an easily-accessible and tangible phenomenon which cannot be adequately explained in rational scientific or even conventional-wisdom terms. If the mass of population were simply hereby persuaded that there are things that science cannot account for, this, in itself, would represent a tremendous consciousness shift.

It is possible that many souls will not be able, for one reason or another, to resonate with all that the new frequency will bring, and will choose to leave by the door of old conflicts or of the climatic or geographical upheavals which are currently occurring around the world. Those who remain and those to come have chosen to partake of the new level of experience and consciousness.

At this very special time, not only is the earth calling on the collective unconscious for assistance, but also it is calling on influences outside our normal frame of reference. These influences have always been there but, because of this period of great change, they have been allowed a closer connection. This whole process of change is being assisted and monitored by an *essence* which could be considered globally peripheral, but has always been an essential part of the wider perspective. Like a mother giving birth to her baby, the earth is calling for assistance in midwifing this new beginning on all levels — from the collective consciousness, to influences outside our normal frame of reference — bringing into play various modes of practical assistance at this crucial time in history. The symbols in England could be considered part of this stabilising process.

Many who understand this level of metaphysics are amongst us, some in physical bodies, giving information and activating the memories of those who have a part to play. That influence has always been here. How can we understand these higher-dimensional aspects from our three-dimensional linear perspectives? Only through our ability to shift consciousness and begin to perceive on all levels. All this is in accord with universal law and in unison with all things, like the wheels of a clock. All aspects are turning full circle, influencing each other to ultimately move the whole. We are about to dust off the pages of history and move toward the dawning of a new understanding of past, present and future, held together as one agreed principle by a fine thread of collective consciousness, in a spiral ever onwards back to the Source.

Has the earth ever gone through this process before? Much of the data in history books and mythology are just faint reflections of a wider past that we are only just beginning to understand. How much of that still has influence today, as more and more examples of change present themselves? What we are witnessing in the crop fields of England is not an end-product but a part, perhaps only a *side-effect*, of a much larger process. Who knows how many people who have a role to play in this process are being given the information that they need, and possibly a tantalising glimpse of another dimensional viewpoint?

It has often been pointed out that the concentration of sacred sites around the globe could correspond to acupuncture points in the earth's energy-field. They have also been referred to as the earth's chakras. The appearance of the overwhelming majority of crop circles at one particular point indicates the current focus of healing and growth, and it is clear that this focus could change, or continue on a level which would lead to the cessation of the visible phenomena. Of course, one wonders what other symbols and wondrous phenomena are in store for us in another dimension, yet to be revealed as the evolving crop circle process develops.

OHANA — THE FAMILY

As time went on, Dean found his travels following a path where the itinerary seemed already set — each place he visited, he found people who all seemed to have input into his ever-widening story. He felt a 'pull' to Maui Hawaii, and shortly after his arrival was invited to go to a luncheon attended by many people. At the end, as he was leaving, Dean noticed a Hawaiian woman (whose name turned out to be Pua) sitting in a corner. Their eyes met, and she jumped up and said "Dean? What took you so long?" This was interesting, for no one knew of his coming to Hawaii. Soon they sat down as if old friends, and got into an exchange, in which she said she did not see him as a white man, but as a person who had had a role to play in Hawaii long ago. She said that the first thing he must do is go up the mountain and into the crater of Haleakala, the volcano, to find the place where he should be, and to meet the guardians there. This he duly did: approaching the summit (by car), he felt overcome with energy to the point where he had to be helped out of the car to sit on a rock. After a couple of minutes he had a strong picture of himself and another group of beings trying to touch each other — there was a feeling that the veil between them was very thin, and that they could nearly touch. Dean broke down with emotion, and after a while felt very light and complete — next day he was amazed at the brightness of the colours of everything and the sharpness of his sight. He came back down from the volcano with an enhanced sense of the universality of the jigsaw which was emerging.

Like the Wessex Triangle, and the Sedona area in Arizona, Maui is a place where legend and phenomena abound on the inter-dimensional comings and goings of supernatural beings, and some look on it as one of the gateways into global grid configurations. Many in Hawaii still understand the old ways, and can utilise *mana*, the universal life-force, as once did the builders of Stonehenge. They have a saying in Hawaii that if you are unsure, look back to the Source. Their cultural heritage goes back a very long way. They too have an Atlantis legend, and claim that the spirit of *aloha* and the well-known Hawaiian healing energy go back to that period. They too regard our present day as being a time of great change. The ancestors, with whom they communicate, have talked to them about this thinning of the veil between the worlds. Promises were made long ago that this time would come and that many signs would precede this change. One of the signs was what came to be called the Harmonic Convergence (the period of intensity in August 1987), and another was the cosmic dance over Hawaii of the total solar eclipse of 11th July 1991, which was reckoned to

herald a major move into a new frequency. They also felt that the circles were part of the coming changes, feeling a great affinity for them and regarding them as harmonising with their own cultural traditions.

They see the eclipse as a representation of the Mother and Father coming together, and of the reuniting of the family of humanity. They believe that all beings came from the same source, and that over this period the many dimensional worlds will come together. The veil will become thinner and eventually all will become part of the Ohana (family). They believe that the different realms (dimensions) will come from above, below and from within, and that the changes will eventually become powerful enough to extend into the physical, as well as the spiritual, and that the lands that once were part of the Hawaiian's heritage will rise once more.

Hawaiians say that those who once lived in ancient times are now assisting with the changes, and many are with us now. Some in spirit, but also many have been born into this time to become teachers, and are being drawn back to their homeland, although they might not possess the same colour skin. Those who have the ability can recognise them for what they really are.

The Hawaiian vision is of a time of great harmony and understanding from which we all came — the Source. We are currently living through a process which will bring us back to that original state, after a period of great upheaval, and we can all once more live in perfect attunement with each other, completing the circle.

There has clearly been a high concentration of energy at these particular points on the global energy-matrix for several millennia at least — as is attested by the presence of sacred structures themselves. Perhaps this has led to a thinning of the veil between the worlds, and, indeed, many of these well-known power-places have been considered as gateways in a multi-dimensional sense. It is also possible that the designation of these sites as gateways should be taken in a literal sense — that they were actually made use of to travel between dimensions, or to communicate through other dimensions to other places and people in different places in our dimension. These places also abound with legend and myths of beings who were once in great numbers, but whose viability was jeopardised by a change in the collective unconscious brought about by earth's cyclic changes and the advent of organised religion.

People still go to these sites and experience a wide variety of experiences on a number of different levels, dictated perhaps by the preconceptions of the individual and also upon what they are capable of accepting. The ability to make proper use of these power points relies on the individual's capacity to transcend the limitations of three-dimensional thinking, and to comprehend the interwoven tapestry of a far greater story. Many cultures still regard these sites with reverence and understand how they fit into the sacred geometrical configurations, how they are an integral part of the creative pattern. Many believe that these sites are now being reactivated as support mechanisms for the alignment of the energy-grid system.

SYMBOLISMS

We have to be very careful as to how we approach the symbolism of circles, for it is possible to get trapped in the interpretation game, and to lose sight of the goal. We need to change our perspective and allow ourselves to feel the essence of the symbols as they relate to our own spiritual position — all interpretation must be based on the development-stage and expectations of the individual.

The information that we need is within us, encoded at the genetic level — what some refer to as cellular memory. The reason why societies with an older cultural tradition are able to accept and understand more of the multidimensional universe is that they have developed techniques for assessing this information and making use of it. Our predecessors who built and used the sacred sites found in such profusion in Britain almost certainly employed the same, or similar, methods. Our society lost the means of entering into the genetic memory in a purposeful manner, but the information is still within us — we simply have to open the door to it.

Language is a very low-density form of communication, often leading to confusion and misunderstanding. Even after the written word became common in Wales and Ireland, the traditional bards refused to allow their stories to be written down, implying that writing them down 'killed' the power of the stories. If their stories were part of a wider, performance-based magic which they used to acquaint their audiences with a higher truth, they were perhaps correct to have this view. Symbolic and pictorial communication is a higher medium of communicative resonance and allows more of the essence to come through. The combined oral and pictorial tradition of such cultural groups as the Hopi, for example, has allowed them to transmit and make use of information throughout thousands of years without the distortions and loss of meaning which generally happens over centuries of linguistic communication and translation — does Shakespeare really mean the same to us now as it did to the Elizabethans? Or even to the Victorians, for that matter? This is because the information is not contained in the symbols and pictures, yet they are used to point the way to the information. This technique of 'collective thought', operating at the genetic level, is a most effective form of information-transfer, aided by graphic representation but not relying on it.

When we talked with the Hopi we were struck by the way their traditions harmonised with much of what we would term as 'new age' and metaphysical philosophy. They too are aware that there is much more to be seen than we allow ourselves to see and there is a far greater picture than the one that we can perceive.

To the Hopi or the Maya, symbols do not contain knowledge and understanding in and of themselves.

They are signposts to the greater truth, which cannot be accessed by means of three-dimensional thinking. Like all signposts they can be misread — the map can be mistaken for the territory.

As we enter this exciting new stage of development it is possible that we will not only witness new phenomena but that we will be able to re-evaluate the old. We will be able to read the signs which have been around us for a long time and form part of a wider truth. The crop circles are another link in a continuous chain of information that is available to anyone who recognises their own ability to access it. The greatest lesson that we can learn from the ancient cultures is that we can read this information for ourselves. It is written down for all to read but is stored in a form which can only be reached by a shift in consciousness.

When one begins to 'see' that information, much of what would be termed 'mysterious phenomena' begins to take shape and to move into a logical and coherent pattern. People from the industrial western cultural tradition for the most part regard the pictograms with uncomprehending recognition. Those from the older cultures seem to react with a much more sophisticated interpretation of their significance because they were able to regard them from a spiritual and intuitive standpoint — those that we talked to spoke of their meaning within a wider context of historical progression, while not attempting to give us a 'translation'.

The crop circles are part of a process, not an end in themselves — and they should never be regarded as such. They are caused by a combination of several cooperating agencies, united by the wider issues of planetary evolution, and are an integral part of the tapestry of life which binds us together in the universal plan. They are a combination of several factors coming together, united by the wider issues of planetary growth, and are an integral part of the thread which binds us all together in the tapestry of life, woven from the finery of the universal plan. We have spoken of the view of sacred sites being gateways to a higher reality, but the most important gateway for the human spirit lies elsewhere — within us. It is within ourselves that we will find the means to solve the crop circle enigma, and to realise that they involve a greater quest than a three-dimensional search for meaning.

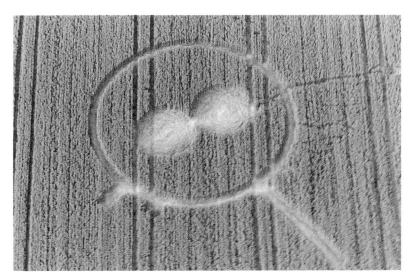

'Two eggs in a pan' at Ogbourne Maisey, near Marlborough. This fitted exactly into the 'interrupted triple ringer' on Longwood Warren 1990. (*Crop Circle Enigma*, p.94) (*Busty Taylor*)

6. Earth energies, leys, megalithic man and grids

DAVID TILT

ENERGY, WATER AND QUARTZ

WE LIVE IN A WORLD where energy and water are fundamental to all forms of life. As the earth orbits the sun, life and many of the physical aspects of our planet are responsive and constantly influenced by cosmic events. In many respects the earth is a living body in a constant state of change. Although the level of magnetism on earth goes through a definite cycle each year, this regularity can be affected by factors occurring elsewhere in our solar system. Sunspots and solar flares increase magnetic activity and can affect the biorhythms of all living creatures and plants[1]. A more commonly known effect is the widespread disruption of radio communications.

Our satellite the moon not only controls the ebb and flow of ocean tides — its gravitational pull also affects the land mass, particularly at fault-lines in the earth's surface where there can be a build-up of pressure between geological surfaces. Where quartz is trapped underground between opposing surfaces, the mineral is squeezed and an electrical charge is generated. Quartz is a *piezo-electric* mineral — it has a natural ability to accumulate a substantial electrical charge when subjected to pressure. Quartz radiates eight outward-flowing energy-lines which can be located by dowsing. A strange fact is that this energy-pattern (type A) always aligns itself in relation to magnetic north — this is known as a *polar factor*. Therefore each underground point where quartz is under pressure is a natural power centre, a source of electromagnetic energy.

The gravitational pull of the moon has the same effect on underground water — which also has its own electrical field, consisting of a series of concentric rings of energy. This energy-pattern (type B) can also be located by dowsing. The electrical field of underground water is weaker than the electrical charge from quartz. Nevertheless it is another natural source of earth energy that is related to lunar periods.

The levels of electromagnetic energy in quartz and the electrical energy in water peak at new moon and to a lesser extent at full moon. The moon's effect on underground water may also contribute to the build-up of the energy-charge in quartz wherever it is trapped in close association with water. The *As Above, So Below* relationship between earth energies and the cosmos is further emphasised by the fact that lunar and solar eclipses also affect the level of energies at these natural power centres.

In a scientific sense the apparent link between the human psyche and earth energies could be caused by quantum inseparability. Ever since I commenced dowsing earth energies I have experienced an extraordinary series of coincidences, of which there have been far too many for them to be dismissed as

Type A dowsable energy pattern.

Type B energy pattern

just 'chance' events. Generally these have involved information connected with my research arriving synchronistically with the arising of my need for it, often not consciously sought, and coming from totally unexpected and apparently unrelated sources. Even my wife Ann, who has not been actively involved in my research, has commented about the odd way so many facts and connections involving people, places and events have just dropped into place.

It has long been recognised that the moon's phases can affect human behaviour and consciousness. This could be because every human being has an energy-field, and a significant part of the human body is water. Energy and water are somehow linked to consciousness, and it is probably the interaction between human and other energy-fields that affects human perception and consciousness. Earth energies appear to give some people a sense of spiritual awareness, which suggests that a living earth has an ethereal body with a consciousness of its own.

Many different peoples throughout the world — for example, the Australian Aborigines, Native Americans and Celts — have for a long time regarded quartz as magical, as a means of communication with other persons at a distance, and with other levels of existence. Offerings of quartz stones were made at holy wells in Wales, and in both Wales and Scotland charms of quartz and rock crystals were used to give the water of healing wells a magical potency[2]. The structure of water is unstable and subject to major changes as a result of even very low-level energy-influences[3]. Placing of crystals in relation to water has a parallel in the modern day practice of healing with crystals.

In folklore and tradition, water in the countryside has a close association with nature spirits — which although it may be difficult to believe in their existence, are probably a natural phenomenon of the living earth. Some other deities associated with 'water cults' are probably a creation of human belief and emotion, which can implant a sense of well-being or unpleasantness at a particular place.

Archaeologist and dowser T. C. Lethbridge referred to the human energy-field as the *psyche-field*, and the electrical energy of water as a *naiad field*. He believed that water was particularly responsive to emotion and could retain images of certain feelings and events. These could be triggered by someone else's psyche-field perhaps years later, and that person would experience the original feeling or event that was recorded there[4]. There is considerable evidence that quartz energy in association with water can retain and periodically replay 'sounds' from the past.

Many prehistoric sites are located near water. In his book *The Stone Circles of the British Isles*, Aubrey Burl points out that "Where an avenue of stones is associated with a stone circle it almost invariably leads from a source of water, indicating the importance of water in the ceremonies that took place in the rings". In Wiltshire, a long avenue links Stonehenge to the River Avon, and both the avenues at Avebury are close to water[5]. Glastonbury is thought to have been an island surrounded by water in the past, and the Tor is known to have spring-water flowing up underneath it. Silbury Hill has often been surrounded by water, and Michael Dames sees Silbury as a 'primordial hill' rising from the waters[6]. Dames believes he has found the whole body of the Earth Mother or goddess centred on Silbury Hill in Wiltshire, where 27 Neolithic monuments (such as long barrows, causewayed camps and stone circles, together with the natural features and contours of the landscape) form a "33-mile topographic image"[6], an outline of the Earth Mother[7]. Dames sees the hill and its encircling moat as "the Great Goddess in her pregnant state", giving birth annually at Lammas, when harvest begins[8]. Of course all this relates to surface water and does not take into account the possibility that all these sites of prehistoric antiquity were originally constructed in relation to the electrical fields of underground water.

LEYS

A significant fact is that Stonehenge, Avebury, Glastonbury, and Silbury Hill, are prominent places on *ley alignments*. It was Alfred Watkins who first used the term '*ley*' in his book *The Old Straight Track*, to describe the alignments he perceived in a sudden vision while out riding across the hills of Herefordshire. Watkins noticed that there seemed to be a network of lines or tracks linking prehistoric sites, ancient mounds (including those on which churches have been built), standing stones, beacon hills, old moats, ponds and holy wells. He concluded that many tumuli and round barrows that were often surrounded by water had been used as reflection-points to aid the sighting of a ley. The publication of Watkins' book led to the formation of *The Straight Track Club*, whose members searched for leys on ordnance maps, and then went on organised field-trips to investigate ley-alignments in the countryside. The exact number of features in the landscape that constitute a true ley is still disputed, although it is generally accepted that at least five points on a line are acceptable, and the length of a ley can be from one mile to several miles.

The archaeological establishment has never accepted Watkins' thesis that some prehistoric features in the landscape had been aligned in relation to each other on a series of straight lines, even though some professional archaeologists have found evidence to support his thesis. The main objection is over Watkins' description of leys as *trackways*, and the fact that many of these so-called ley-alignments often cross inaccessible and difficult parts of the countryside (such as mountains, the steepest part of hills, cliffs, and the widest sections of rivers). It is true to say that ancient tracks usually follow the easiest route, but it does not rule out the possibility that leys have a hidden meaning or purpose.

Archaeological opinion is also critical about the wide variety of sites and features that can constitute points on a ley. It is argued that anyone examining a map will easily be able to discover an alignment of many different landscape features because the choice of features is so wide. There could be a grain of truth that statistically this is possible, but if you limit the choice to prehistoric and sacred sites, of which a considerable number exist that have been precisely aligned in relation to each other, then a totally different picture emerges.

Alfred Watkins was convinced that many leys were also astronomical alignments, aligned to the rising or setting of the sun or to the track of a star. This led him to believe that the overall principle behind leys was mystical, and probably related to ancient religion. Anything suggesting the mysticism of leys has always been rejected by the archaeologists. It seems that Watkins, towards the end of his life (he died in 1935), had modified his straight-track thesis, and he appears to have foreseen the course some ley research would take in later years.

In 1939, Arthur Lawton published a pamphlet entitled *Mysteries of Ancient Man* in which he claimed that ancient sites, of the kind used as ley-markers, fell into patterns in which set distances and angles were involved. These measures resulted, Lawton believed, from the effect of a subtle force being marked out by the site builders, and he suggested that dowsing might be one way of detecting this primordial energy[9].

Also in the late 1930's, a leading ley-hunter and dowser, Major F. C. Tyler, made an observation that puzzled his fellow enthusiasts: that leys often consist of two parallel tracks. This hardly seemed to make sense; why make two tracks close together when one would suffice? It seemed to suggest that Watkins could have been mistaken about the whole straight track theory[10].

After the interruption of the war, interest in leys declined until the 1960's when leys were more widely seen as magnetic lines of force, and an important feature of Earth Mysteries research. The concept of leys carrying an unknown force that is linked to the earth's natural magnetism was brilliantly expounded in John Michell's masterly work *The View Over Atlantis*. Michell wrote: "It was as if some flow of current followed the course of these man-made alignments". Having studied Watkins' thesis and *feng-shui*, a Chinese system of geomancy, Michell identified leys as the western equivalent of dragon-paths, *lung-mei*, and the magnetic current they carry as the dragon pulse. *Feng-shui* treats nature as a living entity, and believes that man must learn to conform to it if he is to be happy. According to *feng-shui*, the surface of the earth is a 'dim mirror' of the powers of the heavens — the stars and planets[11].

In 1978, Tom Graves, a well known dowser, wrote *Needles of Stone*, a fascinating book which explored the whole spectrum of Earth Mysteries. Like Michell, Graves suggested that prehistoric sites, megaliths, and their associated lines of force are like a system of acupuncture on the body of a living earth[12].

For a long time, opinion has been sharply divided as to whether leys are lines of energy or purely alignments. There is ample evidence to show that each of these viewpoints is true in different cases. Most leys, whether alignments or energy-lines, can be related to the megalithic era. However, there are also alignments that appear to belong to other historical periods, such as church alignments. A good example of a pure alignment is the Devereux and Thomson 'Holy Hill' alignment at Wilmington, Sussex[13]. There is need to continue Watkins-style ley work because I believe it is the only way possible to fully evaluate the very complex pattern of alignments across the landscape.

Work of this nature can sometimes yield some surprising results, especially in relation to lines of energy. A ley-hunter, Mr D. G. Whiteside, using a map, pencil and ruler, discovered 22 alignments centred on a churchyard mound at Berwick, Sussex. In 1975, he wrote to the Sussex Archaeological Society requesting them to look into the matter. As far as I know nothing was done regarding this interesting information. Fortunately the Society did file his letter, of which they gave me a copy in 1983.

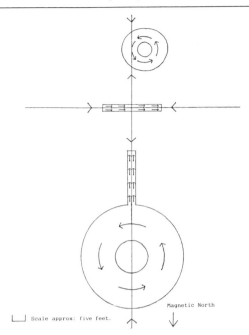

WILMINGTON, East Sussex, formation in barley, late July 1990. The small circle has 16 energy lines radiating from its centre, and the large circle has 24. Arrows indicate the direction of flattened or swirled crops. The configuration appeared at the intersection of two energy-lines, the direction of flow (shown by arrows), reverses 3ft above ground. (*David Tilt*)

This happened because I had contacted the Society after tracing a powerful line of energy from a henge site several miles away to the churchyard mound. I had also discovered that nineteen lines of energy radiate from this mound to other church mounds, tumuli, and long barrows. In checking these energy-lines an interesting fact emerged: the magnificent Windover Hill barrow does not have a line of energy to it or from it, and yet Hunter's Burgh and Long Burgh barrows which are situated to each side of Windover, are both connected by energy-lines to the churchyard mound[14]. More recent work has revealed that some of the energy-lines which radiate from the mound are lunar alignments, and that four energy-lines go to former stone positions at a stone circle site in a field adjacent to the church[15].

Linear alignments are a feature of many countries.

Tony Morrison's book *Pathways to the Gods* describes the existence of 'old straight tracks' across large parts of the landscape of South America. These Indian pathways link the same type of sites, shrines, holy wells, and others, as Watkins' leys.

Recently, I had an interesting discussion with an Australian who told me about his travels with Aborigines and how they 'sing' their way across the landscape. The sacred paths they follow are known as *song-lines*, and link magical centres where sacred rites are performed, which can activate the life-force and increase the fertility of the land. Megalithic remains of standing stones and stone formations on alignments, sometimes north-to-south, have been found in New South Wales, Australia. Apparently compasses often go crazy at these structures. The Aborigines say they were built by a mysterious race of white-skinned 'culture-heroes' who had existed in the long-ago dream-time[16].

MEGALITHIC SITES

Megalithic structures are a feature of many countries, with an extraordinary variety of sites in Great Britain and Ireland. Why were they built, and what was their purpose? Theories abound, yet the megaliths and their builders remain the great enigma of prehistory.

In the late 1800's and the early part of this century, Sir Norman Lockyer (1836-1920), a scientist and astronomer, did some important research concerning the orientation of megalithic monuments in Greece, Egypt, and Britain. Lockyer was convinced that many megalithic temples and structures, including the Great Pyramid at Giza and the temple of Amen-Re at Karnak, had been deliberately aligned to the sun and stars. At Stonehenge, he discovered astronomical alignments which appeared to be related to solar calendar dates.

Lockyer also noticed that two straight lines could be drawn through Stonehenge which, when extended, passed through features that were proba-

bly of great antiquity. One line passed through Sidbury, Stonehenge, Grovely Castle, and Castle Ditches; the other passed through Stonehenge, Old Sarum Mound, Salisbury Cathedral, and Clearbury Ring. In addition, the lines were so arranged that Stonehenge, Grovely Castle, and Old Sarum Mound formed a 'perfect' equilateral triangle. Yet another curious feature was that one side of the triangle extended onwards and aligned through Sidbury, Stonehenge, Grovely Castle, Castle Ditches forming the midsummer sunrise alignment he had found at Stonehenge[17].

Lockyer's work at Stonehenge provided the basis for seeing this classical monument as an astronomically-aligned temple designed as a calendar to determine precise dates throughout the agricultural year. It was not until more recent years that more detailed and systematic studies of the alignments at Stonehenge were undertaken by several researchers. In 1964, an amateur astronomer, Mr C. A. Newham, published a booklet entitled The *Enigma of Stonehenge and its Astronomical and Geometrical Significance*. This was the result of several years study, which turned out to support Lockyer's findings. Newham wrote: "There is not the slightest reason to depart from the belief that the outlying features of Stonehenge were ingeniously arranged in order to provide a calendar by which the religious and social activities of the peoples concerned could be arranged"[18].

Meanwhile, Dr Gerald Hawkins, Professor of Astronomy at Boston University, had been feeding a computer with astronomical data related to prehistory. Hawkins was puzzled by the fifty-six 'Aubrey holes' on the perimeter of Stonehenge. Data from the computer revealed that the 'Aubrey holes' could have been used as a calendar to predict eclipses. A full account of this research was published in Hawkins' book *Stonehenge Decoded* in 1965[19].

Professor Alexander Thom, who made a lifetime study of the geometric arrangement of megaliths, had a major impact on archaeological thought when he published the results of his meticulous surveys of megalithic sites throughout Britain[20]. Thom's work revealed that megalithic people possessed constructional and geometrical skills of the highest order, and that a wide variety of sites had been constructed to a standard unit of measurement — the megalithic yard of 2.72ft. Thom believed that many megaliths had been built for use as celestial observatories because a common feature at most of these places were astronomical alignments which related to either the sun, the moon, or stars. Interestingly, some, like the stones of Callanish, on Lewis in the Outer Hebrides, had been aligned north-to-south.

A dowser, Guy Underwood, spent several years surveying prehistoric sites, the results of which were published in his book *The Pattern of the Past* in 1969, five years after his death. He had arranged this in order to save his colleagues any embarrassment, as he thought his work would probably invoke criticism from professional archaeologists. Underwood's book is important because it is the first really detailed work to establish a connection between the location of ancient monuments and the presence of underground water.

The impetus for this research came from two water diviners, Captain Robert Boothby and Reginald Allender Smith. Boothby had claimed that barrows and prehistoric sites were crossed by underground streams, and that long-barrows had a stream running along their full length. Smith had asserted that at the centre of every prehistoric site a spot could be found from which a number of underground streams formed a radiating pattern. He called these spots blind springs. Underwood was able to confirm Boothby's and Smith's findings. There is now a general assumption that Underwood was looking for water, and to a certain extent, this is what he dowsed, but he also found something different, which he thought was some kind of magnetic force in the ground because it gave a different dowsing response to that obtained by locating water.

"Its main characteristics are that it appears to be generated within the earth, and to cause wave-motion perpendicular to earth's surface; that it has great penetrative power; that it affects the nerve cells of animals; that it forms spiral patterns; and is controlled by mathematical laws involving principally the numbers three and seven. Until it can be otherwise identified, I shall refer to it as the 'earth-force'. It could be an unknown principle, but it seems more likely that it is an unrecognised effect of some already-established force, such as magnetism or gravity. The earth-force manifests itself in lines of discontinuity, which I call 'geodetic lines', and which form a network on the surface of the earth."

This is very interesting, because Underwood surveyed many ancient sites that are on ley-alignments — including Stonehenge, in which he had a special interest. At most of these places he dowsed different types of parallel lines, some of which he called *water lines*. He also found (type B) concentric-ring water patterns, and a variety of spiral lines and patterns. I say this because, although he called the spirals he found around standing stones 'water spirals', many dowsers have detected a line of energy spiralling upwards from the ground around standing stones. These stones have usually been erected to stand on straight energy-lines, either at stone circles where the lines link individual stones, or where a solitary stone has been placed on an energy-line crossing the countryside.

Underwood also surveyed many churches and cathedrals, which also appear to have been built and precisely aligned in relation to underground water. The patterns and effects that he dowsed once more indicate the presence of another type of energy or force besides that of water. This confirms my own findings that many churches have been built on prehistoric sites of ancient sanctity. Bayham Abbey near the border of Sussex and Kent has been precisely aligned in relation to a much earlier site. Fifteen energy-lines converge on the altar in the presbytery, where I also dowsed a type-B water pattern. One of the energy-lines to the altar goes exactly down the centre of the presbytery, quire, and the nave[21].

Underwood also researched two well-known hill figures which are thought to date from prehistory: the White Horse of Uffington and the Cerne Abbas Giant. It is possible that the Uffington White Horse is actually a dragon, because a great circular artificial mound below this hill-figure is known as Dragon's Hill. According to Underwood, both the horse and the dragon had great mystic significance to the ancients. The dragon was associated with creation and life-giving. The lines, patterns, and spirals that Underwood dowsed at these hill figures, and also at Dragon's Hill, once more give a clear indication of energy and water at all of these places. With his comprehensive and rather complex dowsing surveys Underwood believed he had discovered:

"a principle of nature that exists, but is unknown to, or unidentified by science. The philosophers and priests of the old religions seem to have believed that, particularly when manifested in spiral forms, the earth force was involved not only as a catalyst with the construction of matter but also with the generative powers of nature; that it was part of the mechanism by which what we call Life comes into being; and to have been the 'Great Arranger' — that balancing principle which keeps all nature in equilibrium."

Underwood's work at hill figures is of particular interest to me, because a few years ago I discovered that the famous chalk hill figure in Sussex, the Long Man of Wilmington, has seven energy-lines going into the base of the figure — one to each of the staves, one on each side of the figure at a point midway between the figure and each stave, one to the crotch, and finally one to each of the feet. Significantly, the energy-line to the left foot goes to the pre-1874 position of that foot, when it is believed the foot pointed westwards.

The discovery that the Long Man appears to be an energised hill-figure became especially significant when I was tracking energy-lines in the vicinity of Firle Beacon, Sussex. I found a point at the base of the Beacon where there were energy-lines that appeared to align with other energy-lines from tumuli on top of the Beacon. I decided to carry out an infra-red photo survey there. This resulted in the discovery of a lost chalk hill figure — a pillar-type figure with a pointed head and what appear to be three arms on each side of the central column.

My interest in dowsing energy-lines was the result of a chance happening in 1983. I was working on a Roman site with a colleague when we noticed that several energy-lines crossed the area we were dowsing. The lines appeared to originate from an area in an adjacent field. A subsequent search revealed that a large number of energy-lines were radiating in all directions from this spot. I thought at first this unusual place could be explained purely in geological terms, so I decided to trace one of the energy-lines. Much to my surprise it travelled a considerable distance before terminating at the churchyard mound at Berwick, which I mentioned earlier. My second surprise was the discovery that the mound had other energy-lines radiating from it.

The following few weeks were spent on what proved to be a difficult task, tracing many of these energy-lines to places along the downland ridge. With my curiosity at boiling point, I decided to return to the area from which I had traced the first energy-line, and to carry out a full scale dowsing survey. This proved more difficult than I imagined, but during the next fifteen months, it soon became apparent that I had discovered a henge site where the radiating lines of energy had been tapped in a numerical sequence which relates to 56 pits on the perimeter of the site — similar to Stonehenge.

The discovery of this site with a type-A energy-pattern provided the basis for tracing many lines of energy across the countryside to other sites, and landscape features associated with a vast circuit of energy. The creation of this energy-system appears to have been achieved by constructing many prehistoric sites in relation to underground water with its type-B energy-pattern, then linking them with lines of energy. I include stone circles in this category, but the mounds appear to be the most important feature in forming a network of energy, because, like the churchyard mound at Berwick, they usually have a supply line of energy flowing in from a henge, and other lines flowing out. Some of these go to tumuli, where they connect with more energy-lines from other places in the energy-system.

Silbury Hill, the largest artificial mound in Britain, is similar to the mound at Berwick because it has a considerable number of irregularly-spaced energy-lines radiating from it. This suggests that these lines, like those at Berwick, have been aligned to flow to other prehistoric landscape features some distance away. Recently, I confirmed that nine lines of energy flow from Silbury Hill to the West Kennet long barrow, and another powerful line of energy from a different direction goes through the entrance into the chamber. The purpose of a mound appears to be to boost and supplement the energy from a henge before distributing it elsewhere.

The henge that I discovered in Sussex is situated on a geological boundary, and is also in an area where there is quartz from Pleistocene drift deposits — this implies that the source of the energy there is probably quartz under pressure in a natural setting.

As far as I know, no one has yet determined how megalithic people were able to tap or draw off energy, and to run lines of energy across the landscape. The little archaeological evidence available suggests it may have been done by using shaped slithers of flint. Whatever the method, there appears to be some extraordinary knowledge behind it. I feel certain that because the energy-lines have been put into some of the hill-figures and long-barrows, the energy was seen to be a life-force. I also believe that megalithic people must have possessed an acute dowsing ability in order to locate these natural sources of energy. It may also be that because they had a considerable understanding about the mysteries of the universe, they may also have had a greater psychic awareness than we have, with our more material outlook.

CROP CIRCLES

One of the most interesting aspects of my work at the henge, and also in relation to energy-lines, is the phenomenon of crop circles. The primary cause of these mysterious circles appears to be the type-A energy-pattern found at the henges, and its apparent periodic energy-discharges. At certain times, the energy-charge becomes so great that it overflows and discharges itself. When this happens, air which is normally non-conducting becomes a conductor in the vicinity of the strong electrical field and carries the charge away from a number of places on the type-A energy-pattern. This causes what is known as an electric wind which can make crop circles at henge sites, if they are covered by a tall crop.

When a discharge occurs the energy also overflows along the main energy-lines from the site — this can cause a circle to appear away from the site, at energy-line junction points, and at places where tumuli have been removed (tumuli are like electrical distribution points). It is highly probable that the more complex circles where the crop is flattened in clockwise and counter-clockwise directions, are caused by almost simultaneous energy-discharges at different locations, and the resulting conflicting energy-flows. What I find so interesting is the apparent intelligent use of the energy in the formation of some crop circles.

During the night of 27/28th July 1984, a set of five crop circles in the shape of a cross appeared in a field of wheat at Rathfinny Farm near Seaford, Sussex. I had been working on a henge site further inland until the afternoon of the 28th. The energy-level at this site had increased to an unbearable degree, making it extremely unpleasant to continue dowsing there. Under these conditions disorientation, dizziness, and difficulty in concentration are experienced, and this type of site is best left alone until the energy decreases to a more tolerable level.

When I returned there on 3rd August, I was certain something unusual had happened, because the energy-level was exceptionally low. At the back of my mind was the similarity between the crossed alignment of crop circles which had appeared at Rathfinny — with the largest circle at the centre — and the type-A energy-pattern at the henge site. There were no visible signs at the henge because the site was covered by short grass. However, about 320 metres away on one of the main energy-lines from the site, there is a T-junction energy-line tapping point where another line has been run off in a different direction. This point is in an isolated spot which at the time was overgrown with long grass. The T-junction can be dowsed as a square pit about 1 metre across. In dry conditions with little grass it is visible as a square indentation in the ground. I subsequently discovered that the grass surrounding this tapping point had been flattened in a clockwise spiral creating a perfect circle some 2 metres in diameter. Another clockwise circle 3.35 metres in diameter, appeared in wheat at the same place in July 1990 — this coincided with the appearance of some other crop circles elsewhere in Sussex at the same time.

This caused problems because I had to decide whether to visit all the circles briefly, or to devote more time to just a few of them. In the end, I carried out a detailed examination of three crop circle configurations: the first at Lewes, then at Wilmington, close to the Long Man, and finally at Falmer. All of these configurations had appeared in relation to energy-lines. The circles at Lewes had a certain beauty and precision, but were extremely unpleasant to work on. I spent three days there and had a constant thundery headache. At the end of each day I felt completely exhausted — this tiredness lasted

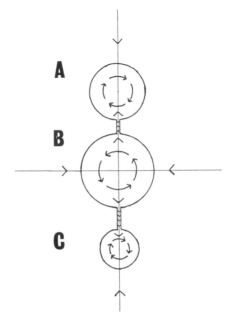

FALMER, East Sussex, three circles in wheat, early August 1990. Circle A (diameter 12ft) has 16 energy-lines radiating from a circular area at its centre; circle B (diameter 24ft) has 20; circle C (diameter 6ft) has 9. The configuration appeared at the intersection of two energy-lines — arrows denote the direction of flattened or swirled crops, and energy flows in the lines reverse 32ft above ground. (*David Tilt*)

about a week. Tom Fenn, the photographer who spotted these circles while taking aerial pictures on a business assignment, could not remain in any of the circles for longer than ten minutes without feeling sick.

After the crop was harvested, I was able to trace the energy-lines converging on the area where the circles appeared. Some time later, Tom Fenn took some friends to show them where the circles had been. They were standing close to the still-visible outline of the small circle at the centre of the configuration, when some of them experienced a strong tingling sensation. Later, they realised the only people who felt this strange effect had been standing in a north-south direction each side of the circle.

This seems a good point to state the obvious: a

Lost hill figure, NE side of Firle Beacon, Sussex. This figure, and another lost chalk hill figure of a giant at Firle, facing north, were located by tracking energy-lines, followed up with infra-red photo surveys. Both figures were energised by lines at the top and base, whereas the Long Man of Wilmington is energised solely at the base. The figure may have a face, but the detail is insufficient to prove this. It may also have a base, again difficult to establish, possibly because of hill-slip. (*David Tilt*)

hoaxed crop circle can be instantly recognised by a dowser because *there is no energy present*. There are other subtle differences that an experienced crop circle researcher can detect between a genuine circle and an artificial one. I do not propose to mention these details, except to say that a hoax, however well-executed, has an unnatural appearance.

In July 1989, I examined a crop circle at Cheese-foot Head, Hampshire. This circle appeared where a tumulus had been removed — eleven lines of energy radiated from an area approximately 2.5 metres in diameter at the centre of the circle — this is similar to the tumuli I have examined in Sussex. Almost a year later, I carried out a detailed examination of a dumb-bell-shape crop circle configuration at Cheese-foot Head. This had appeared on an energy-line which flows from the direction of the Longwood Estate. Prior to my arrival, another dowser, Richard Andrews, had also made a detailed examination of this configuration. Richard specialises in dowsing a layer or level of energy above the ground while I have always been primarily concerned with the archaeological layout of energy-lines in the ground. When we compared our respective plans of this configuration they were remarkably similar, except for one interesting fact: the energy-line flow in the upper level was the reverse of that in the ground.

Since then, I have discovered that the energy from

an energy-line fans out in an upward flow to approximately one metre above the ground, where it connects with another layer or level of energy. Continuing its upward flow above this level, the energy fans inwards until it reaches a further layer or level of energy about 2.1 metres above the ground. In other words, the flow from the ground to the third level assumes a diamond shape. The energy-flow alternates in each level[22].

During the past five years, I have been using a diode receiver (the modern version of a crystal set) coupled to a tape recorder to monitor the very strong pulsating signals that can be detected at the henge, and at some of the mounds elsewhere in the country-side — particularly those, similar to tumuli, with radiating energy-lines from their centres. The sound detected is very similar to that picked up accidentally by a BBC film crew within a crop circle in Wessex[23]. Naturally I was very interested to take recordings of the two energy-levels above ground. The results

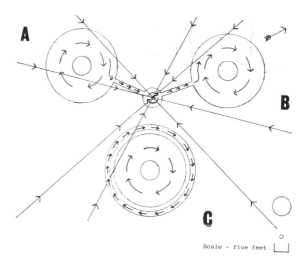

Circles in wheat at Houndean Bottom, nr Lewes, E Sussex, late July 1990. Circle A has 16 energy-lines radiating from its centre, circle B has 17 and circle C 19. The small circle in the middle (diameter 8ft) has four energy-lines crossing its centre, with a tightly-banded swirl of wheat. Circle C had a 3ft wide outer band of flattened wheat. (*David Tilt*)

revealed a difference between the signal pulses at ground level, and those in each of the two levels above ground — those in the first level above ground are faster, and the pulses in the highest level are extremely rapid. I have obtained similar results at Avebury, where I have taken recordings at some of the larger and smaller standing stones, and also on and above the energy lines which link the stones.

I believe these two different levels or layers of energy could have important implications in relation to the height of some megaliths, where for a long time dowsers have been finding different bands and spirals of energy. I do not think this is just because standing stones contain quartz, but probably because the stones link these different levels of energy.

The energy-lines and patterns that I have dowsed at crop circles are *in* the ground. Every circle I have examined had energy-lines radiating from the centre. Some circles also had a Type B energy-pattern — these circles have probably appeared at places where mounds and round barrows have been constructed over underground water, and removed in more recent times. Generally, dowsers have found a variety of different energy-patterns at crop circles, ranging from spirals to an assortment of geometric shapes, including star patterns.

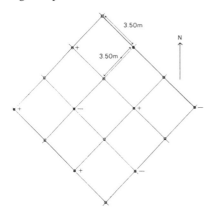

CURRY NET, of terrestrial origin, spanning the globe. Alternate charging and discharging lines. Distance between lines 10–12ft in central Europe, 12–15ft at Equator. (*Journ. Brit. Soc. Dowsers*)

This reminds me of the interesting time I spent dowsing energy-lines and patterns at several prehistoric sites, with a friend of mine, Mike Collier. Mike is an extremely sensitive dowser, and is the first person I met who could dowse with his hands — although, like me, he normally uses angle rods. I was often puzzled when Mike would occasionally find something which contradicted my own findings. He would talk about energy-lines which were increasing in width, and places where he could dowse mysterious circles which were only just forming. I remember he found several of these circles when we did a dowsing survey of former standing stone positions at Rushy Hill, near Peacehaven, Sussex. These findings are very similar to those of dowser Richard Andrews. Richard says he can tell where a crop circle is going to appear, by the shapes and patterns that are forming at certain places. He also mentions the variation in the width of energy-lines at particular times.

Dowsers are often criticised about the conflicting results they obtain, but the fact that an energy-level exists a little over halfway up the average dowser's body, may to a certain extent explain why there is such a variation in the results. Generally most features in the ground including energy-lines remain static, whereas everything in the first level above ground is in a state of flux and subject to change. Richard Andrews has noticed that the energy-level above ground has increased markedly in recent years, whereas I have not detected any increase, other than the normal variation in the energy-level below ground. I believe that some kind of interaction between these two energy-levels — particularly after energy-discharges from the type-A pattern — may hold a key to understanding some of the intelligent-looking crop circle formations. Many parallel energy-lines in this first level appear to be very similar to some of those found by Underwood.

Plate 33. HACKPEN HILL, near Marlborough. Formed 12th July 1991, the anniversary of the Alton Barnes double pictogram of 1990, it has the same 2:1 proportion in spacing of the circles along the axis. (*Busty Taylor*)

Plate 34. A pole shot of the Hackpen Hill Pictogram. (*Busty Taylor*)

34.

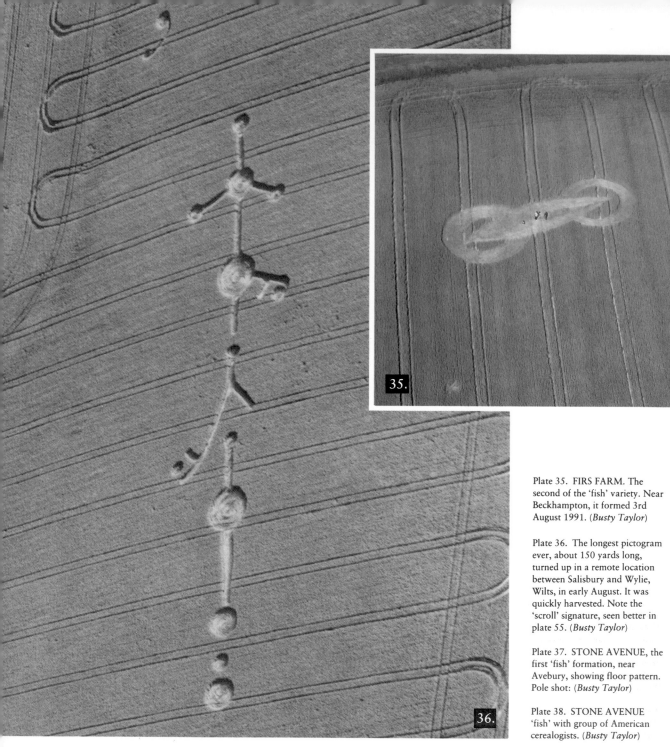

35.

36.

Plate 35. FIRS FARM. The second of the 'fish' variety. Near Beckhampton, it formed 3rd August 1991. (*Busty Taylor*)

Plate 36. The longest pictogram ever, about 150 yards long, turned up in a remote location between Salisbury and Wylie, Wilts, in early August. It was quickly harvested. Note the 'scroll' signature, seen better in plate 55. (*Busty Taylor*)

Plate 37. STONE AVENUE, the first 'fish' formation, near Avebury, showing floor pattern. Pole shot: (*Busty Taylor*)

Plate 38. STONE AVENUE 'fish' with group of American cerealogists. (*Busty Taylor*)

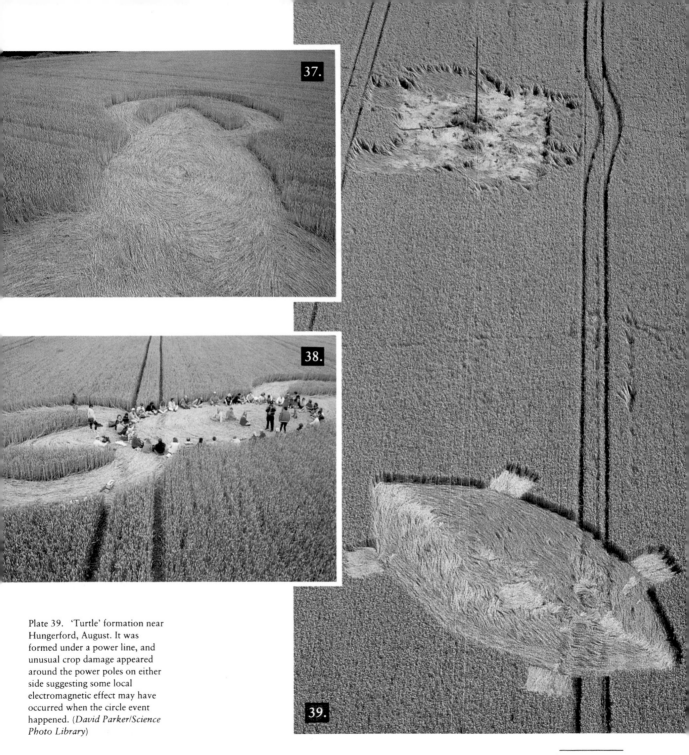

Plate 39. 'Turtle' formation near Hungerford, August. It was formed under a power line, and unusual crop damage appeared around the power poles on either side suggesting some local electromagnetic effect may have occurred when the circle event happened. (*David Parker/Science Photo Library*)

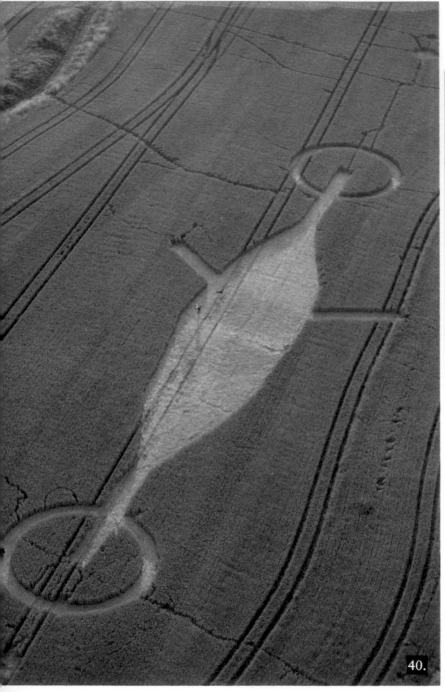

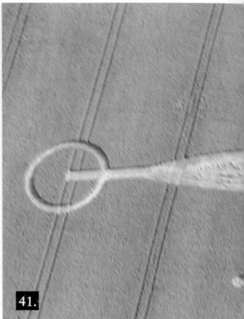

Plate 40. LOCKERIDGE, near Marlborough. The first of two identical 'whales'. Formed 30th July 1991. (*George Wingfield*)

Plate 41. FIRS FARM, Beckhampton. Close by, the second 'whale' appeared on 1st August 1991. (*Busty Taylor*)

Plate 42. FIRS FARM 'whale' floor pattern. Pole shot: (*Busty Taylor*)

Plate 43. HUNGERFORD, August. This looks more like an airship than a whale, but has similar features.
(*Alick Bartholomew*)

Plate 44. A third type of 'fish' at the Firs Farm, Beckhampton, early August 1991.
(*George Wingfield*)

42.

44.

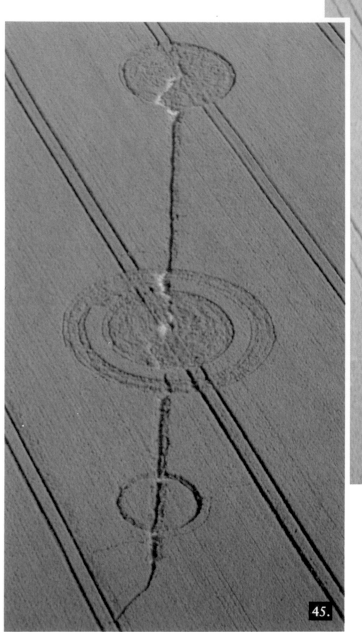

Plate 45. LOCKERIDGE. This large pictogram was found on 21st July 1991.
(*Paul Greenaway*)

Plate 46. Another 3-in-line at Roundway Hill, near Devizes.
(*George Wingfield*)

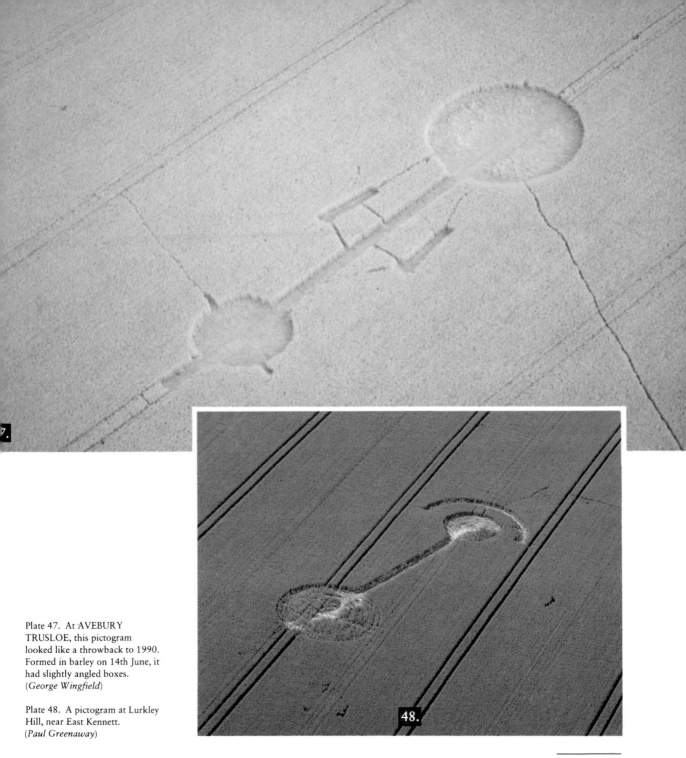

Plate 47. At AVEBURY
TRUSLOE, this pictogram
looked like a throwback to 1990.
Formed in barley on 14th June, it
had slightly angled boxes.
(*George Wingfield*)

Plate 48. A pictogram at Lurkley
Hill, near East Kennett.
(*Paul Greenaway*)

Plate 49. SILBURY. A pictogram right under Silbury Hill. (*Alick Bartholomew*)

Plate 50. SPALDWICK, Cambridgeshire. A wheel cross formation. (*George Wingfield*)

Plate 51. CLENCH COMMON, near Marlborough. This has been claimed as a hoax, and resembles the previous one above. (*Alick Bartholomew*)

ENERGY GRIDS

The most interesting feature of this first level above ground are the energy grids — a natural geomagnetic energy-system that we know little about at present. Various people have made attempts to systematise them (for example, Curry, Hartmann and Cathie), but the picture that emerges is clearly not the whole story.

The two most well-known grids are the Curry Net and the Hartmann Net. The Curry Net was discovered by Dr Manfred Curry as a result of his research into the human energy-field. It has a very regular grid pattern. The grid-lines span the whole world, running from south-west to north-east and south-east to north-west. The net is of terrestrial origin — magma radiation, earth magnetism, earth rotation.

The Hartmann Net is also referred to as the Global Grid. The grid lines run from north to south and from east to west. The Net is said to be of cosmic origin (some mention the Van Allen belt) and seems to be more unstable than the Curry Grid. It has a

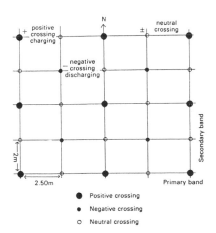

HARTMANN NET, of cosmic origin, with phase changes every 6 hours at sunrise, noon, sunset and midnight, during which the waves sometimes disappear for a few minutes. Intensity of radiation influenced by sunspots, fullmoons, seasonal and meteorological changes. Some say the N–S lines are discharging or *yin* lines, and E–W lines are charging or *yang* lines. (*Journ. Brit. Soc. Dowsers*)

phase-change every six hours: at sunrise, noon, sunset, and midnight. During this phase-change the energies sometimes disappear for a few minutes. The intensity of its radiation is influenced by sunspots, full moon, seasons, and like the Curry Net it is influenced by meteorological conditions[24]. The Germans have done considerable research on the possible health effects for people living on negative energy-lines, and much more needs to be done[25].

A New Zealander, Bruce Cathie, claims to have found a grid of rectangles each 45 square nautical miles in area, set up on mathematical coordinates based on the harmonic relationships of gravity, the mass of the earth, and the speed of light. This grid is claimed to be an energy grid for UFOs[26].

Ever since 1984, when a large crop circle with four satellite appeared at Rathfinny Farm in Sussex, I have been certain the crop circle phenomenon is related to an energy system associated with some prehistoric sites and landscape features, and the lines of energy connecting these places. All the subsequent research I have undertaken has substantiated this viewpoint. Anyone who has seen a pictogram or any of the other complex formations which are evolving, in its natural setting, cannot fail to be impressed, nor can they really question, that some form of intelligence is involved — even though it manifests itself in an energy form. I often think about the vortices of energy that I dowsed in the dumbbell-shaped crop circle configuration (the 'Gaia' pictogram) at Cheesefoot Head, Hampshire, in June 1990. The vortices were noticeable in four rectangular impressions in the crop, and also in a narrow band around the perimeter of the circle where the crop had been flattened in an alternate direction. There is plenty of evidence that the builders of prehistoric structures like the stone circle at Avebury, and Silbury Hill, knew a great deal about some extraordinary aspects of earth energies. Even though this knowledge appears to have been bypassed by *science*, I feel certain it can be related to the physical sciences.

Life today seems a contradiction in the way that

vast sums are spent on space research, yet there is so much to discover concerning the earth's ethereal body. The clear relationship of the crop circle phenomenon to the various energy systems are raising people's awareness of earth energies. Clearly we need to study them in much greater depth to understand the changes taking place in the world today.

REFERENCES

1. Gauquelin, Michel: *The Cosmic Clocks*, Paladin–Granada 1980.

2. Bord, Janet and Colin: *The Secret Country*, Paladin–Granada 1978.

3. Gauquelin, Michel: *The Cosmic Clocks*, p 180, 'Trigger Effects'.

4. Graves, Tom & Hoult, Janet: *The Essential T C Lethbridge*, Granada, 1982.

5. Bord, Janet and Colin: *Sacred Waters*, Paladin Grafton Books 1986.

6. Bord, Janet and Colin: *Earth Rites*, Granada Publishing, 1982 (Book Club Associates Edition), photo caption, p 8.

7. Bord, Janet and Colin: *Earth Rites*, Granada 1982 (Dames, *The Avebury Cycle*).

8. Bord, Janet and Colin: *Earth Rites*, (Dames, *The Silbury Treasure*).

9. Pennick, Nigel & Devereux, Paul: *Lines on the Landscape*, Robert Hale, 1989.

10. Wilson, Colin: *Mysteries*, Panther–Granada Publishing, 1979.

11. Wilson, Colin: *Mysteries*, p 125.

12. Graves, Tom: *Needles of Stone Revisited*, Gothic Image, Glastonbury, 1989.

13. Devereux, Paul & Thomson, Ian: *The Ley Hunter's Companion*, Thames & Hudson, 1979.

14. Tilt, David: 'A Ley Henge in Sussex', *British Society of Dowsers Journal*, No 209, Sept 1985.

15. Tilt, David: 'Some Notes from Sussex (2)', *BSD Journal*, No 220, June 1988.

16. Gilroy, Rex: 'Stonehenge is Here!', *Australasian Post*, Feb 17th 1990.

17. Lockyer, J. N.: *The Dawn of Astronomy*, 1894. Also: *Stonehenge and Other British Stone Monuments*, London 1909 (2nd ed).

18. Brown, Peter Lancaster: *Megaliths and Masterminds*, Robert Hale, 1979.

19. Ivimy, John: *The Sphinx & The Megaliths*, Turnstone Books, 1974.

20. Thom, Alexander: *Megalithic Sites in Britain*, Oxford 1967. Also: *Megalithic Lunar Observatories*, Oxford 1971.

21. Underwood, Guy: *The Pattern of the Past*, Museum Press, 1969. Abacus edition 1972.

22. Tilt, David: 'Some Notes from Sussex' *BSD Journal*, No 218, Dec 1987.

23. Further details of this, and the dumbbell-shape configuration are in 'The Cereologist', *Cereological Dowsing*, Issue No 3, Spring 1991.

24. Tilt, David: 'Monitoring Ley Energy' *BSD Journal*, No 220, June 1988.

25. Pope, Ilse: 'A View of Earth Energies from Continental Europe', *BSD Journal*, No 217, Sept 1987.

26. Cathie, B. L. & Temm, P. N.: *Harmonic 695*, Reed 1971. Also: *Harmonic 33*, Reed 1968.

David Tilt with Busty Taylor with the Long Man of Wilmington in the background. (*Ann Tilt*)

7.   Nature's timely intervention

JOHN MICHELL

THE MOST INTERESTING THING about crop circles, practically speaking, is the effect they have on people. There is obviously some meaning behind these markings, and it is also clear that the circle-making intelligence has a purpose, knows what it is doing and is acting in the most effective way to achieve whatever it intends. It should be possible, therefore, to learn the meaning of the phenomenon by observing the nature of its influence on those who study it or become aware of it.

The simplest and most superficial way of seeing how crop circles are affecting people is to go to one and talk to the other visitors. Everyone one meets at the 'scene of the crime' would first of all like to know who or what did it, and they either produce some tentative theory or confess themselves baffled. There are always a few dogmatists who know that crop circles *must* be caused by whirlwinds, crop sprays, space brothers, earth spirits or the souls of the dead, but most people seem happy to accept the mystery while enjoying its beauty. Young children, who are not much concerned with the causes of crop circles, seem to enjoy them most of all.

How remarkable is this phenomenon! Not only does it write large across cornfields in the symbols of an unknown code; not only does it flout the conventions of rationalism, the pretensions of science and the territorial prerogatives of government; it manages to do all this, to demolish the world-view of materialism, without upsetting and panicking those of us — all of us — who were brought up with that world view and live in a society which is dominated by it. Not only has nobody yet panicked, but many people have been delighted by the phenomenon, have found pleasure and interest in it, have been inspired by it and changed in their outlooks. A common feeling among those who have been affected in this way — including virtually all the experienced crop circle researchers — is that they have been relieved of the prejudices which constricted their previous ways of thinking and have become more attuned to the realities of our spiritual existence. At least one veteran cereologist has developed the gifts of a healer and medium, and others have been influenced, though less dramatically, in a similar direction. Most of the leading researchers have adopted the dowsing rod and become sensitive to the energy fields at crop circle events. All of them admit to having undergone changes. These vary with each individual, but the common theme in every expression is that life has gained new significance and interest through the appearance of crop circles.

Gradually and tactfully, remorselessly and with the greatest possible economy of action, the crop circle phenomenon has forced itself upon our attention. If we judge its intention by its results, attracting attention was its first priority. At the same time, it was clearly not its intention to frighten or dismay us, for its effect has been the opposite. It began, enigmatically, in the 1940s and '50s with the first UFO reports. Strange lights and objects were seen in the sky, followed by strange encounters which altered the minds and outlooks of those who experienced them. In a certain sense, everyone was influenced by these rumours, for, together with the hard realities of space exploration, they introduced to general consciousness the idea of extra-terrestrial or non-human intelligence.

The breach was made, and the forces of rationalism made haste to close it. Geologists, astronomers and psychologists each found different explanations for the entire UFO phenomenon. Though different and often contradictory, these rationalisations each sounded convincing, and many of the more sophisticated ufologists fell prey to one or the other of them and lost their enthusiasm. The excitement of the early UFO-spotting, alien-hunting days brought its own reaction and gave way to the cynicism of the 1980s.

As one door closed, another opened. As the 1980s began, the phantom reality of UFOs developed into the concrete reality of crop circles. The earliest contemporary records of crop circles, in the 1960s, came from UFO investigators. Circular areas of crushed corn or grass, in Australia, Britain and elsewhere, appeared in association with mysterious lights and other UFO-type phenomena. The first name popularly applied to these circles was 'UFO nests'.

In 1981 crop circles gained scientific attention when some examples in Wiltshire were investigated by local savants. One of them, the meteorologist Dr G. Terence Meaden, while agreeing with the others that crop circles and UFO phenomena were closely related, theorised that UFOs were a natural atmospheric product and that crop circles could therefore be said to have a meteorological cause. Meaden's first name for that cause was 'stationary whirlwind'. Later he identified it as a 'plasma vortex'. Neither of these concepts is in fact known to science, but a plasma vortex has a more scientific ring to it than a UFO, and Meaden's theory gave comfort to many who might otherwise have been disturbed by the new phenomenon.

Most of the other crop circle investigators were dissatisfied with the simple meteorological explana-

tion, and their doubts increased as successive years brought new, more elaborate patterns, featuring multiple rings and geometric formations. Yet during the period when the crop markings were invariably circular in form, Meaden's theory retained a certain plausibility. Then, in 1990, came the first rectangular shapes, symmetrically ordered in association with a series of repeated symbols. These clearly were the product of no known or hypothetical natural force. The new pictograms were in no way random effects, but derived unmistakably from some form of organising intelligence.

Apparently in 1990 it was decided, somewhere, that the meteorological theory had served out its purpose and was no longer needed. The prop of science was removed, the materialistic world-view was publicly exposed as inadequate and we were confronted with a wider prospect of reality than our scientific conventions had previously allowed.

Thus gently but firmly we have been led across a watershed, from one world-view to another. The guiding intelligence, whatever it is, has left no loopholes, no ways back into the old rationalisms. It is a bold, radical change that we are asked to undergo, and there are obvious dangers and uncertainties in the process. Yet it is equally obvious that the modern materialistic world-view, the fundamental cause of the multiple crises which threaten the modern world, has run its course and desperately needs a replacement. The changes to which we are being impelled are timely, necessary and inevitable.

Who or what, then, is guiding us? That is a very pertinent question, for the world of spirit has many levels and those who know something of that world constantly warn of its perils and deceptions. "Believe not every spirit", says the New Testament (I, John, 4, 1), "but try the spirits whether they are of God, because many false prophets are gone out into the world". The test in these matters, as given by Jesus (Matthew, 7, 16), is: "Ye shall know them by their fruits". By that test crop circles, which are beautiful, harmless and inspiring, are clearly of divine rather than diabolic origin. They have earned our trust and surely we are justified, though ever cautiously, in following where they lead us.

The crop circle intelligence works anonymously, but its proper name is not beyond conjecture. As revealed in its activities, its nature is subtle, artistic, communicative and . . . mercurial. Patrick Harpur ('Mercurius in the Cornfields', *Cereologist*, no. 1) has already made the identification. The being that inscribes mysterious symbols on cornfields is no mere rustic imp or mischievous spirit; the quality of its communication ranks it far above the gibbering spooks that squeak and scribble at spiritualist seances. It is more powerful than us, for it manipulates our minds and we can neither control it nor discover its methods.

In traditional terms, the superior, intelligent forces in nature are called the gods. Through them the world is governed by the Great Spirit that subsumes them all. Their attributes were studied and expressed in myth by the theologians of all ancient religions, and the attributes of the crop circle intelligence point directly at a certain aspect of divinity, recognised and variously named in religious systems worldwide. It is the god of communication and enlightenment, the Greek Hermes and the Roman, alchemical Mercurius. Sometimes called the most daimonic of the gods, he is identified with the wandering, noctur-

nal spirit of the earth, whose mysterious, flickering flames were known in old England as 'Hermes lights'. He is a notorious trickster, specialising in the deflation of human presumptions, and crop circles bear his hallmark. Depicted with winged feet and a serpent-entwined caduceus, Mercurius is the messenger of the gods. When Mother Nature has something to communicate she sends for Mercurius. According to his legend, he was the inventor of writing. He introduced the first symbols, adapted by the various races to form their alphabets. No one has yet been able to interpret the symbols in the cornfields; they are unlike any known form of writing, but everyone who sees them is dimly reminded of something, as if they were looking at a script once known but long forgotten. Perhaps we are seeing, in the developing range of crop circle shapes and symbols, a new revelation of the primal, Mercurial handwriting.

When a god speaks directly, it is no light matter. Nature and her messenger have some important business with us, and we all have a perfectly good idea of what it is that they are bringing to our attention. If Nature is ever to speak, now is indeed the moment, and we can hardly be surprised at what has now come to pass. We must surely welcome this intervention, be grateful for it and adapt our lives and perceptions in accordance with its guidance.

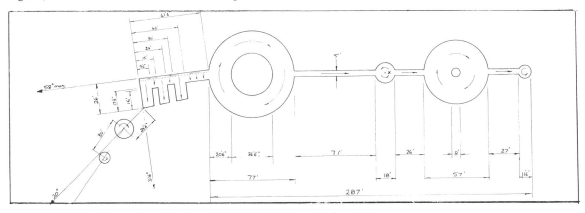

ALTON PRIORS, Vale of Pewsey. Formed in wheat 19th July 1991 (*J.F. Langrish drawings*)

8.   The language of the circle-makers

MICHAEL GREEN

Those who would speak with the Gods must use the language of the Gods. DJWHAL KHUL

THE MYSTERIOUS INSCRIPTIONS

ON JULY 31, 1988 Ludovico Granchi, a resident of Itacunuca, near Rio de Janeiro, Brazil, had a visitation at four o'clock in the morning[1]. What was later described as a UFO stopped over his house at a height of about 200m. To use his own words . . .

> it suddenly emitted a brightly lit white panel with writing in black letters on it. The borders of the panel were also black. On impulse I ran to fetch a pad and pen, and I started to copy down what I saw. This phase must have lasted for about ten minutes, during which time I did my best to copy faithfully what I was seeing, and as if guided by an invisible hand to take down the message. I cannot tell whether my copy was a faithful one. I was in a panic. It was a strange sensation. It was as if the world were about to end.

As Irene Granchi, mother of Ludovico reported, her son has not discovered the meaning of what he copied, and has not been able to decipher the signs (Fig. 1A). As soon as he had finished copying the signs, the light on the panel went out, and the UFO departed. Ludovico was in his late thirties at the time. This would appear to be a genuine paranormal experience, and indeed conforms to many similar accounts of UFO encounters.

Irene Granchi, a *Flying Saucer Review* consultant, is recognised as a sensible and reliable reporter of phenomena. Ludovico is clearly a psychic, since he

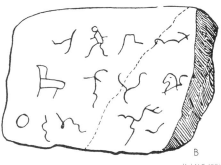

Fig.1a. The Granchi symbols. Fig.1b. Huaytara glyphs, Peru.

had had a UFO encounter as a young child, and again in September 1988 when a more conventional 'abduction and examination' experience took place involving small humanoid beings who "chirruped like crickets".

The message is written lineally in six lines with cursive characters, although whether from left to right or vice versa is unclear. Forty-two signs are shown of which ten are repeated, suggesting a phonographic alphabetical system rather than a syllabacy (multi-consonantal signs). The beginning of the third and fifth lines have characters (a dot within a circle, and a spiral) which look more like *semograms* (ideograms) which are concerned with 'sense' or 'meaning' rather than with 'sound'. The ancient Egyptian hieroglyph for sun is a logogram of a dot within a circle.

Why should a communication like this appear to a young man in a poor township in Brazil, and why should he be expected to understand it? The answers to these questions will be evident as we proceed.

Now this is not the first time that similar inscriptions have appeared in South America. A petroglyph on a rock at Bajo de Canota, Mendoza, Argentina has similar glyphs, and better examples came from Peru[2]. An account by De Rivero and Von Tschudi illustrate a three-line inscription (Fig. 1B) which they comment on as follows:

In the province of Castro-Vireyna, in the town of Huaytara there is found in the ruins of a large edifice, of similar construction to the celebrated palace of old Huanuco, a mass of granite many square yards in size with coarse engravings . . . None of the most trustworthy historians allude to these inscriptions or representations, or give the smallest direct information concerning the Peruvian hieroglyphics, from which it may be inferred that in the times of the Incas there was no knowledge of the art of writing in characters and that all of these sculptures are the remains of a very remote period. . . In many parts of Peru, chiefly in situations greatly elevated above the sea, are vestiges of inscriptions very much obliterated by time[3]

During the third quarter of the nineteenth century a French archaeologist exploring a remote island of the Canaries found petroglyphs similar to those from South America[4]. S. Berthelot comments:

A site very little frequented, designated by the name Los Leteros, appears to have been inhabited in very ancient times . . . on the island of Fer. At a distance of about three quarters of a league from the coast, all the land, sloping and broken by volcanic mounds, extends in undulations to the edge of the cliffs which flank the coast. It is on this desert site, that inscriptions are found engraved on an ancient flow of basaltic lava with a smooth surface, over an extent of more than 400 metres.

Not only do these strange petroglyphs show many of the cursive characters noted by Ludovico Granchi, but included amongst them were a larger range of semogram types. These latter are of particular interest to the investigators of the crop circle formations, or agriglyphs, appearing in England during the last decade, since they are identical to many of the simpler designs or components of the larger ones (Fig. 2).

Now what could be the link or common factor between a mysterious script revealed in a paranormal experience in Brazil, ancient petroglyphs found on both sides of the Atlantic and the strange crop circle formations? The answer appears to relate to what lies between them, beneath the vast rolling wastes of the ocean: the lost continent of Atlantis.

A VIEW OVER ATLANTIS

Atlantis, the lost civilisation: no subject is considered more unfashionable, indeed disreputable, amongst the archaeological community. To adapt Christopher Marlowe "*It is the fact that sank a thousand reputations*". For generations it has been the playground of the occultist and antiquarian dilettante, who felt all too free to speculate when the evidence lay safely out of sight a mile below the surface of the Atlantic. For it has to be stated at the outset that it is commonly perceived that there is not a shred of hard archaeological evidence that Atlantis ever existed. And yet it has remained one of the most potent myths

Figs.2a. Fer semogram glyphs. 2b. Agriglyphs. 2c. Fer cursive glyphs.

of western civilisation ever since the Greek philosopher Plato set out the tale in the two works *Critias* and *Timaeus*, a transcript of conversations between Socrates and his disciples, which was written circa 340BC. A review of this material lies beyond the scope of this study, and the reader is therefore referred to Sir Desmond Lee's translation, which is one of the more accessible available.[5]

According to Plato's account the tale originated when the philosopher Solon visited Egypt, circa 590BC, and paid a call on the then administrative capital of Sais, in the delta of the Nile. A priest of the temple of the goddess Neith teases Solon about the Greek ignorance of antiquity, even the history of their own country. He then goes on to recount an incident which took place, purportedly, nine thousand years earlier when the Athenian state checked a great military power which had advanced from its base in the Atlantic ocean to attack the cities of Europe and Asia. The priest states:

There was an island opposite the strait which you

call the Pillars of Hercules (Gibraltar), an island larger than Libya and Asia combined . . . On this island of Atlantis had arisen a powerful and remarkable dynasty of kings, who ruled the whole island, and many other islands as well and parts of the continent; in addition it controlled, within the strait, Libya (ie. north Africa) up to the borders of Egypt and Europe as far as Tyrrennia (ie. Etruria in North Italy) . . . At a later time there were earthquakes and floods of extraordinary violence, and in a single dreadful day and night . . . the island of Atlantis was swallowed up by the sea and vanished; this is why the sea in that area is to this day impassable to navigation, which is hindered by mud just below the surface, the remains of the sunken island.[6]

Critias develops the subject of Atlantis, giving an account of its geography, natural resources; together with a detailed description of the topography of the ancient metropolis and harbour works. This extended overview ends with an analysis of the political, religious and social structures of Atlantis. There then follows an account of the moral decline of its people, "tainted with unrighteous ambition and power", which results in Zeus calling a council of the gods; at which point the account abruptly breaks off.

Plato's story of Atlantis is something of a *tour de force* worthy of the Greek 'father of history' Herodotus, writing a generation earlier. There are internal inconsistencies between the different sections scattered through the two books, suggesting that the account represents perhaps a composite gathering of material from various sources. There is also the problem of transmission. Solon died around 560BC, and the ostensible reportage of the Atlantis material took place before the death of Critias in around 403BC, a gap of over 150 years — during which period an oral account passed through various named people. However, there is an intriguing reference to a manuscript of Solon which gave the Greek version of various proper names in the story (which had been transcribed into ancient Egyptian), and that the manuscript was still in the possession of Critias. Certainly the detailed topographical references bear the hallmark of a written transcription. Plato's attitude to the historicity of this material appears to be ambivalent. He makes Socrates say, perhaps with irony, that the tale "has the very great advantage of being a fact and not a fiction". Posidonius, a leading Hellenistic philosopher and scientist (c.135-50BC), records Plato as having said: "It is possible that the story is *not* an invention".[7]

Much turns on the purported Egyptian origins of the material, and indeed there is internal evidence of great interest in this connection. The old Egyptian priest of Sais in telling the tale to Solon comments:

in our temples we have preserved from earliest times a written record of any great or splendid achievement or notable event which has come to our ears whether it occurred in your part of the world or here or anywhere else.

The problem is that nothing bearing the faintest resemblance to the Solon account has ever been found amongst the voluminous ancient records of dynastic Egypt. Indeed the whole format of Plato's Atlantis account bears a strong resemblance to the *logos* principle of Herodotus, that is a structured story or account to point a moral. This is a peculiarly Hellenistic literary device, and is not reflected in the records of Ancient Egypt.

However there are two features about the Egyptian connection which may be significant, one is locational, the other temporal. The city of Sais, capital of the Fifth Nome (administrative district) under its tutelary deity, the goddess Neith, was the seat of the Twenty-sixth 'Saite' Dynasty (664-525BC). Sais was linked with the neighbouring city of Buto, capital of the Sixth Nome. Both places had pre-dynastic shrines where according to the Pyramid texts the worship of Osiris was already firmly established. Buto has good claim to be regarded as the oldest city in Egypt.

Recent excavations have revealed monumental architecture using decorative motifs of a distinctly un-Egyptian type, indeed more typical of late fourth millennium Mesopotamian architecture. Unfortunately the lowest levels of these cities are below ground-water level of the Nile, and will therefore never be accessible to the archaeologist. If any cities in Egypt might have retained ancient records of Atlantis these would be they. There is however another possible source for this information.

It is to Herodotus that we owe the account of the Phoenician voyage round Africa commissioned by the pharaoh Necho II (610-595BC).[8]

He sent Phoenicians with ships, bidding them sail and come back to Egypt. The Phoenicians therefore set forth from the Erythraean Sea (Red Sea) and sailed through the Southern Sea (Indian Ocean); and when autumn came they would put to shore and sow the land wherever in Libya (Africa) they might happen to be as they sailed, and then would wait for the harvest; and having reaped the corn they would sail on, so that after two years had elapsed, in the third they turned through the Pillar of Hercules (Straits of Gibraltar) and arrived again in Egypt. And *they reported things which others can believe if they want*, namely, that in sailing around Africa they had the sun on the right side (that is, they sailed south of the Equator).

Now there is much about Plato's account of Atlantis which is reminiscent of a seaman's tale, nautical descriptions of the sea coasts and islands and the detailed account of the complex harbour works of the great city, Atlantis. These latter are of a type which were coming into vogue in the sixth century BC amongst the Phoenician settlements of the Western Mediterranean, and are known as *cothons* or inner harbours. An example is known from the west-Sicilian island of Motya[9], and a bigger version has been found at Carthage.

I believe that the scenario may have been this. Solon visited Egypt about 590BC, just a few years

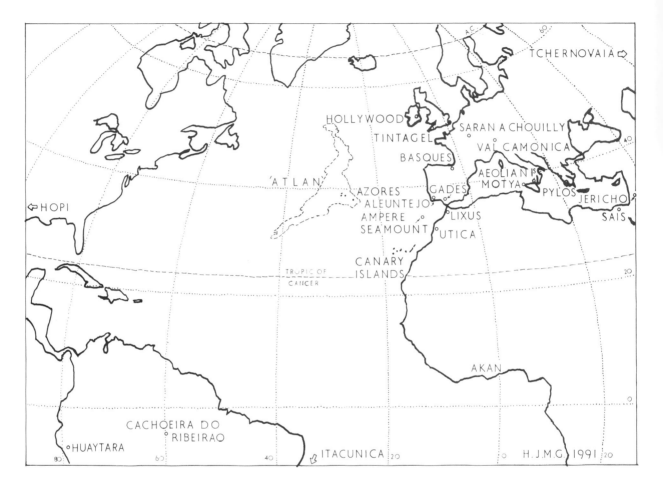

Fig.3. The North Atlantic in prehistoric times. (*Michael Green*)

circumnavigating Africa. An account of the expedition would undoubtedly have been lodged in the
temple archives of the Neith sanctuary at Sais, the
administrative capital of the dynasty. (An Egyptian
log of an earlier official journey written on papyrus
has survived: this involved a Theban priest Wen-
amon, c.1130BC, and the trouble he had in the
eastern Mediterranean[10]).

I suspect that the priest produced for Solon a
miscellaneous collection of material amongst which
were stories from the recent Phoenician trip mixed
with an account of an inundation involving ancient
Crete in 1628BC (recent dendro-chronological evidence) when the island of Thera erupted. Certainly
much of the descriptive material in connection with
bull-worship on Atlantis has marked parallels with

ancient Minoan cultural practices in the second millennium BC. Included amongst the material were the traditions of an ancient war between the Minoan civilisation and Mycenean settlements in Greece, including Athens, with echoes perhaps of the troubles that the Egyptians had had with the Sea Peoples. But most haunting of all was perhaps the Phoenician account of tales heard in their colonies of Gades (Cadiz), Lixus and Utica in North Africa, reflecting indigenous traditions of the peoples of the western Mediterranean, of a great island empire in the Atlantic which had been destroyed by earthquake and flood in a day and a night. It may be significant that the geographer, Strabo (44BC-AD21), in his third book, speaks of 2,600 year-old travellers' tales of the people of Turdetania (earlier known as Tartessos, in south-west Spain), whose records went back 7,000 years before *their* time (Strabo, 3.1.6).

Solon assiduously made notes of all this material, transposing the Egyptian topographical references into Greek, and took it back to Athens with the intention of working it up into an epic on the theme of primeval conflict, with Athens having the starring role. An unfinished version of this composition evidently survived to be handed down in the family of Critias, and thence to Plato.

If this were all, then Plato's evident scepticism about the Atlantis material might be well grounded. After all, tales of lost lands sunk beneath the sea abound, and occur commonly in folklore amongst the Celtic peoples of north west Europe. The most famous of such traditions refers to the land of Lyonesse, said to have extended west from Cornwall as far as the Scilly Isles, but drowned in a major cataclysm in the distant past.

It was mentioned above that there is generally considered to be no hard archaeological evidence for Atlantis as a physical as opposed to a mythological fact. This is not quite true, for what is urgently required is a radical reassessment in the light of new archaeological evidence. In a recent study[11] there is a report by a Soviet deep-sea expedition carried out by the *Academician Petrovsky* in 1974. Soundings, purportedly in the vicinity of the Horseshoe Archipelago, 300 miles west of Gibraltar, took place in an area of underwater mountains. Underwater photographs said to be of the Ampere Seamount appear to show extensive remains of masonry ruins and steps.

But there is also another line of evidence which lies in the field of parapsychology, particularly relating to channelled material from mediums over the last hundred years. Now the sceptic might well object that such revelations merely beg the question: that they only reflect the unconscious state, indeed the private mythologies, of the individuals concerned. The same might be claimed also of remembered reincarnation experiences as an Atlantean reported by mystics such as Christine Hartley, Dion Fortune and Murry Hope. However the persistent and homogeneous nature of the channelled material is impressive, and more importantly, in my view, comes from sources that at a metaphysical, indeed spiritual, level have shown themselves to be true and reliable in other contexts. Amongst these should be mentioned Alice Bailey, Tony Neate and Grace Cooke.

Does a consideration of the geological, geographical and archaeological factors totally rule out the possibility of a physical reality behind the mythology? The first question concerns the location of Atlantis. Plato's account is unambiguous: it lay beyond the Straits of Gibraltar in the Atlantic Ocean. Geographically there is an obvious candidate, allowing for the fact that, at the height of the last Ice Age, sea levels were some 200m lower than at present. The Azores plateau would have formed a compact land mass with archipelagos running to north and south along the Mid-Atlantic Ridge. At 200m below present sea level it would have covered an area approximating to the British Isles.

The second question is: under what circumstances could such an island have been drowned in the way described in the myth? An analysis of ocean core samples indicates a major rise in temperature at the end of the last Ice Age, 10,300 years ago[12]. The

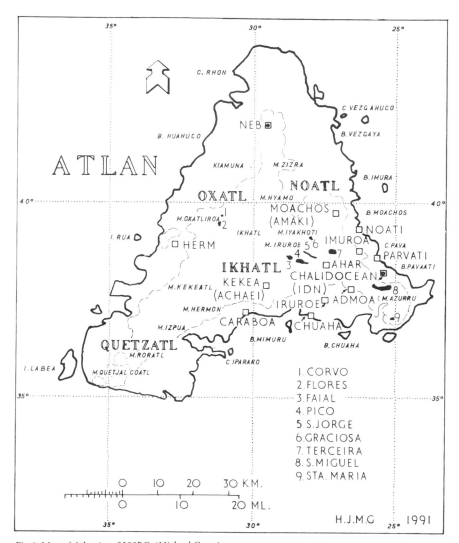

Fig.4. Map of Atlantis, c.8300BC. (*Michael Green*)

melting of the ice sheets led to a last precipitous rise in sea level of over 140m. The continental shelves on both sides of the Atlantic were flooded, and so was the Azores Plateau, leaving only the tips of the highest mountains, the present island chain, protruding.

If this was indeed the location of the island of Atlantis, then its inundation can thus be accounted for in hydrographic terms without calling into play the special seismic factors which form such a prominent part in descriptions of the catastrophe. However seismological evidence suggests that this area at the junction of the North American, Eurasian and African tectonic plates is highly unstable. Indeed there is a concentration of active submarine volcanoes in the vicinity of the Azores: San Jorge Island, Santa Barbara, Maraco Bank, Pico Island, Sete Bank and the Don Joao de Castro Bank. The nine islands of the Azores group are almost entirely of volcanic origin, pockmarked with craters and calderas, and are subject to frequent earthquakes. In this connection therefore the evidence of ancient ruins associated with lava flows located by the Soviet soundings is of considerable interest. Murry Hope quotes circumstantial evidence to suggest that the *Academician Petrovsky* may have been a spy ship operating clandestinely off the Azores in the area of NATO bases, and not in the region of the Horseshoe Archipelago at all!

Until recently it was believed that there is no archaeological evidence for civilised communities at this early date — the ninth millennium. However discoveries in the eastern Mediterranean indicate that there were walled cities in existence during the 9th and 8th millennium BC, of which the notable example is Jericho[13]. Other examples will no doubt be identified at deep levels of the Near Eastern tell and tepe sites as they come to be excavated.

The concept of a physical reality for Atlantis in Platonic terms is, therefore, a real possibility.

WHAT SONGS THE SIRENS SANG

When Sir Thomas Browne posed this leading question in 1658 he went on to exclaim, "although puzzling Questions, are not beyond all conjecture". The same is true of the language of the crop circle formations, whose glyphs appear to be related to Senzar, the ancient sacerdotal language of Atlantis. This has been made quite explicit in recent channelling to the Maitreyan organisation: "[The crop circles] are all ideograms, and if you were familiar with the ideography of ancient Atlantis you would recognise some of them."

Atlantis and its civilisation was destroyed, but before this happened, according to Plato and various other sources, many groups left the continent and settled in other places on both sides of the Atlantic.

> Mass emigrations took place from the ill-fated continent to such places as Egypt, the Middle East, Europe and part of South and Central America. The emigrants carried with them some of the Atlantean lore, although much was to be lost . . .[14].

Now the movement of ancient peoples and cultures is a well established phenomenon in archaeological studies, and the first thing that a student looks for are patterns of related artefacts and structures that are termed 'type fossils'. The search for these elusive cultural links in connection with possible Atlantean migrations has been a burning issue for over a century.

If a late ninth millennium BC date is set for the end of Atlantis, then obvious cultural pointers such as the pyramidical structural form (which is so often quoted) is simply not applicable in the light of established archaeological research. In the Old World such structures, whether for temples or tombs, do not appear before the first half of the fourth millennium BC, and in the New World, the middle of the third millennium BC. This is not to say there is no relation, indeed the evidence from the *Academician Petrovsky* soundings suggests that the steps that were found belonged to a pyramidical structure akin to the Aztec temple type. The credibility gap of several thousand years, however, would appear to rule out a direct cultural link for such structures, and indeed for the better known established civilisations on both sides of the Atlantic. The demographic factor that may be at work, I believe, is the reincarnation of large groups of former Atlanteans in various centres who re-established old cultural patterns.

One important area of possible Atlantean cultural

parallels lies in the field of petroglyphs, which survive on both sides of the Atlantic from the Upper Palaeolithic period into historic times. One of the most intriguing cases concerns a reference by Edgar Cayce[15] to settlers from Atlantis who. . .

> entered the Pyrenees, and what is now the Portuguese, French and Spanish lands. And there still may be seen in the chalk cliff there in Calais the marks made by the (Atlantean) followers, as attempts were made . . . to create a temple activity for the followers of the Law of One.

I know of no petroglyphs at Calais, but one such has been found at Saran a Chouilly, Marne, France, again dug out of chalk[16]. A wholly unique three-chamber tomb or temple of hypogean type has on the outer jamb of the inner chamber a relief carving of a ritual sun staff (Fig 5A).

A true type fossil, the only absolutely unequivocal example known to me, is the labyrinth symbol which appears on both sides of the Atlantic (Fig 5B). In

Europe it appears as a petroglyph in Val Camonica, Italy (2nd millennium BC), Pylos in southern Greece (c.1200BC) and became a widespread symbol across the classical Mediterranean. In north west Europe it occurs as a petroglyph at Tintagel, Cornwall and at Holywood in Ireland, and a major grouping lies around the Baltic Sea coast of Scandinavia.

In the United States, the classical labyrinths in the Hopi lands of northern Arizona are called TAPUAT (Mother and Child), and they occur also amongst the Nasca Lines in South Western Peru. The symbol itself is one of the most profound spiritual mandalas in existence, and sets out the Mysteries of the Great and Little Turnings, or to put it another way, the archetypal paradigm of spiritual development for mankind. Now the point about the Three and Seven Circuit Labyrinths is that these are specific, complex patterns whose distribution must be the consequence of cultural diffusion from a single source. This in my opinion must be Atlantis. There are also other ancient petroglyphic symbols to be found on both sides of the Atlantic, of which the most prevalent one the spiral and the 'cup and ring' type illustrating the Sacred Marriage[17]. These also appear amongst the characters found as petroglyphs on the island of Fer in the Canaries.

As has already been noted these petroglyphs also appear in conjunction with an ancient language using a semi-syllabic writing system whose glyphs were ideograms — the communication system known as SENZAR. Djwhal Khul comments:

> Senzar is the name for the secret sacerdotal language or mystery speech of the initiated adepts all over the world. It is a universal language and largely a hieroglyphic cipher[18].

In the *Secret Doctrine*[19] there is a more expansive treatment of the subject:

> Tradition says that various ancient treatises were taken down from one small parent volume in Senzar, the secret sacerdotal language, from the

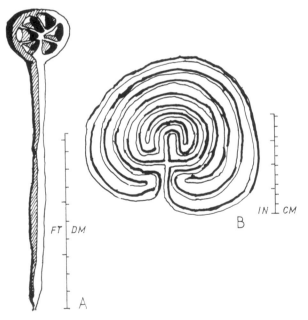

Fig.5a. Ritual Sun Staff. Fig.5b. Labyrinth Symbol

words of the Divine Beings, who dictated it to the Sons of Light in Central Asia at the very beginning of the Fifth (our) Race. There was a time when its language was known to initiates of every nation, when the forefathers of the Totec understood it as easily as the inhabitants of the lost Atlantis, who inherited it in their turn from the sages of the Third Race, the Manushis (Inner Buddhas), who learnt it direct from the *Devas* of the Second and First Races.

However we are still faced with a linguistic puzzle worthy of the Rosetta stone, since these extracts tell us nothing of the detailed ideographic system or their derivative cursive characters, not to mention the actual language itself.

Some twenty years ago a medium in Cornwall, Dr J L P, channelled a considerable amount of information from purportedly a former Atlantean priest, Azmuru[20]. This material agrees well with other information from similar sources, but also includes two features which are of the greatest interest to this study. Azmuru provided a phonographic semi-syllabic system using what may in origin have been ideograms, much as in the case of Egyptian hieroglyphs. He also supplied a detailed map of Atlantis, or Atlan as he calls it, which exactly fits the topography of the Azores Plateau. The cartographical information is included here, and is indeed substantiated from other sources, in the hope that future underwater explorations in the area may identify some of the named sites (Fig 4).

When the Atlantean characters are set out alongside other ancient western systems (Fig 6) the family relationship is immediately evident. In the same way that Phoenician was derived from proto-Sinaitic/Canaanite sources, and these in turn owe their inspiration to the Egyptian system (both in terms of similarities of signs and the basic acrophonic principle), so the earliest Egyptian hieroglyphs relate to the Atlantean alphabet.

But how do we know that Dr J L P did not simply invent an alphabet working on the same principles? There is interesting confirmatory evidence coming from a source unknown to J L P which suggests that this Atlantean alphabet is genuine. In 1971 the Atlantean Society, under the leadership of Tony Neate, were looking for a suitable new symbol. Their spiritual guide, Helio-Arcanophus gave them the symbol of the *ankh* within the blazing sun which symbolised the balance of the positive and negative vibrations of the planet[21]. Now the *ankh* is an ancient Egyptian symbol which means 'life or living' and is derived from a stylised representation of the Earth Goddess, Gaia[22]. On the face of it it would not appear to have much to do with Atlantis. However the Azmuru alphabet has it as the first letter A of the Atlantean alphabet, carrying perhaps the connotation of the Vedic AUM, the great initial creative sound.

The cursive writing of the inscriptions is more difficult to unscramble, but may well represent a hieratic development of the original semograms. They would still appear, however, to represent a form of Senzar. Any non-human entity making approaches to a human being who was sufficiently sensitive to be aware of their vibrations would assume that such a person would be conversant with all forms of Senzar, this being the *lingua franca* of planetary initiates. Hence therefore Ludovico Granchi's experience in 1988: unfortunately Ludovico was no initiate.

Now there is an evident family relationship between the hieroglyphs of Old Egypt (c.2650-2135BC) and the Azmuru glyphs (Fig 6), but it would be incorrect, I think, to suggest that there was a direct *cultural* link, for the time-gap reasons given above. If there were early colonies of Atlanteans around the Mediterranean basin and along the Atlantic seaboard, some evidence of Senzar glyphs might be expected to survive from a much earlier period, if only as magical symbols. And indeed this is the case.

Excavations[23] on the Aeolian Islands of Sicily of the Bronze Age Capo Graziano culture of the third millennium BC have revealed a regular vocabulary of incised signs on the local pottery (Fig 6).

Another early script is known from the Aleuntejo (type 1) grave stelas in southern Portugal, where it constitutes the earliest (c.1300-900BC) of four main writing systems of the Iberian peninsula[24]. Although there is a family relationship to the Phoenician signs, its distribution lies outside the Phoenician cultural zone called Gadir. It also differs from the Phoenician system of 32 alphabet characters, in having a semi-syllabic structure of 28 signs (Fig. 6).

It is evident from the phonetic values that the Iberian language involved was not Indo-European or related to any Celtic system. The only culture which would appear to have similar phonetic values is the Basque language, whose heartland in the Pyrenees is one of the Atlantean settlement areas specifically mentioned in the Edgar Cayce channellings.

The ancient language of Crete in the early second millennium, and its associated script, Minoan Linear A, is another mysterious writing system, perhaps to be related to Senzar. Its successor, Linear B, is an archaic form of early Greek, using a combination of ideograms and numerals; but Linear A appears to be another non-Indo-European language system.

All these semi-ideographic systems from the Mediterranean seem to have parallels with the glyphs of Senzar, and are clearly related to the Phoenician alphabet. Now it is the received wisdom that the Phoenician alphabet was derived from a proto-Sinaiatic/Canaanite source c.1700BC, which in turn borrowed its glyphs from Ancient Egypt[25]. A few of the signs undoubtedly owe their origin to Egyptian hieroglyphs, but the majority do not, although there are parallels amongst the systems of the central and western Mediterranean.

What I am proposing is that there was in the Mediterranean basin, from an early period, the scattered remnants of a semi-ideographic syllabary amongst various cultures, based on a non-Indo-European language. Certain early cultures, such as that of Lower Egypt, adapted and developed their own hieratic hieroglyphic system retaining some of the original ancient glyphs. The Phoenicians encountered this ancient Atlantean syllabary during their trading with and settlement of the central and western Mediterranean, but with a rare stroke of genius transformed it into a true alphabetical system, which is the basis of most surviving scripts today, including defunct European systems such as the Runes[26].

Did this writing of Atlantean Senzar survive anywhere else in the Old World? By a remarkable chance, traces of a clearly related system of glyphs survived in the old African coastal kingdom of Akan, now the Ivory Coast and Ghana[27]. These remnants of some ancient Atlantean landfall have not survived as a coherent script, but only as magical symbols. What did survive, however, was a related numerical system, which may be the only surviving clue to that used in old Atlantis (Fig 6).

This evidence for Atlantean colonisation or exploration in the southern hemisphere is matched by similar glyphs discovered in Brazil by the explorer Franz Keller in 1875, along the central reaches of the Amazon and Madeira rivers[28]. (Fig 7A)

In early August 1991, an agriglyph appeared at Stanton St Bernard, Wiltshire (Fig. 7B). It consisted of a single line of glyphs (12–15 feet high) similar to those from Brazil. At each end are *determinative* semograms carrying the sense 'Deity'. There are two words separated by vertical spaces, written from right to left, of 5 and 6 characters each and using 6 different glyphs. The letters appear to have an archaic Senzan syllabacy, and read PH.EH.TH.I EA–E.CH–CH.E. Although the language is not known, the first word is cognate with PTAH, the Creator God of Ancient Egypt, and the second to the Sumerian deity ENKI (EA), God of Wisdom and lover of mankind. I believe that these are the essential attributes to that Being I have termed *Archon*.

In purely symbolic terms *Archon* is represented by the Mandelbrot Set at Ickleton (pl. 1). The primal triad of the mandala is shown by 3 circles of which the largest is *heart* shaped, while the secondary Ray triad of *Aspect* is symbolised by an equilateral triangle of 3 smaller circles and the quatemic Rays of *Attribute* by a square of even smaller circles. Science and mysticism meet in the Mandelbrot Set.

This still leaves the problem of the language of Atlantis, which on the face of it would appear to be an insuperable difficulty. Could it, by an absolute miracle, have survived anywhere amongst the colonists from the sunken continent? It has, but perhaps in a demotic form rather than the sacerdotal structure of Senzar. Many of the channelled messages speak of settlements in the area of the Pyrenees "where there are ruins of early settlements, still to be uncovered"[29]. The Pyrenees are the home of the Basque people, who have a unique language structure unrelated to all the other Indo-Aryan languages of Europe and incapable of classification by normal linguistic criteria. It is not quite time to say that there is no parallel language system, since there may be Amerindian links. The Basque historian Esteban de Gaubay writing in 1571 notes that Basque sailors had been able to converse with the Indians with the greatest of ease, and the latter, despite a lack of education, proved able to learn Basque with extraordinary facility[30].

LATIN	ATLANTEAN	AGRIGLYPH	EGYPTIAN	P.CANAANITE	PHOENICIAN	EARLY GREEK	ETRUSCAN	RUNE	AEOLIAN	IBERIAN	AKAN
A											1
B											2
C											2
D											3
E											3
F											4
G											4
H											4
I											5
J											5
K											6
L											6
M											7
N											7
O											8
P											9
Q											9
R											9
S											9
T											
U											
V											
W											
X											
Y											
Z											
CH											
TH											

H.J.M.G.1991

Fig.6. Alphabetical & Numerical Systems. (*Michael Green*)

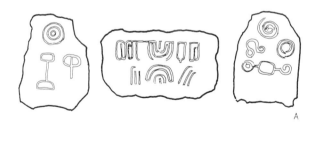

Fig. 7a. Amazon Petroglyphs; Fig. 7b. Milk Hill Agriglyph

THE RINGS OF TIME

At the beginning of this paper it was suggested that the crop formations of Southern England were reproducing the symbolism, indeed the very characters evident in written Senzar (Figs 2 & 6). In an earlier study I traced the developing symbolism evidenced by the crop circle formations during the 1980s[31]. There gradually developed seven basic circle types, defined by varying numbers of satellites, which clearly relate to ancient Celtic planetary symbols. In 1987 these were supplemented by certain thematic formations representing metaphysical principles. In 1990 symbolic figures of the Sun God (Solar Logos) and Earth Goddess (Planetary Logos) appeared with a range of attributes illustrating their different functions. At the end of 1990 three great formations appeared in the vicinity of Alton Barnes (Wiltshire) which represent a new level of teaching about the nature of Deity.

At this point a word is necessary to define the Timeless Wisdom's concept of God. The motivating principle of any system, human or cosmic, is symbolised by a single vibrant point indicative of monadic (soul) life. The life principle or seed germ — the 'Jewel in the Lotus', to use the ancient oriental appellation — encapsulates in embryo all that that life has been, is and will become for that entity. For us on this planet it is the Earth Logos, " . . . in whom we live and move and have our being" (Acts 17:28). The earth *logos*, however, is but one centre in the make-up of a greater entity, the Solar Logos. His centres or chakras are formed at a physical level out of the planets of the solar system. But the Solar Logos is in turn only one focus of a still more transcendent Being, which is an aggregate of certain star systems in this part of the galaxy. This Being I term *Archon*, in the sense that Paul uses the expression *Archai* for 'supernatural powers' (Romans 8:38). The galaxy itself, made up of innumerable such entities, is a spiritual Being whose complexity and dimensions lie beyond our comprehension, yet this too is part of a greater Being, and so it is throughout the Universe. At the limits of our understanding, and yet still within the manifested form of the cosmos is the etheric structure of that unknown entity to which esoteric science gives the name *Space*, and which in the classical world was called *Aion*.

For every material manifestation of Deity performs within the created karmic matrix which we call Time, and every manifested life-form is on a path of spiritual development from Atom to Aion. Although the earth *logos* and upwards are all from our viewpoint perfect, in cosmic terms they are imperfect Gods on a path of progressive unfoldment. Each is subject to the constraints of its weakest component. None can 'graduate' until all aspects of its make-up have achieved fulfilment.

Whence then is Deity? This great system of Being is but an expression of the One, the Good, the Unmanifest God of Whom it is profitless to speculate. As Krishna proclaims:

> the three Gunas came from me: peaceful light, restless life and lifeless darkness. But I am not in them — they are in me
>
> (*Bhagavad Gita* 37).

These perceptions about the truth of theogeny are to be found in every age and culture where the Timeless Wisdom has been taught. Indeed they are not merely heuristically valid but are the very experience of sage and mystic. It cannot be truly understood in purely intellectual terms, indeed for those locked within the conventional orthodoxies of the great religious systems, a true appreciation of the Mysteries requires, literally, a cosmic shift of consciousness. It is this that humanity is now experiencing as the New Age dawns, and the symbols of the true nature of Deity, the cosmic paradigm, symbolise this expansion of consciousness in the phenomena of the cornfields of England, and increasingly across the world.

This digression on the nature of Deity is necessary for it illustrates the possible varying metaphysical levels and theocratic directions from which the crop formations may be derived. There have been a few of the simpler designs in 1991 reflecting the patterns of previous years, but the vast majority are totally new, of immense size and complexity. The Barbury Castle formation in particular, which appeared on 16 July 1991 near Swindon, Wiltshire, and the Ickleton formation which appeared on 12 August 1991 in Cambridgeshire, present the researcher with the need to make a quantum leap in understanding the phenomenon. It really is no longer intellectually honest for even the most blinkered scientist to pretend that those extraordinary formations are either hoaxes or the consequences of freak weather effects.

No two formations are identical, but there are certain groupings of designs which can be distinguished. Their interpretation is of course another matter, and the views expressed here necessarily represent a strictly personal perception, which, as in my earlier study, is presented only as a working hypothesis.

The Logoi formations

That great entity *Archon*, through its various centres, is in the process of laying down an energy matrix in southern England. The purpose of this energy-field, which is using the geodetic etheric structure of the planet, is to raise the level of consciousness of humankind. This major exercise has been brought into play at the specific request of a number of spiritual groups, large and small, across the world (and significantly in England) in recent years. The geodetic grid, familiar to dowsers, has an analogy at the microcosmic level with the acupuncture points and meridians of the human body. There is considerable evidence that the whole process of raising human consciousness is meeting with some success across the world in the last couple of years.

The mechanics of laying down the energy-matrix is based on a relatively simple system of electro-magnetism, using what is known occultly as the 'triangle of power' principle. Each energy-field of the seven centres (chakras or rays) of *Archon* — which at the physical level are solar systems in this part of the galaxy — is putting down a carefully-ordered system of triangles marked at the apexes by major crop formations. The sides of these triangles are two or three miles in length, and the overall structure acts as a great coil or battery and combined transformer, which is effectively plugged into the geodetic grid of the planet. The triangular base or distributing centre at ground level is the lowest point of a process which brings the emanating energy from an *Archon* centre, stepped down through three planets of our solar system, to a receptive force centre which synthesises the responsive point of negative energy. The resulting energy is then passed through a secondary triangle at ground level.

So that humanity can understand the process, our own Solar Logos has kindly provided a detailed blueprint showing the structure in plan form in the formation at Barbury Castle (pl.5). A diagram and discussion of the principle involved has also been set out by Djwhal Khul in his study of cosmic energies[32].

In 1990 these formations forming a triangle of power were put down at Alton Barnes, Stanton St Bernard and East Kennet. The energy concerned from *Archon* is that of Ray II (Love-Wisdom) which emanates from *Ashna*, a planet of the binary solar system of Sirius. The symbolic claws and tail of each formation appear to symbolise one of the two intelligent life-forms of that planet, the *Paschals*[33]. Each of these formations produced by the Solar Logos of Sirius is characterised by a small ringed circle set at the head of the formation, symbolising the planet *Ashna* and its sun, Sirius, respectively.

In 1991 the same process has continued for other centres of *Archon*. During July, three formations of Ray VI (Abstract Idealism) were put down on Preshute Down, Alton Priors and West Kennet (pl.56). The principal life-form in the solar system of the star Fomalhaut is piscine, and the formations therefore symbolise this by providing a fin-like tail and a head with a large fish-eye. In March 1991, a mystic, Libby Valdez, envisioned these particular formations appearing, communicated personally to me in the following passage:

I saw a fish that was swimming through the blackness of the depths of the earth. The dark depths of the earth were also the depths of outer space, and the fish was simultaneously the star Fomalhaut, and many earth elementals collected together in an organised and purposeful fashion . . . From the mouth of the fish, deep under the earth, a stream of bubbles emerged as it swam. These slowly rose to the surface of the earth where they broke (like bubbles breaking on the surface of a lake) and formed crop circles. There was a sense of the circles being seeded now (ie. March 1991) by the fish, and of the bubbles/circles rising slowly, sequentially, through the earth, through time and the crop seeds, from the time of the dream onwards, to break in their fullness on the surface of the land when the crops are ripe

Another major formation which formed in 1991 was the *Dolphin formations* in the Beckhampton area (pl.38, 39), which reflects an intelligent life-form on the solar system of the star Capella (Ray IV, Harmony, Beauty and Art). The twin circle-markers appear adjacent to these formations as they do on all the others of this type.

An important group of five or more formations appeared early in the 1991 season in the Winchester area, and spread across to Salisbury Plain, where the last examples occurred immediately south of Stonehenge (pl.15). Each has the basic triadic form representing spirit, matter and synthesis[34], but are further characterised by horns and a ladder construct at the 'tail' end. These ladders appear also in prehistoric ring-and-dot petroglyphs from the British Isles[35]. The Logos responsible for the formation at Litchfield, (pl.24) which is designated by the twin-circle signature, is that from Alcyone of the Pleiades, whose serpentine intelligent life-form is known as the 'blue

people'. The ladder form is symbolic of the sequential form of a snake, and should be compared with the Bronze Age serpent bones of the Mediterranean basin, which date back to the third millennium BC[36]. In the Djwhal Khul system, the Pleiades constitute Ray III (Active Intelligence) of the centre of *Archon*.

Other centres of *Archon* are also represented by formations in 1991. A triple formation with double solar haloes symbolising the binary system of Alpheratz (Andromeda constellation) appeared at the foot of Hackpen Hill, Wiltshire, on 11-12 July 1991 (pl.32). The life-form from the associated planet is basically humanoid, and the system represents Ray VII (Order) of *Archon*.

A complex formation originating from a planetary system of the star Aldebaran (constellation Taurus) appeared on 30 June 1991 at Newton St Loe near Bath (pl.28). Aldebaran is Ray V (Science) of *Archon*. As a formation it is closest to the Alton Barnes group of 1990, but it is distinguished by a 'winged' circle at the bottom end which is symbolic of the avian intelligent life-form of this system.

Ray I of *Archon* from the Dubhe binary star system (Ursa Major) has appeared near the avenue at Avebury. A ring appears at each end of a fish/bird body. (pl.35).

Rods of Power formations

The sceptres of initiation are wielded by the Logoii at every level of the universe and act as a focusing and transformative agent of cosmic energy. In the etheric realms they are not merely symbols of power, as displayed by royalty to this day, but have the specific purpose of "dynamic stimulation of all the subordinates in office who come under their touch, thus inspiring them to increased activity and service"[37]. What then is initiation in cosmic terms?

Initiation is (in its simplest definition) an understanding of the Way, for understanding is a revealing energy which permits you to achieve. Initiation is a growth of experience and the attainment thereby of a point of tension: the initiate sees that which lies ahead. Initiation permits a progressive entry into the mind of the creating Logos. . .[38].

In tradition and iconography the Rods of Power have the threefold structure of Deity, and survive in this form as the *vajra*, the esoteric thunderbolt of the Aryan tradition. The Solar Logos is represented as carrying a rod in each hand, one for the initiation of humanity and the other for the initiation of the devic (nature spirit) world, which is a parallel line of evolution. The sun god on the lintel of the Gateway of the Sun at Tiahuanaco in the Andes holds the two rods, which are also snakes, a reminder that the classical Caduceus of Mercurius has its origin in this form. The three-eyed solar deity found at Tchernoraia in Eastern Europe also carries the twin rods, which in this case are tridents. Nearer home we have the Long Man of Wilmington Hill figure, in Sussex, who also carries the two rods.

The rods of power formed out of the living crops have certain common features to distinguish them from the other formations. Notably they have two small circles on the left-hand side of the rod, evenly spaced between the central and the outer circles. At Ogbourne Maizey (10-11 July 1991) and Alton Barnes (1-2 July 1991), the rods are very similar with a ring at the head (symbolising spirit), a circle at the foot (symbolising matter), and a synthesis of the two with a large ringed circle in the middle. The central rod runs through the head circle giving it the impression of an open cage. This would have held the 'flaming diamond' of tradition, which is characteristic of that used by the One Initiator, the Lord of the World or the earth *logos*.(pl.62, 63)

This rod, through its surmounting diamond, focuses the three fires (the vital divine spark, the spark of mind and the twofold blending of the kundalini) in the same way that a burning glass reacts to the sun, and causes a conflagration by which every centre is vitalised, every impurity is burnt away, and the goal is reached[39].

The twin rods of the solar *logos* have also appeared at Lockeridge and Upton Scudamore, Wiltshire. The Lockeridge formation (pl.43) is basically the same as those of the earth *logos*, but have rings at both ends. The Upton Scudamore formation, however, has the true trident associated with devic initiation (pl.50).

The Senzar glyphs are to be found associated with all these different types of formation. The Alton Barnes formations of 1990 tended to have them attached to the main formations, but what has been termed the 'hand of God' also occurs as separate structures attached to a circle in 1990 and 1991. Increasingly in 1991 they tend to be placed as separable features alongside the main pictograms, and now represent a number of different ideograms (fig 6). These ideographic letters are undoubtedly of significance in defining the character of the formations — that is, if we could decipher the Senzar language. More importantly, however, like the formations themselves, they are timeless mandalas which reach the deepest levels of the human subconscious. For the 'language of the gods' is not a spoken language at all, but the conveyance of ideas at the thought level between those who are on the same spiritual wavelength.

Now it has been shown elsewhere[40] that the agriglyphs are directly related to the geodetic structure of the earth and in particular the acupuncture nodes now represented in many cases by sacred sites. The grouping of particular types of agriglyphic symbols round certain foci serve to define the etheric character of that particular energy source. In old Atlantis, an understanding of the etheric structure of this geodetic system was well advanced, according to channelled sources I have encountered, and the wrongful exploitation of these great centres of metaphysical energy was one of the reasons for the destruction of the Atlantean civilisation.

As the final days approached, the reigning Arcanophus summoned all the powers used by the priesthood on the Atlantean vibration. He sent priests to seed that power in various parts of the world; and then, by means of certain rituals, he sealed the rays so that none could call upon them until the time came when there would be once more people incarnate on Earth who would possess the right knowledge and wisdom to unseal them. The key to this seal be placed in the land you call England. Its symbol is the sword of St Michael, or the Excalibur of Arthur, and its withdrawal signifies the emergence of the new Atlantean race[40].

The rays were released in 1989, making it possible for various great cosmic powers to join with humanity and the *devas* in revitalising the planet. This process constitutes, I believe, the formal beginning of the New Age, or 'Second Coming' in Christian parlance. The crop formations are the visible sign to humanity that the Kingdom of God is upon us.

REFERENCES
1. Granchi, I.: "A pleasant encounter in Brazil with 'Human-Looking' little people", *Flying Saucer Review*, Dec 1990, pp20-21. I am indebted to George Wingfield for this communication.
2. Mallery, G.: *Picture Writing of the American Indians*, Vol 1, Dover, NY, 1972, p15.
3. Mallery, G.: *Ibid*, p159.
4. Mallery, G.: *Ibid*, p183.
5. Lee, D. (trans): Plato *Timaeus and Critias* Penguin Books, 1986.
6. Lee, D.: *Ibid*, pp37-38.
7. Posidonius, in Strabo II, p102.
8. Casson, L.: *Travel in the Ancient World*, Book Club Associates, London, 1979, p61.
9. Guido, M.: *Sicily, an Archaeological Guide*, Faber & Faber, London, 1972.
10. Casson, L.: *Ibid*, pp39-43.
11. Hope, M.: *Atlantis, Myth or Reality?*, Arkana, London 1991, pp83-88.
12. Calder, N.: *Timescale*, Chatto & Windus, London 1984, pp213-214.
13. Renyon, K.: *Excavations at Jericho*, Vols 3 & 4, London, 1981-2.
14. Dean, M. (ed) & Neate, T.: *The Guide Book*, Gateway Books, Bath, 1986, p119.
15. Robinson, L.: *Edgar Cayce's Story of the Origin and Destiny of Man*, Berkley Books, NY, 1976, p71.
16. Briaid, J.: *Avant les Celtes*, p21. Musee Departemental Breton, Association Abbaye de Daoulas, 1988.
17. Noyes, R (ed) & Green, H. J. M.: "The Rings of Time: the Symbolism of the Crop Circles", in *The Crop Circle Enigma*, Gateway Books, Bath, 1990, pp144-5.
18. Bailey, A. A.: *Initiation, Human & Solar*, Lucis, NY, 1984, p224.
19. Blavatsky, H. P.: *An Abridgement of the Secret Doctrine*, Quest Books, Wheaton, 1966.
20. I am indebted to Frances Evans for this communication.
21. Wilson, A.: *Where There's Love*, Gateway Books, Bath, 1986, p67.
22. Noyes, R.: *Ibid*, p152.
23. Holloway, R, R.: *The Archaeology of Ancient Sicily*, Routledge, 1991, p28.
24. Harrison, R. J.: *Spain at the Dawn of History*, Thames & Hudson, London, 1988, pp140-43.
25. Healey, J. F.: *The Early Alphabet*, British Museum, London 1991, p16.
26. Page, R. I.: *Runes*, British Museum, London, 1987, p9.
27. Briard, J.: *Mythes et Symboles de l'Europe Preceltique*, Editions Errance, Paris, 1988, p148.
28. Keller, F.: *The Amazon and Madeira Rivers*, Philadelphia, 1875, p65.
29. Robinson, L.: *Ibid*, p63.
30. Collins, R.: *The Basques*, Blackwell, London, 1990, p258.
31. Noyes, R.: *Ibid*, p147, *passim*.
32. Bailey, A. A.: *Esoteric Astrology*, Lucis Trust, NY, 1982, p459.
33. Hope, M.: *The Lion People*, Thoth Publications, London, 1988.
34. Noyes, R.: *Ibid*, p147, *passim*.
35. Noyes, R.: *Ibid*, p167.
36. Holloway, R. R.: *Ibid*, p26.
37. Bailey, A. A.: *Ibid*, p129.
38. Bailey, A. A.: *The Rays and the Initiations*, Lucis Trust, NY, 1965, p557.
39. Bailey, A. A.: *Letters in Occult Meditation*, Lucis Trust, NY, 1985, pp186-7.
40. Noyes, R.: *Ibid*, p170.
41. Neate, T, & Dean, M.: *Ibid*.

This strange script appeared near Milk Hill, Wiltshire a week after an American cerealogist had inscribed in a field of grain the message 'Speak to us'. Very strange though it was, most of the researchers felt it was genuine. (*Jürgen Krönig*)

9.   Devas, crop-circles and earth energy

GLEN WALL

MY FIRST EXPERIENCE of crop-circles occurred in July 1988 in a wheat field adjacent to Silbury Hill, Avebury, Wiltshire. On a warm summer's evening I sat down to meditate in a large circle surrounded by four smaller circles in a 'quincunx' or quintuplet formation — which, according to Carl Jung, is an alchemical symbol of wholeness or unity. In the spiritual tradition in which I was trained we are taught to investigate the meaning of symbols by using them as meditational glyphs. I visualised a white quincunx on a black doorway, and imaginally passed through the symbol. Immediately I found myself in communication with an entity belonging to the order of beings called *Devas*, after an old Persian term used by Hindus — 'Shining Ones', alluding to their appearance as glowing lights.

This *deva* was a very powerful, beautiful being, and our communications took the form of an exchange of pictorial impressions. I was shown that, in antiquity, Silbury Hill (which is reputed to have been a four-sided white chalk pyramid) was used by the ancients as a vast storage battery for earth energy — terrestrial serpent power. The *deva*'s function was twofold. It was both the guardian of this sacred site, and it was responsible for mediation of cosmic energy from the star Sirius, the constellation Ursa Major (the Plough or Great Bear), and elsewhere, into the Silbury Hill mound. From here and other sacred sites, these energies would flow through the earth's network of energy-leys, and have most important effects in the evolution of humanity.

The energy-patterns of crop-circles exist, and may be dowsed, before the circles themselves appear. The reason they have become so conspicuous in recent years is because the human race is being given the opportunity to go through a mass initiation formerly only available to comparatively few individuals.

This same energy flows through our bodies as well as through the earth — I usually call it *kundalini*, another Hindu term. It is the great force of evolution and the basis of all forms of existence. When it begins to rise from the base of the spine, where it tends to lie dormant, it opens the energy-centres of the subtle body, causing dramatic changes of consciousness, and, eventually, an enlightened, blissful state of being in which all opposites are reconciled.

In ancient times this process was initiated in caves, barrows and special chambers such as may be found in the Great Pyramid of Cheops, which itself is a powerful storage battery for cosmic and earth energy. These secret places are a thing of the past — the new initiation chambers are out in the open, and for the use of everyone. Crop circles are the *chakras* or energy-centres of the earth, and every one that I have visited is pulsating with energy.

As a teacher and student of Kundalini yoga, I am used to handling and recognising this energy. My experience is that it is a benign, profoundly transformative energy. Initial exposure to *kundalini* may, in some cases, cause headaches or dizziness as the body adjusts itself to accommodate this powerful life-energy, but these effects soon pass and are super-

Grapeshot at Alton Barnes. (*Paul Dexter*) — try to hoax this one!

seded by wholly beneficial effects on both mind and body — unless this process of accommodation is actively resisted.

It is hardly necessary to explain why a worldwide consciousness-raising is crucial if we are to survive the millennium without destroying ourselves. This year, crop-circles and related phenomena have appeared in many countries besides England. Also, during the past few years more people than ever before have experienced spontaneous awakenings of life-energy (myself included).

This profound spiritual energy is the one thing which can save our planet. The message of the crop-circles is clear: we are all to be raised an octave. Let us go to them, make ourselves open and receptive, and pray to receive as much light and wisdom as we are able. And let us return again and again, secure in the knowledge that now, more than at any other time in history, our prayers will be both heard and answered by the Absolute, whose nature is Love.

10. Word from the Watchers

Editing and commentary by Palden Jenkins

ISABELLE KINGSTON

PREAMBLE

ISABELLE KINGSTON IS one of several sensitives around the world who is receiving specific information about crop circles — she happens also to live in the Avebury area, where there is a plethora both of megalithic sites and of crop circle phenomena. Excerpts from her channellings are included in *Harbingers* to give an idea of the kind of material and perspectives which can come forward in this form of investigation. Of the full range of investigative means, laboratory science represents one end of the spectrum, and channelling work represents the other. Whether or not you live easily with the notion of channelling, the material itself has, for any discerning person, a way of linking things together, and giving the crop circles a cosmological backdrop. Since all things in the crop circle world have to be taken open-mindedly as *possible realities*, it does no harm to juggle around some of these ideas to see where they lead.

Isabelle receives these communications while in a state of trance (in which she is unconscious of her behaviour and utterances, maintained and driven, as it were, by another presence), or semi-trance (in which she is conscious, lucidly 'dreaming', in a highly relaxed or inspired waking state). She never does channelling work in crop circles themselves, for the energy is, for her, too strong, and counter-productive for such a purpose. Communications are taped and transcribed for the record. I have leafed through these transcriptions, extracted what I feel is valuable to this book, and have changed phrasing, but not

meaning or emphasis, in cases where readability or clarity needs to be enhanced. There is no sequential order to these communications: they are arranged more by theme and tone. Take each paragraph independently — it does not necessarily follow along from the previous one.

There appear to be different sources coming through Isabelle at different times, with recognisable linguistic patterns and styles, and no doubt different qualities of presence. It should be pointed out that, in most cases of channelling, the source is communicating by *proto-thoughts* which are then translated into expressible words through the mind of the channel, which acts as a kind of intelligent dictionary and syntax-processor, often with perceptible energies (such as love or stillness) coming through too. Channelling is a *total* activity, requiring a profound level of conscious surrender and trust — something anathema to many of us. This is not the place to go into a detailed discussion about the validity or methods of channelling, but, as one with considerable experience in this field, I can vouch that the material, and the personality of the medium, Isabelle, strike me as being genuine, and genuinely derived from sources other than the unconscious of the medium. Usually, I find it possible to detect even a sophisticated psychic hoaxer, or simply one who has an inaccurate understanding of what they are doing, quite quickly. Living in a place (Glastonbury) which is thick with people with outrageous claims (and others with equally plausible ones), I am not easily fooled! But the main issue is not so much the *medium* as the *material* which is produced. Look this material through, and form your own conclusions.

Isabelle strikes me as a person who, while leading an unusual life, applies sense at every turn, and is remarkably free of the shifty kinds of certainty, self-appointed greatness, mysterious powers or other-worldliness which some mediums display. She seems jolly, straightforward and honest. I met her for the first time only when I visited her to collect this material for editing. "By their deeds shall ye know them". I believe this material to be of value to anyone, regardless of their metaphysical standpoint or ways of rationalising things!

Note: The emphasis to certain statements has been given by the Editor.

ABOUT THE CIRCLES

• There are some formations which link with your natural elements. There are some working within the bowels of the earth. You have often forgotten energies at play contained in the confines of the outer shell [of earth]. There are some formations linked with the higher consciousness of the universe. With others there is also a link with the knowledge of your Old Ones. Therefore each formation is different. Some say that you have the inner understanding to feel the difference.

• The circles at Silbury [1990] — the Watchers helped with this, but this time there are also elemental aspects involved, because this is what is important at the moment. We have in fact to a degree stabilised the planet, but now the natural elements need help.

• This ancient land holds the balance. It is the key to the world. Many of these places are being cleansed, as if made bright, so that they are channels of the new energy. Many lights have been placed there, but it is as if it needs a cosmic force to actually turn the switch. It is right for many groups to tend the lamp and get ready for the input of power.

• The pyramid of power which surrounds this country is the key — in your words a button to press to activate. You are the immune system of your planet, the healing system which will create the changes, but also there are other keys which will need to be activated. *This country* [England] *is a testing ground* — it has to be right before the whole can be lined up with the other dimensions. Things changing at Stonehenge — a field of energy is above the stones. [Some] corn circles are the exact dimension of Stonehenge — circles have appeared as a blueprint for humankind to mark that place as a place of power — it is as though those places are being unlocked, turning and being unlocked. Centres are being awakened — it is part of the Plan.

• We give indications of energy [in the circles], and yet *even if the secrets were never divulged, they will have changed many, many souls.* If you wish to truly enter the spirit of the formations, then stand a little away, project your thoughts to that place, connect your mind with the universal mind of understanding, then you will know whether these circles are of light beings or of man.

• We can only link when conditions are right, and we are sorry we cannot make things more plain at the moment. Understanding has to grow before acceptability becomes possible — so think of the symbols given, and you will know that we are with you.

• We give signals in the corn and we give sound in the ear. Changes in eyes, different aches and pains around the body — as though being re-aligned. Sounds in ears, like morse code. Information being programmed in for a later date. Always the right ear. Also a two-way exchange at an unconscious level.

• More circles will be coming very shortly [this was 1989]. There will be a circle within a circle showing first, and then more. This will bring about more energy, and the input is most necessary. Your earth cries with tears, and we feel the pain and sorrow of humanity's misunderstandings.

● Formations different? There is always change, for the energies flow and move, always interacting. Sometimes the same point, but as a tune of music, sometimes it is not easy to hit the same note. There is a music of the earth and of the universe, and a note will be revealed. Gradually the music will be completed and you will recognise the tune. *The corn circles are like a score of the music between the earth and the cosmos.* You do not at this time need to learn to read the score. *The best is to feel it.*

● Vibrations have to be acceptable for the formation to form in the correct way.

● Your Silbury Hill lies in a field of energy which is an area which draws cosmic power. There are leylines running through the earth, and at various points lines of power are energised. It has happened mostly in this part of the country. You lie in the triangle of power which will be guiding humanity's understanding. Similar circles have appeared in other countries. There have also been energy-healings to Peru, and the Himalayas and the West Coast of America — all places set down many many earth years before. We have come many times but humanity's awareness did not recognise the signs.

● The energy has been put through [into circles] through thought-processes, with light beams rather like your national grid system, so we input power into the earth's grid. This is to stabilise the energies in the earth, to stop the earth destroying you. This has been going on for some time. You have been told of the purpose of the Hill of Silbury: if we placed the circles elsewhere you would not have recognised it [the connection between the energy of ancient sites and that of crop circles].

● It is an intelligence of elemental energy which is linked to other solar systems. You cannot conceive of the energy relayed at this time, but you have experienced sound waves transmitted at high frequency. Change the tempo of the sounds and in this will emerge the code. We will be giving different sounds at this time. It is affirmation of facts which is necessary. You have physical form: matter has form in its being. Matter is not just energy and light, but also molecular formations. These are a print-out being shown in the circles, therefore you are being given the body of a form. Each entity shows itself in the formation, therefore you can communicate with these.

COUNSEL FOR INVESTIGATORS

● I want you to go to the hillsides and call upon the Brethren. Link yourselves with the cosmos and draw the energies in to help. Become as lightning conductors. Channel the light into the very soil. Transfer it into pure love and wait for the explosion.

[This channelling was a request to Isabelle and her group to draw energy into the Marlborough area, received on 10th July 1991. The work was done the next day (11th July), and during the following 24 hours, dramatic pictograms appeared at Ogbourne Maizey, Temple Farm and Barbury Castle — all within the vicinity of Isabelle and her group. On 12th July 1991, the group was led to Silbury Hill, asked to draw a line in visualisation between the moon and Avebury: a circle appeared that night in the vicinity, made up of two circles joined by a line. This piece demonstrates ways in which we may begin to interact creatively with the circle-makers.]

● You can facilitate the circles happening by sitting in a circle, sending out light and opening your hearts.

● You have before you symbols of the two worlds, combined with the essence of the cross [referring to quintuplet formations in 1990]. The matrix symbolising the power from all directions. The two worlds are now coming closer within the symbolism of the circles you talk of. However you must in your investigations remember that the two worlds are coming closer and that negative vibrations, and vibrations seeking for monetary gain will in fact hamper the progress of any souls investigating. There must be pure thought and seeking of knowledge for the benefit of humankind, and not for a select few who seek power, withholding information. Therefore keep open your heart centre and send the thought to those investigating for them to see the way of light clearly. You must not allow your mind totally to seek the energy that is being transmitted, but rather understand that it is being transmitted seeking the hearts of humankind, and opening minds in love.

• Keep your feet on the ground. Do not allow your minds to mislead you. Allow yourself to open, but not to close your mind: do not allow your imagination to override the visions being given. You have been conditioned to accept certain visions: do not expect the expected, but rather, open and let whatever is right flow through.

• How we would like you to understand the mysteries in true clarity — but the minds of many have yet to open fully, and thus the work is painstaking and slow. We regret that much [frivolous] interest has been shown, and in some ways this is contravening the energies. Seek not in the physical, but seek in the spiritual, for this is where the imbalance lies. You also must realise that the energies being transmitted at this time are a combination of all elements and all elemental beings as well as inter-planetary information. There is a coming-together, therefore *one source is not the whole picture, and many varying types of information might well be given*. It is a time for all to work together — thus all must pool their information and find that a vein of pure gold will run through.

• There is a new code of understanding being transmitted. Seek not to accept the barrier [of rationality]. It is a blueprint of a new energy-coding [that is] coming on to the planet. We have communicated

before many times: it is usually through thought-processes, but now it needs to be seen. Changes are occurring in all people — this sometimes stirs up anxiety and strife before the operation is complete.

COSMOLOGY AND TECHNOLOGY

• Open your minds. Cast aside your limitations and the thought-processes you normally use. An atom of intelligence touches your world and gives you a message for you to unlock. You sit in the centre of an isle of light, and you have been given the task to unlock ancient doorways. The information given to early man has been stored, and we again come to pass the messages on. Part of you still holds the ancient civilisations, and through your genes you have received this passed on information. Within you you have the blueprint to raise consciousness, to see the unseen, to link telepathically. Each one has through the choice of your birth incarnated with these abilities, and that small gene vibrates and grows within and is passed on. You have all walked on this earth many times but you know you came from other civilisations, other planets. You must protect your world, for many will follow you. Therefore we give you the help, therefore we give you the key to heal. But it is the task of others on your planet to reconstruct the information that we are giving. Secrets will be passed and transmitted and it is your task to help and transcribe those messages. We are those whom you might call the magical beings.

• You ask the meaning of your circles in the field. You have been made aware of the presence of the Watchers. Watchers is a name of a collective intelligence which guides you mortal humans. It is an intelligence from outside the planet, linked to angelic beings, part of cosmic consciousness — what you might understand as beings from outer space. We have been linked with humanity to bring the power necessary to build the New Jerusalem. We have been coming for years and years, and this has happened many times before, but the significance of the triangle of light and energy has been guiding us to give more power to you humans. Your country lies in the centre of the great pyramid of light which encircles your world, and the energies of the Watchers bring love through magnetic channels.

• The Aboriginal people understood the dimensions of the dreamtime, and although the information is lost, the understanding still remains. There was a time when many walked upon the earth and could link into many dimensions. That facility was lost, but can return at the point of the change-over [consciousness shift].

• The satellites given — the small circles — contain the code that will be understood. Although the great shapes show signs of power, as always the smaller gems contain the greatest light. These formations came before your planet was as it is now. The formations are like molecular structures and blueprints — like a form of morse code — and someone will be used to unravel this information, and scientists will be able to use it and put it into practice. It will be possible to use this new form of energy within your lifetimes — in seventeen summers [from 1990]. The unravelling will start before then.

• This new source of energy is now being created, and certain beings are being prepared to understand the messages being projected at this time. Some scientists are very close to the answer — an energy machine. This energy is only partially linked to magnetism. It is linked to the illusion of time. Rather like thought-transference, man will be able to change the molecular structure of things, including himself. Within the energy-pattern of the circles we give you this information. You humans do not believe your dreams and inspirations, so other methods have to be used. This will happen by the right people being drawn into the understanding. Some of you will be necessary to sit at the sidelines injecting love and light, and only a few will be involved totally.

• We stood with you, the three that stood upon the hillside yesterday, and you remarked on the feeling of the holy place on which you stood. We confirmed that what you call the Avebury Sanctuary is alive with pure energy which like a network links all the places of power around the globe. The building of the place you know as the Hill of Silbury was in fact directed by a higher intelligence — by the Watchers and by one that you refer to as Beings from other areas.

• In all things you are linked — an invisible web joining all to all and us to you. Therefore work is done for those who may be weaker links in the chain. Spiritual power, power from other dimensions, is drawn down to the Hill of Silbury — the word *Sil* derives from the word which means Shining Being. It is the hill of the Shining Beings which showed themselves to the ancient seers and started the work in earnest. The temples that remain were in fact meant to last until this cataclysmic time in earth's history. Therefore the foundations were laid to help humanity at a later date.

• Amidst all its struggles, humanity does not seem to want to accept that love great and powerful is encircling the world and being transmitted. It is most essential to create the right atmosphere for enlightenment into the grid system of the planet. Power is being created though the intellect of the scientist — knowledge is being awakened. Those who bring knowledge and understanding are here again. We are known as the Watchers, because we can only aid and help. We have not the will to change the world — this, my friends, is your work. *Do not always look upward, for there is much to love below.*

11. The Voice of the Earth

LUCY PRINGLE

May the light of love shine over the land,
May the waves of love pour through the sea,
May the song of love be carried on the wind,
May the flow of love enter the hearts of men,
And may this purest love heal the wounded earth.

TEHANETORENS

I AM THE MOTHER of A-ro-senh and Jenh-ni-doh, young braves of the Mohawk tribe. I am the voice of their Chief Tehanetorens.

It all began many moons ago when A-ro-senh and Jenh-ni-doh were still with their brothers and sisters, the stars in the Great Sky.

One day a certain boy, young and wide-eyed with the wonder of youth, looked about him, and quickly an idea came into his mind. He was a lively child with an unruly mop of tousled brown curls. He was fleet of foot. On this morning he had managed to escape from his governess, and before she had a chance to find him, he had disappeared into the forest. His heart soared high with the thrill of freedom. In his excitement he chased the dappled sunlight and darted from rock to rock, from tree to tree. The very birds and animals seemed to join in the game, sensing that they need not fear the boy, for he was, on this day, as much a part of them as they were a part of him. Deep and still deeper into the forest went the boy, filled with a new feeling that made him glad that he was alone with the creatures of the forest, his friends.

He felt very small amongst the towering trees, he had a feeling that the animals deep in the forest knew him to be a boy and yet were not afraid of him. He was glad he had left his governess at the house, for she would not have understood what he was feeling now.

Never before had he had a chance to *listen* to the

sounds about him, the song of the birds, the grunts and squeals of the animals, the soughing in the branches and the rustling of the leaves on the ground. They all seemed to be *saying* something, a language that he wished he understood — for if only he could, it seemed to him that much of what puzzled him would be explained. He also felt that the very earth was a part of that language, and so he decided to sit down hoping to get a clearer understanding by being a part of it.

He found himself sitting on the edge of a small pool of crystal-clear water. It was protected from the full glare of the sunlight by the branches of the towering trees. He dabbled his toes in the water, watching the ripples spread ever outwards. He had started off that morning being just himself, now he knew that he was also a part of everything else and that oneness stretched as far as each extending ripple, continuing on forever.

He gazed at his reflection in the pool and wondered if he looked any different just because he *felt* different. He pulled faces and laughed at the face in the pool. Then he noticed that he had grown a face on either side of his own and they too were smiling. The boy turned round and looked straight into the eyes of a young man on his right and another on his left. His heart gave a tiny lurch in his breast, and quickly stilled itself in the laughter of friendship which broke from the three young faces.

The boy looked at his companions. They were older than he — in fact they seemed grown-up, and grown-ups, as we all know, are old to children. He could see that they were tall and strong like trees, their skin was reddish brown, glistening as though blessed by the sun, and their eyes shone with silent laughter, dark as the pine needles at their feet.

We greet you, child of the still water. We are your Mohawk brothers. We have often seen you walking in the forest with your governess, but we have never shown ourselves as she would not let you venture far, scared by even the tapping of a woodpecker. But today you are on your own, and we have followed you all the way, sometimes in front of you and sometimes behind you. It was good to see that you were not frightened by your tall brothers and sisters, the trees, nor by your small brothers and sisters, the birds and the animals.

And so the boy and the two young braves talked and played and the boy found that he could speak to them of many things, strange mysterious things about nature and being frightened of the dark, which when they were spoken of were no longer strange or mysterious. And they told him how they addressed the Creator.

We return thanks to our mother, the earth, which sustains us. We thank you that you have caused her to yield so plentifully of her fruits, and we hope that she will continue to do so.

We return thanks to the lakes, rivers and streams, which run their courses upon our Mother the Earth. We thank you that you have supplied them with life for our comfort and support. We hope they will continue to do so.

We return thanks to the lives of the medicine plants of this earth. We thank you, Sakoiatison, for giving strength to the medicine-life of this land, helping to keep our bodies healthy and strong.

We return thanks to the Three Sisters — the corn, beans and squash. We thank you for the abundant harvest gathered in during the past season.

We return thanks to the bushes and tree-life of this land. Our daily needs are dependent on your constant generosity, and we hope that the bushes and tree-life will continue to live as our brothers and sisters on this land.

We return thanks to the four winds of this land, which by moving have kept us healthy and strong. We hope that the winds of the north, east, west and south will continue working on our behalf.

We return thanks to our grandfathers, the thun-

52.

53.

Plate 52. UPTON SCUDAMORE, near Warminster. This lovely pictogram had a very feminine quality. Found in barley 21st July 1991. Note the 'cricket bail' boxes, 4 on each side. (*Paul Greenaway*)

Plate 53. The Neptune 'trident' was most unusual. (*Busty Taylor*)

Plate 54. National Geographic film crew at Upton Scudamore. (*Busty Taylor*)

Plate 55. This 'scroll' formed the same day close by. (*Busty Taylor*)

Plate 56. ALTON PRIORS. The second pictogram to form in the area on 19th July. (*David Tarr*)

Plate 57. The fork at Alton Priors. (*Stuart Dike*)

Plate 58. THE KENNETTS pictogram. With its dramatic key, this was one of the grandest pictograms of 1991. Formed on 27th July, the anniversary of its predecessor in the next field, it also pointed towards Silbury Hill. (*Busty Taylor*)

Plate 59. Pole shot of the Kennetts pictogram. (*Busty Taylor*)

Plate 60. The Kennetts pictogram. (*George Wingfield*)

Plate 61. The key pointed to Silbury. (*David Tarr*)

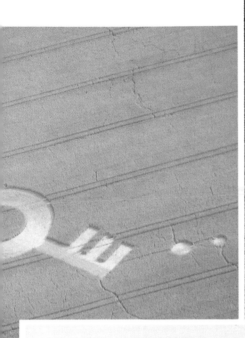

59.

61.

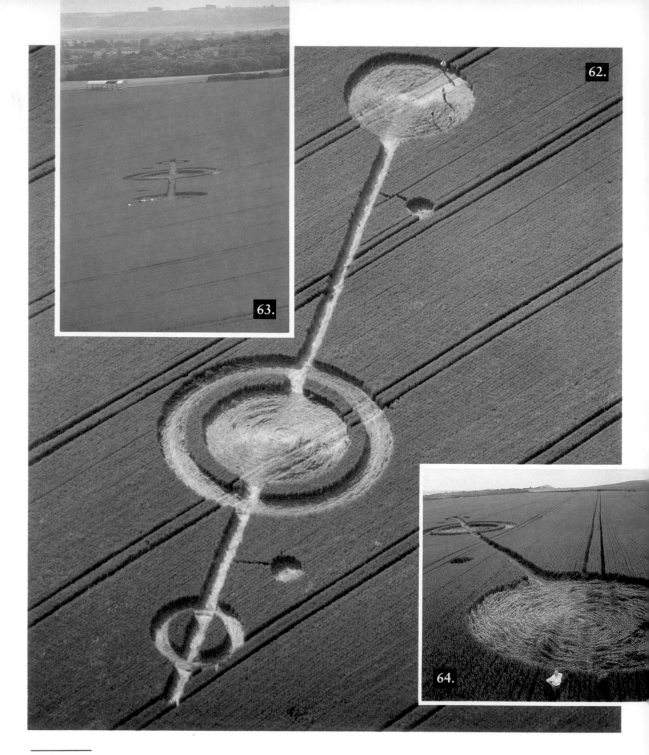

62.

63.

64.

Plate 62. ALTON BARNES I,
2nd July. (*Paul Greenaway*)

Plate 63. Alton Barnes
landscape. (*Alick Bartholomew*)

Plate 64. Pole shot:
(*Busty Taylor*)

Plate 65. MAISEY FARM,
Marlborough. The Alton Barnes' I
twin, but double its size, formed
11th July. (*Busty Taylor*)

Plate 66. Maisey Farm
landscape. (*Busty Taylor*)

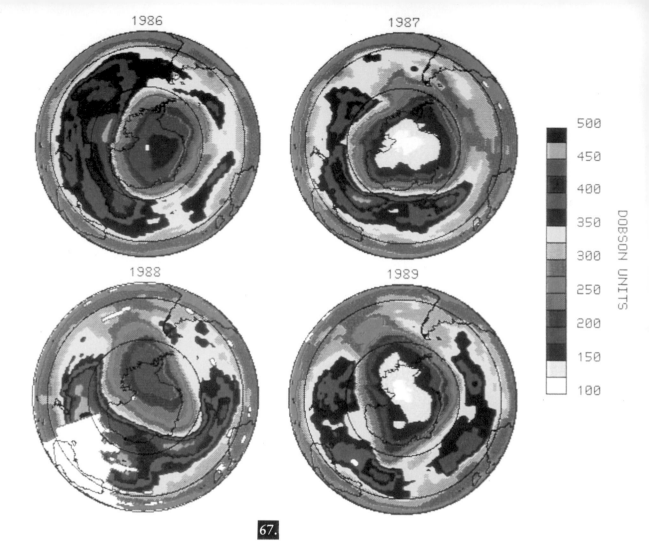

Plate 67. OZONE HOLE: A series of satellite maps comparing the severe depletion in the ozone layer over Antarctica on each 5th October between 1986 and 1989. The hole appears in shades of blue, violet and pink with Antarctica outlined. The colour scale shows total ozone values in Dobson units (missing data is white). The map was made by the American Nimbus-7 weather satellite. (*NASA/Science Photo Library*) (see Chap.2, p.72)

der people. We give our thanks, for you generously provide for our happiness and comfort in causing the rain to fall, giving us water, causing all plants to grow. We ask that you will not abandon us as our protector in our daily lives.

We return thanks to the sun, for looking down upon us with a never-ending smile. We thank you, Sakoiatison, that our brother sun continues to regulate the return of the seasons, and for watching over the comfort of our people. We hope the sun will never hide his face in shame and leave us in darkness.

We return thanks to the moon and stars, which give us light when the sun has gone to the west. We look toward our grandmother moon, for she is still fulfilling her cycle of life as originally ordained. The life of the stars, who shine their light of beauty, we also give thanks for, and we hope they will continue to do so.

Last of all, we return thanks to you, our creator, Sakoiatison, for you are the master of all life. Should my people disobey your wishes in times of confusion, look upon us and help us see the way of righteousness. Restore your traditional teachings to us, for your teachings were the path of our ancient forefathers. Only to them can we now look for an example for our people.

Soon hunger overtook them and the braves each produced a piece of bread, and seeing that the boy had no food, they each gave him some, for that is the Law of their People. As the sun started to go down, the boy realised he did not know the way home, for he had made no note of the path he had taken and had left no markings. He felt stupid and silly in front of his new friends, but they were laughing, having guessed his problem. And so they made their way together to the edge of the forest, telling the boy wonderful stories about the animals and the life of the forest, for all the forest's creatures were brother and sister to them, and each spoke to each with respect and understanding.

The Native American knows that man's heart becomes hard if it is away from nature — he knows that lack of respect for growing things soon leads to disdain for humans too, so he keeps his youth close to its softening influence. Kinship with all creatures of the earth, sky and water is a real and active principle. There exists a brotherly feeling that keeps the Mohawks safe, and so close do some of them come to their feathered and furry friends that they speak a common tongue.

Our people did not kill our animal brothers for sport or pleasure. All life was sacred to us and we knew we were only one part of the life of this earth. If we were hungry we killed an animal to eat and we thanked the spirit of that animal and the Great Spirit who sent it. We killed only what we needed, wasting nothing. Only thoughtless ones boast of killing ability and only cowards lack consideration for the life and feelings of all creatures.

Our fathers spoke to the animal they killed thus: "I am sorry that I had to kill you, little brother, but I had need of your meat. My children were hungry and crying for food. Forgive me, little brother. I honour your courage, your strength and your beauty. Each time I pass this place I will remember you and do honour to your spirit".

As the three friends drew near to the house, his governess appeared and tried to pull the boy away from the young braves, but the boy was resolute and waited until his mother came up to them. "Welcome my friends" she said, "I invite you into my house, for you are indeed my friends, being the rescuers and friends of my son".

So a friendship was struck that, like the great trees of the forest, endured the heat of the summer, the snows of the winter, being as the strong sap running through the heart of everything. The mother was known as A-di-ronh.

The boy grew to manhood and travelled far and wide, and his mother also lived in many distant lands. And it happened in the late summer of her days that she had two grandchildren, and looking upon these children, she thought of her Mohawk friend, one of the young braves of yesterday, Tehan-etorens, with whom she regularly exchanged greetings by letter.

For these children, it seemed to her, were like young saplings, and she felt in her heart that they could grow up as strong trees, their roots in Mother Earth and their branches reaching towards the Great Spirit in the sky.

Thus it came about that the two brothers became A-ro-senh and Jenh-ni-doh as declared by Aren Akweks and Ska-won-ate.

I, Aren Akweks, a warrior of the Mohawk nation, will soon call you brothers. Since Ska-won-ate, a woman of the Turtle Clan of my nation has given her consent to your adoption into her family, I am charged with the duty of conferring upon you the honour of becoming adopted members of this Clan and of her family. You become one of us. You become of our flesh and blood, of our mind and soul, and from now on you will be welcome to sit with the members of your clan when the Great Peace Bowl is set in our lodge and eat of the Beavertail soup, the ceremonial peace-dish of all our clans.

From now on you will be made welcome to the great Confederation of the Ho-de-no-sai-ne, the Long House of one Family. You may travel to other reservations but you must first seek out the home of one of the Turtle Clan. That will be your home during your stay. You must treat the Matron of the Clan as your Mother, the warriors as your Brothers. Should you overtake an elderly Matron or Warrior, you shall escort her until she tells you to pass on. Should you meet any of your Clan who are in distress and in want of food or bread, and you have but one piece, you shall give one half, for it is the Law of our People. It is the command of the Great Spirit, the Giver of All Good Things, and

he has promised to give abundantly to the obedient. And now may the Guardian Spirits guide you and protect you from all harm.

Your names among our people will be Red Squirrel and Little Beaver, or in the ancient language of our fathers, A-ro-senh and Jenh-ni-doh. And now, holding this sacred wampum string and this feather of the noble bird, the Eagle, we declare you duly made members of the Turtle Clan of our Nation. We welcome you, A-ro-senh and Jenh-ni-doh.

And so A-di-ronh entered the winter of her days. It was a long and sometimes lonely winter, when her limbs felt heavy and bent, as the snow laden branches of the forest trees. But nothing is forever.

What is life? It is the flash of a firefly in the night. It is the breath of a buffalo in the winter time. It is the little shadow which runs across the grass and loses itself in the sunset.

So A-di-ronh began the dawn of her tomorrows, and as requested her ashes were taken by her old friend, Tehanetorens, to the sacred mountain of his people, and there as dawn broke and the sun started its path in the sky, they asked that her spirit be returned to the Creator.

Your soul has returned from whence it came, but you have touched the earth, you have let us touch the earth through your wisdom. We set your soul free, but your time here will not be forgotten.

At that moment a golden eagle rose in the sky carrying the spirit of A-di-ronh. The noble bird rose higher and higher until it was lost to sight and thus A-di-ronh began her new journey into tomorrow, to a place in the heavens, beyond the Beyond.

HEALING THE EARTH

And thus it was that I turned to the wisdom of the Mohawks when asked to write about healing the earth. For it seems to me that whilst we are expert at destroying the earth, little is known or practised regarding its healing or regeneration. I am sure none of us are any longer in doubt that we are inextricably one with the earth — "Whatever befalls the earth, befalls the sons of earth."

As humans continue with their wanton damage, the earth cries out in pain. People are devouring her bit by bit, inching closer and yet closer to her heart. In her death-throes the earth staggers and reels in agony, and as a snake needs to slough off its skin in order to revitalise itself, so does the earth. As the dance of death and rebirth begins, many souls might perish, leaving behind those whose energies and vibrations will be in harmony with the reborn planet.

How will we fit into that day? We need to look to the plants and trees of earth, the birds of the air, and the fishes of the sea. We need to learn to breathe with the earth, to see through the eyes of the earth, hear through her ears and feel through her heart.

What can we do with our thoughts? We can seek to link to the supreme Mind, who gave us the power of higher intelligence. We can link to divine Consciousness. We need to understand how small we are when we wander from the true path, when we block our ears, when we cover our eyes — how easily we can cause our own destruction! Imagine what we could achieve if we put that energy into *creating* rather than destroying.

My search has taken me far and wide, not only to the Mohawk Indians on their large reservation stretching from upper New York State into the province of Quebec, but to the Kogi Indians of the Sierra in Columbia, South America, and from there on to Austria to learn the secrets of *living water*, and finally to Bombay to track down a master of terrestrial acupuncture. Is this knowledge so scarce that I have had to travel so far?

LIVING WATER

First come with me on a visit to meet Viktor Schauberger in Austria. He was a remarkable man whose knowledge of nature came from observation. He was a forester, as were his father and grandfather before him. He had only an informal education before going into the service of an Austrian prince in a remote part of the prince's estate. Thus for many years Schauberger was allowed the freedom to bury himself in nature.

He lived his life deep in the forest. He had a profound understanding of nature's hidden relationships and knew that there had to be fundamental balance. Above all else he felt that *water* was the essence of life, that:

the mysteries of water are similar to those of the blood in the human body. In nature, normal functions are fulfilled by water just as blood provides many important functions for mankind. Water in its natural state shows us how it wishes to flow, so we should follow its wishes. This is an immensely important concept and is readily applicable to all nature. First understand nature, then copy it. The task of technology is not to correct nature, but to imitate it.

After some years living in the forest Viktor Schauberger faced a major test. The Prince needed to transport logs from a remote region of his forest. The expense would be great. Schauberger, through his understanding of water, was able to design a method of doing this at a low cost. He had observed how a snake moved in the water, and basing his theory on the snake, he designed a chute, which he placed in the river. When the logs were laid in the chute, the water became agitated in such a way that the movement enabled the logs to navigate the twists and turns of the river with elegant ease.

News of this amazing discovery travelled far and wide and many people tried to duplicate Viktor Schauberger's method but gave up in frustration as he would not produce a formula. He himself needed no formula — his reasoning was based on observation, observation of the characteristics of each river, and therefore the formula needed to be adapted to each new set of circumstances.

As you can well imagine, this caused a deep divide between Schauberger and academics. He was mainly a *right brain* man, using intuition, contemplation and higher consciousness. He *felt*, contemplated and observed.

He used his senses to bring about working harmony with nature. These senses were not dulled by preconceived ideas, for nature is ever-changing — the man who thinks he can predict it is in for many surprises.

Viktor Schauberger knew that nature held secrets which were inaccessible to those who did not speak its language. "Go to a stream and listen to its music." In effect by *listening* to nature and hearing the message it has for us, the destruction of our planet could be prevented. Water is the essence of all things.

I wonder how many of us understand how changes in water temperature affect the properties of the water? Viktor Schauberger again drew a parallel between blood and water. Just as the rise in blood temperature can reveal that a person is ill so it is with water.

He found that water at +4°C reaches its highest quality, and that on approaching +4°C water becomes healthy and alive. He called this water *positive*. Above +4°C he found that the water had a "diminishing energy and biological quality". This he called *negative* water. This was one of his most important discoveries — one on which all further experiments were based.

He also gives much encouragement for regeneration by telling the story of a mountain spring that had been an endless source for supply until the stone structure which covered it was removed, leaving it open to the light and sun. Gradually the spring dried up. Some while later it was decided to replace the stone covering and little by little the spring returned to normal.

Reforestation of the earth would also bring back the water and in its turn recreate harmony and balance. Is that too simple a solution? I think not, for most of the important things in life are indeed the simplest. Reforestation is needed not for the sake of quick commercial gain, but for the salvation of our planet. Not just one species planted for fast growth but mixed planting — for a healthy forest is in fact a strange assortment of vegetation blending together in harmony.

It would seem what we could be giving much more time and thought to the reforestation of our planet, not only to halt damage but to reverse the destructive process. All aspects of nature, if untouched by humanity, combine into a harmonious whole — so indeed should we, as individuals, understand that we are also part of and have a responsibility to the whole.

Technology is being used to supplant the universal laws of nature. People want money, lots of it, and they want it fast. If fertilisers on the land give a greater and faster yield, why bother to consider that this will render the planet barren? If drilling for more oil and felling more trees brings the Earth to its knees, who cares? People say, we will not be here to see it.

Viktor Schauberger understood this clearly[1]. Following the water-chute experiment he developed a simple process enabling him to photograph the spiral movement of water — a spiral movement of energy which runs through all nature. We observe it in the twisting-turning movement of water, in DNA, in whirlwinds, cyclones and hurricanes and even in the simple pineapple, the twisting clematis and sweet pea. It is nature itself.

Having observed this fundamental principle and realising that we live in a three-dimensional world, he had a basis for future experiments. He saw endless potential in the vortex energy in water and insisted that water, if harnessed according to its own harmonic laws, could take the place of much modern technology, which frequently causes friction and damage.

Here once more he saw the need to work *with* nature. He reasoned that knowledge could not be acquired simply by reading books and working in laboratories. The first step had to come from the very *essence* of nature, its spirituality.

Is this spiral force which Viktor Schauberger talks about, also behind the circles in the crop fields? For a long time, in fact so long as they were rotational, it did seem possible. It is intriguing to note that when Viktor Schauberger describes the centrifugal movement in nature as "It forces the moving medium from the centre outwards towards the periphery in straight lines. The particles of the medium appear to be forced out from the centre". He appears to be

describing the Swastika crop circle in almost uncanny detail. Pure coincidence? I rather think not. However as the formations developed in complexity, appearing as rectangles and triangles, it became clear that it was no longer a valid explanation.

THE ELDER BROTHERS

We have much to learn from people whose survival is dependent on the wellbeing of the land, for they listen to what nature has to tell them. One example is the Kogi Indians, a mystical race in Colombia. They see themselves as Elder Brothers, and in order to carry out their task of saving the earth and their Younger Brothers (we of the western world) they have separated themselves from us and gone into self-imposed isolation in the Andean Sierra. Despite the differences in climate and culture, many of their

beliefs run parallel to those of Schauberger. The Kogi say:

> In the beginning all was water, and the water was the Mother. It was 'aluna'. Where there is water, the essence of life, there is memory and potential. The earth, too is the Mother.

So the Kogi explained that water is the link to the life-force, and that what is dry is dead.

> The earth and the water existed from the beginning. In the beginning we were formed in the water. The Mother formed us there. All the trees, that tree, another tree, another tree, all of them had water. When the trees are dried out they can be cut and used for firewood. All types of tree can be used for fire. We all need water. We cannot live without it. We wash in water. We cook in water. And all the mountains we see have water. Everything emerged from water. Water therefore is the raw material of every culture and the basis of every bodily and spiritual development.

Both Viktor Schauberger and the Kogi abhor the misuse of technology. They insist that it goes against the fundamental laws of nature. They have in common a belief in our responsibility to heal the Earth — encouragingly they believe it *is* possible to save the planet and reverse the destructive processes. However their approach is often different, for whereas Viktor Schauberger had an engineering-oriented approach, the Kogi have an intellectually-enigmatic concept of bringing *aluna* into balance and harmony with the earth.

What is *aluna*? It is higher consciousness, its linking with Source, the springhead of our Being. In the beginning there was only *aluna* — Mind.

> In the beginning there was blackness. Only the sea. In the beginning there was no sun, no moon, no people. In the beginning there were no animals, no plants. Only sea. The sea was the Mother. The Mother was not people, she was not anything.

Nothing at all. She was when she was, darkly. She was memory and potential. She was aluna.

All things need to be in balance and harmony in *aluna*. All things have a spirit which is also within *aluna*, and if something is out of harmony it must be acted upon *in aluna* and brought back into balance. *Aluna* is all things — it is the past, present and future, the essential *beingness* of everything. Only by going into *aluna* can the Kogi hope to save the planet. They say:

> We can no longer look after the world alone. The Younger Brother is doing too much damage. He must see and understand and assume responsibility. Now we will have to work together. Otherwise, the world will die[2].

SINGING TO THE CLAY

We in our turn must understand the need for harmony. We must understand the need to go beyond our everyday mind into our higher mind, linking with our Source. In linking we find we are at one with the Universe and in that Universe we hear a '*song*'. This song is tuned so that only those who have attained oneness with the Source may hear it.

As the song travels downward it reaches our planet. Our planet has its own particular vibrational song. Those vibrations ebb and flow, always changing. The song heard may be the singing of the trees, the music of the winds and the oceans, the rumblings of the earth and its overlapping tectonic plates and fissures. The birds and animals tune into the changing vibrations according to the seasons and to weather, and they give forth their sounds accordingly in song, as do the whales of the deep. The plants respond and make their music too.

Unfortunate the soul that cannot hear these songs! Yet fortunate because of the wonder when it awakens and hears!

Each soul gives forth its own magic according to its

vibrations. Each soul needs to attempt to raise its vibrations — according to the personal development of each soul. Some may realise their increased vibrations by listening to music, others by painting, or tuning into nature in all its diversity.

An example of balancing and working with nature is the 'Tonsingen' or 'singing to the clay'. Farmers in days gone by would regularly perform this rite at certain times. The farmer sang at a selected pitch which set up a resonance whilst he stirred the contents of a barrel. This choice of pitch depended not only on the contents but also the shape of the barrel. It was thought that this stirring accompanied by singing would make the contents take on a *neutral voltage*. The general practice was for the ritual to be carried out in the cool of the evening. The contents were stirred with a wooden spoon and the singing either rose or descended, according to the direction in which the spoon was being stirred. Clockwise the notes ascended, anti-clockwise they descended. The water with loam or clay added was then poured thinly over the fields with enormously beneficial results.

As so often happens these traditions were dismissed and scorned as new technology took over, so that the knowledge is in danger of being lost. For fear of derision, a reluctance to pass it down to the next generation has emerged.

EYE OF THE NEEDLE

Viktor Schauberger concentrated much of his research on the spiral and the different effects resulting from the direction of the spiral — clockwise or anti-clockwise. Each direction plays its part in harmonising nature. In spiritual terms clockwise is considered 'the spiral of descent' — the working of the spiritual into the material. Anit-clockwise is the 'spiral of ascent', working the material into the spiritual.

We turn to the Kogi Mama's (wise ones) grave warning to their Younger Brothers:

We are the Elder Brothers. We have not forgotten the old ways. We still know how to dance. We have forgotten nothing. We know how to call the rain. If it rains too hard we know how to stop it. We call the summer. We know how to bless the world and make it flourish.

But now they are killing the Mother. The Younger Brother, all he thinks about is plunder. The Mother looks after him too, but he does not think.

He is cutting into her flesh. He is cutting into her arms. He is cutting off her breasts. He takes out her heart. He is killing the heart of the world.

When the final darkness falls everything will stop. The fires, the benches, the stones, everything. All the world will suffer. When they kill all the Elder Brothers then they too will be finished. We will all be finished.

What would they think if all the Mamas died? Would they think, Well, so what? What would they think?

If that happened and all we Mamas die, and if there were no one doing our work, the rain wouldn't fall from the sky.

The human body is made up largely of water, so is the Earth's biosphere. Again the Wise Ones (Mamas) speak:

We had everything, and Younger Brother took it all to another country.

Now the Mama grows sad, he feels weak. He says that the earth is decaying. The earth is losing its strength because they have taken away much petrol, coal, many minerals.

A human being has much liquid inside. If the liquid dries up we fall with weakness. This same thing can happen to the earth, Weakness makes you fall, weakness.

So the earth today catches diseases of all kinds.

The animals die. The trees dry up. People fall ill. Many illnesses will appear, and there will be no cure for them. Why?

So the Mamas say, no one else should come here, no more ransacking because the earth wants to collapse, the earth grows weak. We must protect it, we must respect it, because he does not respect the earth, because he does not respect it.

Younger Brother thinks, "Yes Here I am! I know much about the universe!" But this knowing is learning to destroy the world, to destroy everything, all humanity.

The earth feels. They take out petrol, it feels pain there. So the earth sends out sickness. There will be many medicines, drugs, but in the end the drugs will not be of any use. Neither will the medicine be of any use.

The Mamas say that this tale must be learnt by the Younger Brother.

Technology is threatening the balance of nature. Humanity tried to make the planet a playground for his superficial needs, turning a deaf ear to nature's plea for harmony. For just as humans are created from nature so must they understand the need to abide by nature's laws. Technology has thrust its way upon us, pushing aside the laws of nature as unimportant and irrelevant, harming the planet as it advances, acknowledging only its own power.

This will lead to inevitable breakdown unless a new understanding of our interrelationship and interdependence with nature comes about. We must try and understand that the planet is a living entity with whom we need to be in harmony. We need to be the guardians of harmonic balance. Hear the poignant and moving words of Chief Seattle, Chief of the Suquamish, spoken in 1851:

How can you buy or sell the sky, the warmth of the land? The idea is strange to us. If we do not own the freshness of the air and the sparkle of the water, how can you buy them? Every part of this earth is sacred to my people.

Every shining pine needle, every sandy shore, every mist in the dark woods, every clearing and humming insect is holy in the memory and experience of my people. The sap which courses through the trees carries the memories of the red man.

The white man's dead forget the country of their birth when they go to walk among the stars. Our dead never forget this beautiful earth, for it is part of us. The perfumed flowers are our sisters, the deer, the horse, the great eagle, these are our brothers. The rocky crests, the juices in the meadows, the body heat of the pony, and man all belong to the same family.

So, when the great Chief in Washington sends word that he wishes to buy our land, he asks much of us. The Great Chief sends word he will reserve us a place so that we can live comfortably to ourselves. He will be our father and we will be his children. So we will consider your offer to buy our land. But it will not be easy. For this land is sacred to us.

This shining water that moves in the streams and rivers is not just water but the blood of our ancestors. If we sell you land, you must remember that it is sacred and you must teach your children that it is sacred and that each ghostly reflection in the clear water of the lake tells of events and memories in the life of my people. The water's murmur is the voice of my father's father.

The rivers are our brothers, they quench our thirst. The rivers carry our canoes, and feed our children. If we sell you our land, you must remember, and teach your children, that the rivers are our brothers and yours, and you must henceforth give the rivers the kindness you would give any brother.

We know the white man does not understand our ways. One portion of land is the same to him as the next, for he is the stranger who comes in the night and takes from the land whatever he needs.

The land is not his brother, but his enemy, and when he has conquered it, he moves on. He leaves his father's grave behind, and he does not care. His father's grave and his children's birthright are forgotten. He treats his mother, the earth, and his brother the sky, as things to be bought, plundered, sold like sheep or bright beads. His appetite will devour the earth and leave behind only desert.

I do not know. Our ways are different from your ways. The sight of your cities pains the eyes of the red man. There is no quiet place in the white man's cities. No place to hear the unfurling of leaves in spring or the rustle of the insect's wings. The clatter only seems to insult the ears. And what is there to life if a man cannot hear the lonely cry of the whippoorwill or arguments of the frogs around the pond at night?

I am a red man and I do not understand. The Indian prefers the soft sound of the wind darting over the face of a pond and the smell of the wind itself, cleansed by a midday rain, or scented with pinion pine. The air is precious to the red man for all things share the same breath, the beast, the tree, the man, they all share the same breath.

The white man does not seem to notice the air he breathes. Like a man dying for many days he is numb to the stench. But if we sell you our land, you must remember that the air is precious to us, that the air shares its spirit with the life it supports. The wind that gave our grandfather his first breath also receives his last sigh. And if we sell you our land, you must keep it apart and sacred as a place where even the white man can go to taste the wind that is sweetened by the meadow's flowers.

You must teach your children that the ground beneath their feet is the ashes of our grandfathers. So that they will respect the land, tell your children that the earth is rich with the lives of our kin. Teach your children that we have taught our children that the earth is our mother. Whatever befalls the earth befalls the sons of the earth. If men spit upon the ground, they spit upon themselves.

This we know: the earth does not belong to man; man belongs to earth. All things are con-nected. We may be brothers after all. We shall see. One thing we know which the white man may one day discover; our God is the same God. You may think now that you own Him as you wish to own our land; but you cannot. He is the God of man, and His compassion is equal for the red man and the white. This earth is precious to Him and to harm the earth is to heap contempt on its creator. The whites too shall pass; perhaps sooner than all other tribes. Contaminate your bed and you will one day suffocate in your own waste. But in your perishing you will shine brightly fired by the strength of the God who brought you to this land and for some special reason gave you dominion over this land and over the red man.

The destiny is a mystery for us, for we do not understand when the buffalo are all slaughtered, the wild horses are tame, the secret corners of the forest heavy with the scent of many men and the views of the ripe hills blotted by talking wires. Where is the thicket? Gone. Where is the eagle? Gone. The end of living and the beginning of survival.

Where then are the guardians of the future of this planet?

We can perhaps pin our hopes on the young of today. The young, with a wonderful clarity of vision that encompasses a seemingly old wisdom of yester-year — when the earth and the heavens knew each other, when communications passed easily from one to the other, when there were no barriers of time or space, when distant travel was commonplace and when thought-forms were realities. It is to these young we must look.

A dawn of spiritual awareness when man will no longer manipulate technology for his own ends and when advancement will only be called progress when it is for the benefit of all. These young are here, and you will not have to look far to find them. Technology that works *with* and not against the harmony of nature will be universally encouraged, old knowledge

wind and water. They are consulted before locating a site where any construction is to take place, be it a city, road, temple, house, tomb, or indeed even where a tree should be planted. This also extended to interior decoration and the placing of furniture within a dwelling. We in the west in the olden days would approach a dowser before selecting a site for a church: this knowledge happily is not lost.

Everything has to be in harmony with the landscape, and in order to do this the geomancers used a compass which carried signs of heavenly constellations and physical elements in addition to giving the polar directions. By this method they detected a force called *ch'i* which flows invisibly in the sky, the landscape and the water — *"that which cannot be seen and cannot be grasped"*. The Chinese also refer constantly to dragons and the *ch'i* force is the dragon force, the lines flowing through the landscape being the dragon's veins. These lines were the force which runs through the powerful current lines, lines of subtle magnetism. The principal of *feng-shui* is to harmonise everything with nature. The *ch'i* is also related to the *Yin* and *Yang*, the *Yin* being passive, receptive, negative, dark and female, the *Yang*, active, outgoing, positive, and light and male. In addition there are smaller lines, the *lung mei*. All play their vital part in the harmony of the whole.

I would like to tell you a little about Khojeste. He is a Zoroastran priest. Zoroastrianism is the ancient Persian religion. Zoroaster lived around 500BC, but the actual dates and place of his origin are uncertain. He believed that the cosmos and history play out the struggle between the forces of light and darkness. The forces of light are led by *Ahura Mazda*, the Supreme Being, and those of darkness by *Ahriman*. He believed that the ultimate victory would go to the side of light but that the ball is still very much in play.

To Zoroaster, man's work for the harmonious enhancement of the earth was an essential function. As happened in Christianity later on, Zoroastrianism tended to relegate the deities of the previous religions to the status of demons. So the myriad spirits of the

of former times will be remembered and be in everyday use.

WIND AND WATER

I now invite you to travel with me to Bombay to meet Khojeste Mistree. Khojeste is a geomancer, an exponent of the flow and harmony of earth energies. Geomancers are practitioners of *feng-shui*, an ancient Chinese science of bygone days, that translates as

Vedic Aryan religion — the Devas — became the demons in Zoroastran belief. Not all 'earth spirits' were looked upon as good.

So we place Khojeste and his ministry in a theological environment. He holds the increasingly universal belief that the earth *is alive*. The earth has energies that need balancing, and his mission as geomancer is to work these telluric energies as did the Egyptians, Chinese and Indians in days gone by. Khojeste calls it *"the art of working from the surface of the earth, to assist in the balance, when the earth needs balancing, it needs healing"*.

There are wholesome and unwholesome forces in every aspect of life. When Khojeste is asked to heal a location, he believes that he must try and harmonise the forces of the place with those of the person. To achieve this, he borrows an article of clothing from the person to *feel* their energy. He then dowses the location to be worked, on a map, using a whalebone rod. He dowses with the help of a woman who must be in a state of 'ritual purity'. The map is dowsed using a three-handed method. The woman holds a pointer in her left hand, with her right hand she holds the end of Khojeste's V-shaped rod. Khojeste places his left hand on the woman's right wrist and holds the other end of the rod in his right hand.

A grid of energy lines is dowsed. It can take several weeks to build up the complete grid. The grid indicates where negative points are located. Khojeste judges these to be good or bad (negative and positive) from the rod's rotation clockwise or anti-clockwise. Clockwise is considered good, and anti-clockwise bad.

Having completed his map survey of the location and having absorbed the energies of the person (from the cloth sample) he is ready to work on the site itself. He chooses the time most carefully, mainly using his intuition. He does not consider it propitious to work three days either side of the full moon and prefers to start around dawn, with the rising of the light and the surge of earth energy. He starts with prayer to establish the sacred context of all such work and to establish light as the guiding principal.

Khojeste sings very beautiful prayers. They are verses from the *Gathas*, the Hymns of Zoroaster. He then walks round the perimeter of the location, sets a light in place, a natural fire lamp with oil, and he prepares rose-water and milk. All these preparations are done as he sings his prayers. Then he goes to the *exact* locations where he considers the energies need adjusting. Iron rods with copper tips are driven into the ground. This is a critical time. Khojeste imagines that he and the rod are one — in the sense of himself as the channel, pinned to the point. It is Khojeste's own energy-field which acts as the healing catalyst.

If indeed he has found the precise *head of the Dragon* spot, the negative forces could make Khojeste violently ill. For this reason ritual purity, an 'earthing' method and his prayers are crucial. He likens the feeling to the capping of an oil well, and

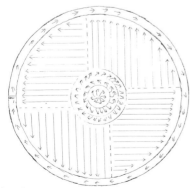

Quartered circle

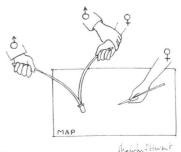

Map dowsing

intuitively knows how far the rod should be inserted before he anoints the spot with rose-water for sweetness and milk for nourishment. Ten, twenty or even thirty rods may be used to achieve the full effect and the process is best completed in one day. A light is left on the site for at least 24 hours, and ideally for up to seven days.

The 24-hour period after healing is the period when the earth *groans* as the energies sort themselves out and the balance is restored. "A uniting of the world above with the world below". As harmony returns, the people often feel happy or elated, the animals are content and the land becomes fruitful and at peace. However this warm feeling is not always permanent and additional balancing work may subsequently be necessary. Similarly to human acupuncture, the first treatment is radical and major, and subsequent treatments are less intensive in order to achieve the correct balance. Khojeste also mentioned that after he had completed his work the PH factor in the soil was found to have changed, but he did not elaborate on this fact.

GUARDIANS

Should we not realise that we are all entrusted to be guardians of the earth, each and everyone of us, and that it should not be the sole responsibility of the Kogi, or the Indians of the Americas, or of Khojeste Mistree? That we in our turn should listen to Viktor Schauberger when he says "it is desperately important to rediscover nature's way if human beings, animals and the land are to be saved from decline, and the earth is not to die of thirst. It is only mother nature who can and must be our teacher".

Many people find the crop circle phenomenon disturbing yet fascinating,in that there is no ready scientific explanation of how they are formed. However we must understand that many aspects of the world in which we live, in nature and in ourselves, cannot be explained scientifically, and that the missing pieces are often found in folklore, myths or ancient custom or beliefs. The essential grains of truth remain there for the seeking.

Many people appear not to stop to think and realise that the planet can do very well without us, but we cannot survive without it. At present we seem to be intent on bringing about its destruction and hence our own. What madness makes us so hell-bent on our own elimination?

How do we approach the problem? First human greed must be restrained and we must bring into being a collective responsibility to the planet. This would in its own turn result in a collective responsibility to mankind. It is immensely encouraging at this particular precarious stage in our planet's history, to be in contact with the many people who demonstrate heightened awareness. They exist for the express reason of bringing new understanding and hope to our present materialistic chaos.

You may ask, with justification, what on earth crop circles have to do with all this? The answer is simple — they bring a message to the many who see them, who witness their absolute beauty — they are inexplicable — they make people stop and think. The circles may in fact be a gateway to higher consciousness. Circles convey many important messages to many people.

Hehake Sapa, Black Elk of the Teton Dakota Indians wrote in 1863:

Everything an Indian does is in a circle. That is because the power of the world always works in circles and everything tries to be round. In the olden days all the power came from the sacred hoop of the nation and so long as the hoop was unbroken the people flourished. The flowering tree was the centre of the hoop and the circle of the four quarters nourished it. The East gave peace and light, the South warmth, the West rain, and the North, with its cold and mighty winds, gave strength and endurance.
Everything the power of the earth does in a circle.

The sky is round and I have heard the earth is round like a ball, and so are the stars. The wind in its great power whirls and birds make nests in circles — for theirs is the same religion as ours, a natural religion.

The sun comes forth and goes down again in a circle. The moon does the same and both are round. Even the seasons form a great circle in their changing and always come back again to where they were. The life of a man is a circle from childhood to childhood. So it is with everything where power moves. Out tipis are round like the nests of a bird and they were always set in a circle — the native hoop.

"But what can I do?" I hear you ask. This is where the crop circles in the field are playing their vital role.

CROP-CIRCLES

I am very conscious of Mother Earth, a living breathing entity. It leads me to understand that there is an energy to all living things, a conscious energy, inter-

acting and interrelating. It is my belief that the energies present in the crop formations are indeed interacting and interrelating with humans and animals according to the energy forces present in them. Just as Khojeste Mistree believes in a harmony or disharmony between a person and a location, so it is with the crop circles.

We have had many reports of the effects felt by people while in, or shortly after leaving, a crop circle. I myself have experienced the healing effects (see *The Crop Circle Enigma*) but I must stress that negative effects seem to be in the majority and I have had several unpleasant sensations, such as light-headedness and headaches. When this happens I leave that area of the circle as fast as I can! Headaches, dizziness, nausea, and disorientation seem to be the main ill-effects, but sudden hyper-activity has also been reported.

Let us consider the energies in the crop fields. I call them *Yin* and *Yang*. There is also a third force which is a force of reconciliation or manifestation. It is not easy to describe the concept behind these three forces for we are not dealing with the material, and the more we try to pin it down the more elusive the concept becomes.

The two opposing forces or principles are all around us, in nature, in ourselves, in everything. The centrifugal and centripetal forces which Viktor Schauberger discusses are also the *Yang* and *Yin*. The centrifugal (*Yang*) disperses, expands, explodes and heats, whereas the centripetal (*Yin*) concentrates, contracts and cools. In our bodies we have the two nervous systems, the para-sympathetic and the sympathetic — the latter dispenses, therefore being centrifugal or *Yang*. Fever is *Yang*, cramp or menstrual pain contracts and is *Yin*. You will see this happening in a tree or flower. The root or seed in the ground being the *Yin* and the expanding branches or flower reaching towards the sky, the *Yang*. The third force brings them into being or manifestation.

In the crop circles I perceive the earth and the macrocosm as being two opposing forces with the third force of reconciliation bringing about the actual manifestation of the formations. Clearly the strength or intensity of the *Yin* and *Yang* energies will vary from very slight at one end, through all stages to a high concentration at the other end of the spectrum.

We then move into the human conditions and find we are also dealing with many categories, the physical, mental, emotions and also indeed the spiritual. They all have a considerable range of fluctuating possibilities. Combine these with the possibilities of the Yin and Yang and you will see what an immensely complex situation emerges! Animals have many of the human emotions, but clearly not so abundantly.

So what is the meaning of the circles and giant formations lying in our crop fields? I do not believe they are placed at random, for there is a reason to all happenings in nature. My son Angus, Jenh-ni-doh, sees the circles as a means by which a mother (macrocosm) seeks to teach her children (earthlings) how to grapple with the lessons they need to learn — using love and laughter as she imparts her knowledge, depicted in symbols. They appear to be universal symbols, intelligible to all mankind.

I believe they have a message for all of us, whatever walk of life we pursue, and whatever language we speak. They portray Universal Wisdom in Universal Tongue. They issue an invitation. An invitation to expand our knowledge and yet respect all other wisdom. It is a message of sharing, of mutual understanding, of unification. A message so profound and yet so simple, it may be missed by many. It would seem that they are indeed heralds of a new era leading us to a greater understanding of ourselves, of the planet on which we live and of the universe in which our planet is but a tiny speck.

It seems fitting to end with this prayer from the Iroquois to the Great Spirit:

O great Spirit whose voice I hear in the wind
And whose breath gives life to all the world —
Hear me.

I am a man before you, one of your many children.
I am small and weak, I need your strength and wisdom.
Let me walk in beauty and let my eyes
Ever behold the red and purple sunsets.
Let my hands ever respect the things you made,
My ears sharp to hear your voice.
Make me wise so that I may know the things that you have taught my people,
The lessons you have hidden in every leaf and rock.

I seek strength, O my creator,
Not to be superior to my brothers
But to be able to fight my greatest enemy — myself.
Make me ever ready to come to you
With clean hands and straight eyes,
So that when life fades as the setting sun
My spirit may come to you without shame.

REFERENCES
1. Alexandersson, Olof: *Living Water: Viktor Schauberger and the Secrets of Natural Energy.* Gateway 1990.
2. Ereira, Alan: *The Heart of the World.* Cape, 1990.

12.   A preparation for the next impact

STANLEY MESSENGER

INTRODUCTION

THIS IS ABOUT understanding corn-circles. These mysterious things have been with us some years now, and several excellent books introducing the phenomenon have been published. I do not wish to repeat the coverage that these books have already given. My purpose is somewhat different.

The appearance of these remarkable figures is comparable with the flood of UFO sightings of twenty years ago, in the sense that it has challenged to the depths the way in which people look at the natural world. In doing so it has polarised observers very clearly into different streams with different attitudes. Like many another phenomenon of nature the thing in itself is straightforward enough. Existential, one might say! There they sit like birds in the wilderness!

What is not at all straightforward, however, is people, their levels of awareness, their background and training, their temperamental dispositions, their prejudices. The more stark the phenomenon the more penetrating the searchlight it directs upon people's capacity for observation and thinking, for emotional honesty, for simple objectivity and non-attachment.

There was once a famous cartoon, probably in an early edition of "Punch" It showed a sturdy Victorian countryman, surrounded by open-mouthed children and a toddler or two, standing in the entrance to an animal stall at the zoo, where a giraffe stood munching its hay. They had clearly been contemplating each other for some time, and it was difficult to say which was the more astonished.

The countryman, better placed to reach a conclusion, finally shook himself, thumped the ground with his stick, and turned to go. "*All I know*", said he, "*is that there ain't no such animal*". So we had with corn-circles a phase of simple disbelief on the one hand, countered by wild fantasising on the other. Either they were all hoaxes, or we were about to be invaded by beings from outer space. Since UFOs had failed to deliver, this was to be the next round of warning signals. So much for UFOs having been as far as possible swept under the carpet by military security! These creatures would not be so easily disposed of. And so forth.

The universal hoax proposal could be summed up in a single acronym: APICHTID. *A priori* it *can't* happen, therefore it *doesn't*! In our scientific age many people don't get beyond this, understandably. As the evidence mounts the position of people whose whole sense of reality is invested in leak-proof materialism becomes tragic. So much is invested in such beliefs that a few people have been driven to establish inexplicable incidents as mischievous artefacts. The alternative for them is a kind of madness.

It is obviously very difficult to assess the wild variety of alternative views which have been put forward. First there was Dr Meaden and the '*plasma vortex*'. Then George Wingfield began to point out serious errors in Dr Meaden's actual physics. The *laws* were correct enough, but the *attribution* was wide of the mark.

In parallel with the activities of those who wanted

to establish mechanical causes for crop circles came the much more numerous efforts of those who sought imaginal causes. The whole range of mythology, symbolism, archaeological and spiritual lore was invoked in an attempt to place the crop circle phenomenon in context with the mysterious and the paranormal. 'Mythological' speculation has grown in a number of interesting ways, but it is not yet robust enough to present a serious challenge to more orthodox approaches. Behind all this, there was a feeling that everybody was standing, hand over mouth, asking *"Whatever next?" "What on earth is happening?"*

This is approximately where matters stood at the end of the 1990 season. The corn-circle phenomena are beautiful, mysterious and redolent of spirit. However, there are energies at work which may be too easily linked in a speculative and undisciplined way with ancient wisdom. We need to get beyond speculation and into attuned discipline. This means being more scientific than scientists. Ancient wisdom demands and deserves this.

In the book *The Crop Circle Enigma* Dr Meaden's theory is clearly described by him, sitting amongst much other imaginative material and factual anecdote, where it offers an uneasy challenge to less thorough but more broadly-based work. Meaden's coherence gains an unfair advantage from its narrower aim. If the work of others is sometimes less thorough, it is because it covers an enormous field of speculation and is only at an early stage of assessment. The balance is bound to alter as evidence accumulates in the years to come.

Many people are worried by crop circle events. As if wars, economic uncertainties, political insecurity, threat of educational and medical breakdown and environmental toxicity were not enough! I want to try and address these fears. But I cannot pretend that this can be done in an undemanding way. It is my belief that the phenomenon itself is exactly that, a demand upon humans to stand up and understand the world in a deeper way.

For many people it is precisely this sort of demand which is so frightening. Read the first chorus of T S Eliot's *Murder in the Cathedral*. We want things to be ordinary. *"We do not wish anything to happen"*. And later on, Thomas à Becket's sad and compassionate conclusion: *"Humankind cannot bear very much reality"*.

All the same there is much misunderstanding involved in these fears. Our education predisposes us to think that we need to be very intelligent to understand the world. Not so. There is increasing evidence that as the world increases in complexity the *heart* proves a more reliable guide than the head. Women seem to have more natural talent for understanding this. But men are often better at articulating it, particularly when it comes to understanding what, for instance, Rudolf Steiner meant when he said: *"Hearts must begin to have thoughts"*.

I think Eliot's Becket was wrong. I think that mankind *can* bear a great deal of reality.

The problem of CCPs (crop circle phenomena) is not simple. Understanding it means setting out upon a path of knowledge. But that path is not meant to be tackled unaided. I try to demonstrate here that in CCPs we are being provided with a new door to go through. We have ignored such doors in the past. We shall ignore this one at our peril. The aid is there within our hearts' intuition.

THE SCIENTIFIC APPROACH

What question does science actually ask about crop circles and upon what assumptions is this question based?

I want to try to break a deadlock which is growing in the way we look at the crop circle mystery.

This deadlock is by no means a new phenomenon, and is in no way special to the crop circle mystery. It is implicit in the whole way in which science impinges on the consciousness of those whose sense of wonder feels its way into the realm of the new. This is not to say that scientists are not themselves imbued with wonder — very little progress would be made if research scientists were not initially awe-struck by the mysteries they unravel.

The direction that science has taken, however, tends to replace wonder by something rather less starry-eyed. As a result *science* has become rather different in tone from *scientists*. Science has grown up in the last three centuries as a monolithic *belief-system*, commanding the same kind of fearful respect once accorded to the Catholic church. It has come to be reified as an authority in itself. Most of the time we forget that this structure is something we have built ourselves, just as we built religion ourselves.

Why has it become possible for us to create this eidolon (fetish), this form we project into our thinking about the world, and call 'science'? It is because the scientific *process* is *real*! The scientific *method* was the biggest leap forward in human conscious achievement for hundreds, perhaps thousands, of years. I want to demonstrate that it has been over-taken recently by an even greater achievement. But this in no way diminishes the stature of the scientific *method*.

In what sense then has science become an eidolon, a belief-system, an idol? Idols can be built only on the solid foundation of true insights if they are to stand up. We can only create the false out of the substance of the true if it is to convince people. In spite of the monolithic structures we build to contain, and in the end to imprison, our spiritual growth being of our own construction, the power they embody is real and effective. All religions are idols in this sense, and scientism is presently the most powerful religion of all.

We need to be clear on this point, otherwise we are in danger of polarising ourselves into a number of different groups and believing them to be mutually exclusive. Is it perhaps because it is we ourselves who have tied ourselves up in such a strait-jacket of limitations to understanding, that realities are pro-voked into breaking out, attempting to re-establish some balance between our observation and our thinking? Are we being required to look again, not at the *methods* of science, which are impeccable, but at the extremely narrow parameters and axioms upon which these methods have been built? Have we not confused the method with the conclusions we have drawn from it?

It is not scientific method which has gone astray. We have failed to re-examine at each stage the *axiomatic assumptions* upon which this method has been based. In this way our judgement of what is real, and the proofs we demand for its establishment, have come to depend on a philosophy of science which we believe no longer needs reappraisal and updating. We no longer basically question the nature of the cognitive process. *We think we know how we know things.* However, as our knowledge grows, questions of how knowledge is acquired grow with it. This understanding has immediate relevance to ordinary observers and thinkers. They deserve something better than a monolithic belief-system.

I can hear cries of protest from generations of hard-thinking philosophers, who believe themselves to have examined how we know things quite exhaustively. I believe many of them have failed to notice, and have built upon, errors of observation and judgement very far back in the philosophical process which accompanied the development of science in the early nineteenth century — in Emmanuel Kant, for instance, with his '*ding an sich*', the thing-in-itself. Kant failed to observe the part thinking plays in the creation of phenomena.

Such errors of observation are never without personal and feeling-based connotations. Even giant minds can harbour prejudices which blind them to simple truths. Very complex systems can be built up on foundations which harbour quite simple errors, which resonate to the tendencies in the age in which they arise. Both mechanistic theories in physical science and behaviourism in psychology are limit-ations of this kind. They carry man's view of the world only so far, and then reality overtakes them.

However, in our crop circle mystery cereologists are dealing with the *outcome* of these old errors at a new, more basic and much simpler point. Ordinary people inherit the results of these high-flown philosophical errors unconsciously. The huge structure of science conceals from them the fact that they no longer know what they actually *perceive*, and how their thinking is related to it. Thus ordinary people no longer know what part of their perception relates, through their thinking, to a real world, and what part is a construct, which they project upon reality in order to conform to the consensus reality they imbibed with their mother's milk from day one.

Post-Freudians like Fairbairn and Winnicott believe that this *sufficient reality* is the only reality mankind is capable of relating to. Almost from the first moment we draw breath, we are actually conned out of objectively examining the inner perceptions we carry through birth into physical life. We accept instead a consensus 'reality' which for the most part we don't question. Until, that is, some apocalyptic event, either through our sense-perceptions or through an inner spiritual crisis — such as a near-death experience — catapults us into facing suppressed memories of early life or even life before birth.

So long as the material world *out there* plays our little game, and pretends to be as real as our projections would have it be, we think we have a usable stability, a consensus reality we can live in. Then along comes something like crop circles!

Dr Terence Meaden's 'reality' is one such creation. It starts with certain assumptions. He shares these with the majority of scientific researchers. There are many other starting points for serious inquiry into reality. If these are ignored we close the door into huge areas of understanding. This is what science mainly does, and this is why it is for the most part no more than a belief-system, a religion like all the others.

However, beyond a certain point this system breaks down. Reality calls our bluff. It is not any longer prepared to play our game — this self-deceiving game in which we say that our thinking, our cognitional process, is not a valid part of reality, and that this observed world has its own separate and independent existence *out there*, separate from the construction we put upon it.

There is no separate reality out there! We create our own reality!

A lot more could be written in this vein, and no doubt needs to be, because the breakthrough of new phenomena is only just beginning. A whole new way of looking at the real world is growing up within human consciousness, and we see it reflected back as an apocalyptic explosion of new phenomena. Before this happens we need at least to begin upon the process of looking within our own consciousness at what we mean by *knowing*. It is a whole science, bearing the formidable and scarcely-used name of *Epistemology* — the study of the method and the grounds of knowledge. Formidable it may be, but we need to have some grasp of it, otherwise this new time will overwhelm us. We will be thrown into a mental and emotional turmoil we can't handle.

In the light of this, can we perhaps begin to look at the situation "Science versus the Rest" in a somewhat different light? This is not a matter of right and wrong explanations: it concerns peoples' way of looking at the world, which is an inseparable product of their background assumptions, and that these remain very largely unexamined!

For those who have developed themselves within current scientific disciplines, only certain questions are valid. There is a prescribed pathway along which these valid questions may be refined, focused and put to the test. The answers arrived at become the new frontiers of "*our*" knowledge. This "*our*" is central to the result. It is the idol or eidolon of scientism. What it chooses to ignore is that "*we*" together don't know anything! Only individualised intelligences know things, and our path of knowledge is our own responsibility.

If we take this individual responsibility, and share its results with others who do the same, wonderful new channels of communication are opened up. We recognise that the channels of communication, like the knowing process itself, take place essentially *within* consciousness. There is real communion of minds. Moreover we then start to recognise that there is a larger mind beyond our individualism. Genuine cognitive questions are raised and sometimes answered, which for the trained scientist would be frivolous and scientifically invalid.

However, it is very important to recognise that the scientist's own questions and the path they lead him on are no less valid. Failure to appreciate this ignores a discipline, and thus exposes wider-based inquiries to charges of turgidity, sometimes childish fantasy, and worse still a nominalistic word-game, a juggling with symbols which never manages to look at the phenomena for what they themselves actually are — within our consciousness *and out there*. In order to look squarely — from a perspective which includes the *whole* range of possibilities opened up by the thoughts I have been developing here — at what science actually asks and answers we have to see clearly that the only thing the scientist asks is *how events take place*.

The scientist asks HOW?

A scientist doesn't actually ask *"What?"* or *"Who?"* or *"To what end?"*. For a student of, and product of the 20th Century scientific-materialist process, these questions are actually meaningless. There are no *things* to ask *"What?"* about, there are only behaviours of energy in an outside world. There are no persons or beings to ask *"Who?"* about. These matters are already pre-decided. *Being* is a sort of 'standing eddy' in the path of certain energy movements. There are no *purposes* to prompt the question *"To what end?"*. *Purpose* is, to a scientist, no more than a subjective projection on to a reality consisting of *processes*: tables and chairs are not things in themselves, but they are energy-processes. It is *we* who make tables and chairs into *things* because we

have an innate knowledge of Being in our spiritual nature. But the scientist denies the reality of this level of Being: this is what being a *scientist* implies.

The above considerations become extremely pertinent to the whole crop circle mystery if Dr Meaden's *'plasma-vortex'* theory, or any other scenarios which seek a mechanical explanation for crop circles, are allowed to dominate the field.

This will only happen as long as we are only asking *"How?"*. However, epistemology itself has a broader base. There are axiomatic starting points, perceptions of the nature of perception itself, and of the thinking which arises intuitively to match it, which open valid paths and such questions as, *"What is this phenomenon?"*, *"Whose consciousness manifests here?"*, and *"To what end do these events tend?"*.

These starting points transcend the axiom implicit in what has become the philosophy of science in our time. They in no way invalidate the question *"How?"*, and they in no way invalidate scientific impeccability. But they do lead into realms of valid knowledge which are closed to mechanistic science. These are realms of wonder and of the miraculous, which also have their reality.

INTELLIGENCE AND INTELLIGIBILITY

What is implied in the proposition that crop circles are the product of intelligence?

I tried in the previous section to defuse the battle that has been developing among crop circle buffs — cereologists — between what we may call *Scientific Explainers* and the Rest. This *Rest*, among whom I include myself, is a far less coherent body, a real rag-tag-and-bobtail of open-ended views, or no views at all. All that unites us is our intuition that, however coherent and consistent the mechanistic view is, there is something about it that doesn't ring quite true.

The materialist asks only one question: "How does this phenomenon work? I seek an answer" says he, "which does not violate the laws of a science which I have, to the maximum extent of my capacity, mastered. I believe myself to understand the parameters, the limits within which man's capacity for knowledge operates. Within these limits only certain questions are valid, and I am only interested in answers to valid questions. The rest is pure speculation, even downright nonsense".

I hope I am not misrepresenting the mechanistic position, because there is great strength in it. It owes its strength to the limits which it sets itself. These are not limits derived from a logical process, they are limits of *choice*. Once that choice is made its consequences can be impeccably logical. But this is only after a certain starting point has been chosen, not frivolously or arbitrarily, but out of a deeply-held conviction that only one view of the world leads to *knowledge of the world*. This is a view which starts with sense-observation and then tests, by setting up a hypothesis, and creating a process in which confirmation or denial of that hypothesis emerges from further sense-observations. This process is named *proof*, and where new phenomena are concerned it can be a long, exhaustive and exhausting process, in which certainty is hard to come by.

The dignity, as well as the arrogance and exclusiveness of science derives from the rigorous training and discipline required. However, in the course of developing scientific discipline, many scientists forget that the original starting point — the conviction that only sense-experience (empiricism) and thinking based upon it constitute valid grounds for certain knowledge — was not the result of a logical process, but of an *intuitive conviction*. It was an axiom, something requiring no proof, but an immediate observation excluding other possible observations, allowing no question to go beyond it or to invalidate it.

Exclusive, self-validating axioms have enormous strength so long as consciousness remains wholly fixed upon them. Look at Euclid's 'a point has position but no magnitude'. Starting from there, and deriving from it secondary definitions about lines,

Circles centres: winter barley at Avebury Trusloe. (*Adrian Dexter*)

areas and volumes, Euclid laid the foundation for the whole of spatial geometry as most of us know it. Had he started instead from 'an infinite sphere has magnitude but no position' he would instead have developed projective or spherical geometry (in which the finite world is perceived as deriving from the infinite). If that had been the direction in which human consciousness had been evolving at the time of Euclid he might well have done so, and changed the course of history. But it was not evolving in that direction, and Euclid also was a product of that fact.

Why is it that the mechanical approach to the crop circle mystery, while perfectly logical and valid, at the same time rings false, violating the intuition with which we react *directly* to the impact of the events seeming to lie behind the phenomena themselves? It is because human consciousness is no longer moving

Centre in green wheat, Alton Barnes I. (*Adrian Dexter*)

tation of sense-perceptible reality — crop circle phenomena.

Dr Meaden's *plasma-vortex* theory, for example, is a description which does no more than brush the surface of this phenomenon. In fact it is precisely *because* sense-perception linked with logical analysis have reached their limit, that this real world has started to behave as it is doing in the crop pictogram phenomena.

It is this behaviour which prompts us to speculate about the part that *intelligence* plays, or appears to be playing, in the production of cereological phenomena. I stress that we should not here be *anti-materialist*. Starting from different axioms about the nature of observation and thinking, our understanding stands *beside* scientific observation as an *addition* to their understanding. So far, for the most part, our grasp is sporadic, muddled, speculative and scrappy. In some respects science can run rings round us — to coin an appropriate phrase! We need to do better than this. Our gut feelings need to be embodied in a much more exact understanding if they are to become something we can claim as *knowledge*.

Efforts in this direction are going to take us very far afield. Ultimately they will lead onto a path of study and research into a science of exact observation and thinking, an exact Science of Realities, or *spiritual science,* which goes beyond what is observable by the senses, and beyond the empirical thinking which can only process sense-observable phenomena. The foundations of such a science of the spirit already exist in the world, and have done so for many decades.

What I hope to convey is that, if a few hints are offered about the nature of intelligence and the way in which it manifests, it will lead people to ask more precise questions about why, with these cereological events, the manifestation of intelligence in the sense-perceptible world is taking a new evolutionary step.

in the same direction as it was, even as little as two centuries ago, when the sense of human evolution was aimed at attaining an ever more exact relation to the physical world.

That process is now complete.

It has been complete for a long time. That is why we have the feeling that further efforts to understand the universe by the methods of physical science have started to move *away* from reality instead of towards it. The language of higher physics moves further and further from anything that the total human being can experience as real. It is *because* scientific method has now overshot the mark of its usefulness, that we now have an intuitive sense of violation when we see science used as a means of corralling, taming the pristine creative newness of an entirely new manifes-

Stages of intelligence in natural phenomena

The first thing to recognise is that intelligibleness is the presence of manifest order which consciousness can recognise. And intelligence, at some level, is awareness of order.

In that sense all that manifests to our senses as matter is ordered and hence intelligible. However, if we take a step further and purport to recognise different orders or kingdoms in nature — mineral, plant, animal etc — we give expression to an intuitive feeling that, as we 'ascend' toward 'higher' orders of nature, we are looking at the operation of different principles. We feel that the difference between a mineral and a plant, or between a plant and an animal, is a difference in *kind*, not just in degree.

Physical science denies this. It says our feeling is at fault here. Science says we confuse the steep increase of complexity in a plant, due to the special chemical character of the carbon atom, with the emergence of a different principle of operation. It is at the frontier between minerals and plants that the conceptual division first appears — between those who believe that in all phenomena everything lies on the surface and can be fully accounted for by what manifests to the senses and sense-based intelligence, and a second group who believe something different. As suggested in the case of the crop circles, the difference is between those who are content to explain everything in terms of how it operates (which is valid in the case of the mineral kingdom) and those who perceive that in a body which can grow, metamorphose, reproduce, and die, the body not only manifests a mechanism of operation, but it also betrays the presence of an element not detectable by the senses.

There is an overriding form, say these people, an archetype, a '*what*' rather than a '*how*', in the plant, which bears a different relationship to time from the linear cause-and-effect sequence operating at the mineral level. Changes in the mineral, like crystallisation or solution or oxidation, can be accelerated or reversed by factors operating from outside. Those happen in the plant too, if a leaf is injured or falls, but they take place in the context of an *overriding formative tendency* which is irreversible.

Our observation of any moment in the life of a plant is like a still picture in a cinematic sequence, of which all the other stills in the plant's past and future exist on another time-scale, invisible to us. Without the total sequence the particular one we are looking at is without its full meaning. The *total being* of the plant exists on a level which is inaccessible to our sense observation. But it is not inaccessible to our thinking. Our thinking takes place as a real event on the same level of existence as the plant archetype. At this level there is no temporal sequence. The whole of time is permanently present, accessible to thinking. At this level thinking is not a processor of successive sense observations, but the direct observer of an extended event within time.

It is this level to which we can give the name 'Etheric'.

It is particularly important that we do not make the error of observation which is made by physical science. If we permit ourselves to let go of the scientific obsession that thinking is simply an energy-response in the brain to what the senses receive from the physical world, then the above description of the way in which exact observation of the whole plant *alters our relationship to time* can become an actual experience for us, instead of just another theory. What starts simply as a new thought becomes a perception of what thinking *is*, and *where* it is. Thinking becomes a perception for us when the extended plant, seed via leaf to seed, becomes a perception in our image-forming consciousness. This is what Einstein did when he arrived at the *unified field*. It is what Sheldrake is doing in his picture of the morphogenetic. Instead of seeing a single moment of a plant in space, and thinking the whole sequence of pictures in time, we start to *see* the whole plant in space-time, with our combined thinking-perception. All the time, what we are talking about is *thinking moving over into perception*, loosening itself from the illusion the brain imposes on it, becoming a reality in itself. This is the path of the *etheric*, and a path to the understanding of crop circles, where they come from, what their challenge to consciousness is, and what we can do about them. These phenomena are warning signals that a fundamental evolution of our perception of the world, and the thoughts we form about it, is urgently overdue.

Etheric manifestations can have physical counterparts, but their origin is *not* physical. When people claim to see auras physically they are not contacting the true etheric level. This can only be perceived by *willed, feeling-imbued thinking*. However, the etheric level of energies can sometimes affect the more rarefied levels of physical energy and transfer its forms to them, often in a somewhat distorted way. Some sensitive observers can perceive these effects physically, the degree of distortion depending on the soul-orientation of the observer — particularly on whether fear or love dominates the feeling.

In the first instance what Rupert Sheldrake is describing as a *morphogenetic field* is a description of the interface between the physical and the etheric levels of manifestation. Active, feeling-endowed thinking can reverse the process of manifestation, elaborate these physical perceptions, raise their energy levels, and move over into etheric clairvoyance.

The etheric, however, is only the first layer beyond the physical. Beyond the plant level there lies the realm of *sentience*, where the animal archetypes operate. Beyond that again is a third level, that of individualised self-awareness, where it is possible to observe what is characteristically *human*. The most important thing to grasp is that these insights and the realities which lie behind them approach you from *inside* your consciousness, not from outside it.

We have an intuitive feeling that intelligence is manifesting in these forms which have appeared in the crops. I have given you a very brief introduction to the etheric realm, not at all to deeper realms. But even grasping this much gives the possibility of a more mature approach to seeking the nature and scope of the intelligence manifesting there.

The question is, at what level is crop circle intelligence manifesting? And why?

THE SICKNESS IN CONSCIOUSNESS AND ITS INBUILT THERAPY

How do we find our own path to healing through cereology?

When something *can* happen in nature or in life, and it *doesn't*, there is a misplacement of energy. Something else happens instead. Often what happens instead is some form of sickness or distortion. The appearance of the capacity for manifestation may, of course, be timely. Then the emergence of the phenomenon is normal and mature. If it is delayed the result appears as a deficiency condition. If it is premature there is a monstrous form.

In the bony system, for example, at the moment when a bony formation should appear, correct timing results in the appearance of healthy bone. If for some reason this fails to happen, the moment passes, the body goes on developing and, for example, cartilage appears but fails to ossify. In the opposite case the impulse to form bone may precede the moment when the developing process indicates that it would be appropriate. This could result in an anky-losed joint or an exosteosis.

Dysphasia (uncoordinated timing) between *potential* and *manifestation* is an inbuilt feature of organic life. Much depends on it. It is not necessarily to be regarded as sick or evil. An example described by Rudolf Steiner in the plant kingdom is such plants as Henbane or Deadly Nightshade (*hyoscyamus* and *belladonna*). The flowering phase of a plant stems from the astral world, one level above the vegetative etheric level. From this world comes the geometrical starry form of the flower, the colour, the perfume, the relation to the insect world, pollination and growth of the ovule, ripening of the fruit, sweetness, flavour and so on. Not till the seed is set do we contact a still higher level.

However, the astrality of colour, perfume etc, may sink below the normal flowering level into what should be purely vegetative. In henbane, for example, the colour purple and some of the chemical processes which would operate normally in the flower and fruit invade the purely vegetative realm of the leaf, whose proper sphere is that of photosynthesis and nourishment. The result is that when the plant comes into relation with animal or man this relation is disturbed. We describe it as poisonous. The relation is distorted.

Consciousness however *may* rise into this situation in a redemptive way. Instead of accepting the destructive, death-dealing effect, we may through consciousness transform its energies into the opposite pole of healing. Henbane may be made into a medicine instead of a poison.

At the present time we have an analogous situation to this in the realm of the crop pictograms.

In a cornfield the normal outcome when physical substances in soil and rain come into relation with the colossal etheric fertility invested in last year's corn-crop is *corn*, millions of tons of the stuff. Crop-circles may be miraculous, but they are nothing like as miraculous as a bursting ripe ear of *corn*! Millions of them stand there every year, radiating the fertile nutrient energy they have drawn from the sun, transmuted by the crystalline, hexagonal, forming might of silica and carbon on earth, into hundreds of millions of fragrant grains of power.

The formative dynamic of silica is essentially vertical. The corn-stalk is nearly all silica, an element which stands between the sun and the earth with an essentially vertical, gravitation-balancing dynamic, stretched like a bow-string and finely tuned to the recording of the subtle forms and movements deployed between sun and earth.

Clearly the provenance of events described in this way lies deeper than the mechanical processes which bring them into visibility. In Sheldrake's terms, the cornfield is a morphogenetic powerhouse, a place in which forms are straining at the leash to manifest. And straining towards them is human thinking, a phenomenon of the same nature as the forces operating in the plant, here manifesting at as high a concentration as anywhere in the plant kingdom.

By remaining too long in the mechanical mode human thinking has strained its capacity to evolve, almost to breaking point. We are seeing a kind of breakdown in the formative process. At a point of minimum resistance there is a kind of lightning strike between human thinking resisting its own expansion into etheric perception, and the plant world thereby forced into producing inappropriate, damaging, even poisonous forms. It is the obstinacy and fear in human thinking which forces these to appear as physical forms, rather than rising to meet them in the etheric.

There is a situation here on earth at the present time which can only be met by expanding consciousness. The human thinking which forms its picture of the nature of physical reality has driven itself into a bottleneck. Increasingly the pictures we form of the processes going on in mineral form, plant life, animal sentience, and human awareness are coming into direct conflict with the actualities. The evolution of earth processes continues apace, and human consciousness remains stuck in a fixed view of reality, now close to bursting point. The pressure by now is colossal.

There is in fact a perfectly organic and healthy way in which humans can keep pace with the present changes going on in earth energies, and in the new etheric forms trying to manifest through them. This is to *loosen up our thinking*. What I have described as *active, feeling-endowed thinking* not only enters the energy-field where the processes which give rise to cereological phenomena are happening. It also starts to *live* in them and *learn* from them. It learns to participate with the energies, breathe with them — also to hold them back from premature manifestation in physical form.

What it amounts to is this. Like the poisonous substances in henbane an element is bursting through from the astral level into physical manifestation where corn is the normal condition. If we simply meet this manifestation with materialistic thinking on the physical level where it appears to be, it can act as a poison. The poisonous effect shows itself in a simple form as headaches, shock symptoms and time-displacements, due to a misplaced relationship with the etheric realm where sequential time originates. One might expect that further developments along these lines would start to affect growth processes, possibly of a cancerous nature, and also damaging effects on the developing embryo.

Nature always manages to produce appropriate remedies whenever an imbalance produces sickness. Materialistic thinking has become mankind's most serious disease. We have the opportunity to heal this sick condition by bringing the thinking down, out of the dead brain-mirror, into the active, feeling-endowed will, and entering the etheric levels from which thinking itself arises. The crop pictograms, bursting into physical form out of an intense organic nourishment source, are being offered to us as a natural remedy for our now extremely serious epistemological condition.

How are we to make use of this remedy?

The first thing to realise is that it is we ourselves who are producing it. One of the signs of this is that the more attention is paid to them, the more crop circles appear. In a comical sense the cereological crazy-gang who insist it is all a hoax have a twisty sort of truth on their side! Without the sick abnormality of our own conceptual life the matrix of natural phenomena would not be producing abnormalities of its own. In that sense it is we who are 'doing' it though not in the crude sense the hoax-boys imagine. But it is certainly we who, by the limited scope of our 'reality-projection', are yanking down the prolixity of etheric formative expressions onto a relatively crude physical level.

So what we think of as the physical world is a hoax??

Not too far out, as some of the more imaginative early science-fiction testifies!

Incidentally, have you noticed how the actual physical sight of a freshly formed pictogram shoots directly into the nervous system, at solar plexus, or even heart level, and administers a most unpleasant and possibly even damaging shock? This shock can be considerably enhanced, as Janet Trevison has shown, if you happen to be holding a bar-magnet in your hand at the time!

It has been my aim in this account to open a path of discovery and healing which every person who encounters the cereological phenomenon can follow. It is important to realise that this path of discovery is unique to each person. It is your own imagination you have to activate and get to work on the visualisation process, not mine. And it will be your own new world you are entering, and your own conceptual and perceptual healing you will be bringing about. The medicine is not off-the-shelf. It is custom-designed for each patient, directly out of the wisdom of that one's own higher being.

Cereological events are no more than one aspect of an apocalyptic explosion of energy changes leading mankind to an immense transition of new consciousness, and into a new time. With crop circles we have a distinct descent into form, *"with such permanence as time has"* (T S Eliot). The challenge to mankind to change his thinking becomes more urgent — to meet reality head-on, to go more than half-way to meet what is presented to our consciousness, and to master it with our hearts as well as with our dying heads.

HEALING OF CONSCIOUSNESS AND HEALING OF PERCEPTION

(a) How to take the medicine offered by crop pictograms

We used Henbane as an example of how a poison can be converted into a remedy. If we try to apply this analogy to the recognition of crop pictograms as potential healers of our cognitional and perceptive processes, we can only take it so far, since both aberrant phenomenon and psychic effect lie already in the etheric, manifesting in the physical only indirectly.

In ordinary chemotherapy a poisonous substance is used in a controlled dosage to counteract directly another chemical process which is perceived as causing an illness. This is a gross over-simplification, but serves to mark the contrast with homoeopathy, where a different principle is involved. To grasp this we have to understand how the operation of the etheric is related to the corresponding area of the physical, to which it is related as formative principle. We could use the analogy of a mould used to cast a clay or metal object. The mould is the inverse counterpart of the resulting object. The object is the substance, the mould is the form, and this form is inside out.

In using a poisonous substance to produce a homoeopathic remedy we reverse the process used in chemotherapy. We contrive a method of producing a kind of anchor which will hold the form which gave rise to the poisonous substance (namely the etheric body of the henbane plant or whatever), while we proceed to dilute the actual substance virtually to vanishing point. The further we dilute the substance the further we extend the etheric form as a sphere surrounding the little lactose pill or drop of dilute alcohol we are using as an anchor.

When we administer the dose we can conceive of this etheric sphere sucking back into itself the henbane-like activities which are manifesting in the patient as symptoms. The form sucks the substance back into itself, so the stronger the symptoms the stronger the suck has to be. That is why the higher, more diluted potencies in homoeopathy are used for the more severe conditions. The etheric form of a poisonous substance retained by a little lactose pill is a true opposite of the substance used in its creation, not just a dilution of it. Hahnemann, who invented homoeopathy, believed, perhaps too simplisticly, that the poison used should exactly imitate the symptoms it was designed to cure. In the scientific belief-system all this is the purest gobbledegook!

Now, how does this scenario relate to the crop pictogram situation? Essentially my notion is that the corn-circle phenomenon is basically an etheric activity which we are not yet perceptive enough to *see*. Nature is screaming out to us that it is high time we *were* perceptive enough. This cry takes the form of a spilling over of the etheric into physical manifestation. This is having a toxic effect on our perceptual field and concepts.

Am I justified, moreover, in going further, suggesting that the phenomenon constitutes a major spiritual-scientific challenge, a challenge to turn the tables on it and construct from it a therapeutic path to heal our whole consciousness, not just that part which misperceives corn circles?

Are we now to overturn pseudo-science and raise our whole consciousness, perceptive and conceptual, onto a higher level? Furthermore am I right in positing that these cereological events have been offered us by nature (of which our own nature is the substantive growing point) for this very purpose?

From another point of view, is this not a manifestation of an attempt at self-healing by nature itself, in its perception that a major aspect of human activity — particularly in the way that humankind perceives events and forms concepts of them — is pathological in it?

We can only begin to answer these questions by doing so in a scientific manner, using the scientific method, which is the golden core of cognition in our time. We shall be using a true spiritual science, based on axioms which take the etheric into account. Without doubt this will also lead us to ask true scientific questions about higher levels of being also. This scientific path of observation, experimentation and thinking will carry from the start a very different mood from much that we think of as scientific in our day. We are also starting out from a much deeper starting point than does most contemporary scientific research. In rejecting the limitations of their axioms, we are in a sense returning to the nursery class.

We are allowing each individual his or her say in what he or she knows. For as I said earlier 'we' know nothing. Only the individual knows things. So we will find ourselves discounting much of what contemporary science takes for granted as common knowledge. After all it is our own very consciousness we are investigating.

We have to start from the admission that we as cereologists know *practically nothing*. We also have a lively expectation that there will be new fields of unforeseeable wonders thrown into our laps every other week. Perhaps one of the chief contributions we will have to offer the scientific world is quite a new dimension of humility. At the same time, in rejecting some of its certainties we are gaining others. We may know nothing, but *we are beginning to know what knowing is.*

(b) Where to start?

As in all science, paths begin with intuitions, wheezes, crazy notions. The rot sets in when the results of these congeal into orthodoxies.

I shall offer here a notion which may turn out to be an insight or may not. It has always niggled at my mind that this loony phenomenon is happening in *cornfields*! We are so busy gawping at strange shapes, electric shocks, and time-displacements that we largely fail to notice precisely where they are happening. These events are busily invading one of our chief sources of nourishment: our daily bread, forsooth!

Please note the following: perception and thinking are grounded in organic bodies — us! Perception and thinking are at the end of their tether. Organic bodies nourish themselves on corn. They eat *bread*.

Perception and thinking are based on organic processes, nourished by something that is going over the top. Perception and thinking are going over the top in places where their nourishment is coming from.

Are these half dozen observations linked by nothing but coincidence? Or are we faced with a coherent sequence here?

How do we hit back?

Suppose, for example, we were to make homoeopathic preparations of corn which has been subjected to forces which have resulted in crop pictograms. Suppose we used as our diluting agent corn which has not been so influenced. In other words we potentise crop pictogram flour in ordinary flour. We could do this at first according to standard homoeopathic precedent, say 6X and 30X (dilutions of 10^{-6} and 10^{-30}).

We then face a wide range of questions. Normally we turn flour into bread and eat it. We, however, are going to make medicine out of flour. Heat destroys homoeopathic remedies. So we can't cook our cereological flour into bread. We shall have to take cereological flour pills. What have we then actually done? The mind boggles. We have taken a substance which has been subjected to forces which have made crop circles out of it. We have used homoeopathic methods to dilute this substance to near vanishing point, using an excipient of the same nature as the presumably altered substance. We hope the formative influences which, in their unhomoeopathised form, acted on our consciousness to produce aberrations in our perception and thinking, will now as remedies have a corrective effect on the latter.

What does that mean?

Does it mean that we now simply revert to our

'normal' way of perceiving the cornfield, where we now perceive no crop circles, experience no buzzing in our ears, no shocks to our solar plexus and heart chakra, no time-displacements, no funny shadows across the field which are not quite parallel? Surely not.

What I am hoping is that we may be giving our organisms, by removing the toxic effect of the assault on our perceptions, the maximum chance to experience the situation at a healthy level. We then maximise our efforts to raise consciousness to a level where we can perceive the realm which gave rise to the phenomena in the first place. It occurs to me to say: "First put upon yourselves the armour of light". I have an idea we are going to need it. This is not a game.

All pathology results from something which at one level or another we have failed or are failing to do. We fail to rise to a certain challenge in our lives, whether to correct some error in how we are living or whether to take some step relevant to the point of development we have reached. As a result of this failure we become ill. We needed the illness in order to seek healing in the form of a remedy which nature at the same time provides. In seeking the remedy we perceive at the same time the step we should have taken, whose failure led to the illness. We are offered another opportunity to take the step.

In this case our failure to rise to a perception of the world, for which foursquare materialistic images and thoughts are no longer adequate, is resulting in an explosion of phenomena into our perceptual field which cause aberrations there. These aberrations have a pathological aspect, both physically and psychologically. Healing of them should open doors of perception, through which a further opportunity would be offered to raise our consciousness. Doors may open, but they have to be walked through. New paths of enlightenment, appropriate to the stage of development mankind has reached, already exist in the world, have done so indeed for the greater part of this century. Not much notice has been taken of them. The doors in general were not walked through. So they have not entirely evolved to keep pace with changing spiritual needs.

Like remedial plants crop circles also have a meaning of their own apart from the therapeutic one into which we shall increasingly be able to enter. I have a strong feeling that the two processes are twin aspects of the same thing, and that this is what the aberrant phenomena are telling us. We have reached a point where we need both the sickness and the cure. If it were not so the phenomena would not have occurred.

So we reach the most challenging conclusion of all, that crop pictograms may well become a next step in the present rapid evolution of channelling pathways, one in which we may be learning to see the written language of the spiritual world, as well as hearing its voice in our speaking. But this demands that we allow the vision to heal by transcending its purely material form and rising to the level in which we can perceive what is being said at the level at which it is spoken. This is the etheric level from which our thinking comes, from which the pictograms come, and from which the corn itself comes.

If we can achieve this out of our own guided consciousness directly we may not even need the medicine. We shall see.

SIBSON AIRFIELD, nr. Peterborough, August 1991.

Index

[Note: Figures in italic relate to illustrations]